# MAAP

# Grade 4 English Practice

## GET DIGITAL ACCESS TO

 **2 MAAP Practice Tests**

 **Personalized Study Plans**

## REGISTER NOW

### Important Instruction

Register online using the link and the access code provided by your teacher.

Enter the access code (for your reference) in the box given below.

**Access Code:**

# Mississippi Academic Assessment Program (MAAP) Online Assessments and Grade 4 English Language Arts Literacy (ELA) Practice Workbook, Student Copy

Contributing Editor - Mary Evans Rumley
Contributing Editor - Julie Turner
Contributing Editor - George Smith
Contributing Editor - Wendy Bundgaard
Executive Producer - Mukunda Krishnaswamy
Program Director - Anirudh Agarwal
Designer and Illustrator - Snehal Sharan

**ISBN 10: 1722793929**

**ISBN 13: 978-1722793920**

**Printed in the United States of America**

## CONTACT INFORMATION

**LUMOS INFORMATION SERVICES, LLC**

 PO Box 1575, Piscataway, NJ 08855-1575
 www.LumosLearning.com

 Email: support@lumoslearning.com
Tel: (732) 384-0146
Fax: (866) 283-6471

Lumos Learning
Step Up Your Skills

# INTRODUCTION

This book is specifically designed to improve student achievement on the Mississippi Academic Assessment Program (MAAP). Students perform at their best on standardized tests when they feel comfortable with the test content as well as the test format. Lumos online practice tests are meticulously designed to mirror the state assessment. They adhere to the guidelines provided by the state for the number of sessions and questions, standards, difficulty level, question types, test duration and more.

Based on our decade of experience developing practice resources for standardized tests, we've created a dynamic system, the Lumos Smart Test Prep Methodology. It provides students with realistic assessment rehearsal and an efficient pathway to overcoming each proficiency gap.

Use the Lumos Smart Test Prep Methodology to achieve a high score on the MAAP.

## Lumos Smart Test Prep Methodology

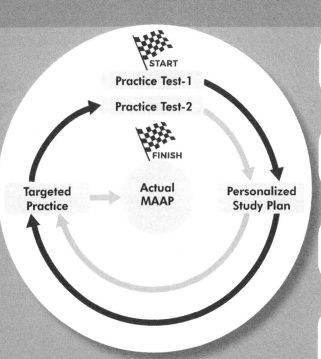

**1** The student takes the first online diagnostic test, which assesses proficiency levels in various standards.

**2** StepUp generates a personalized online study plan based on the student's performance.

**3** The student completes targeted practice in the printed workbook and marks it as complete in the online study plan.

**4** The student then attempts the second online practice test.

**5** StepUp generates a second individualized online study plan.

**6** Additional activities are planned to help the student gain comprehensive mastery for success on the MAAP.

# Table of Contents

# Chapter 1 - Reading Literature

## Lesson 1: Finding Detail in the Story

### Question 1-3 are based on the story below

**After reading the story, enter the details in the map below. This will help you to answer the questions that follow.**

"The Elephant Who Saw the World . . .," Mary started speaking. It was Friday, and the students had to share their creative writing stories of the week.

Mary loved writing, and this was her favorite part of the week, when they were able to make up stories for creative writing. She enjoyed it so much that she became really good at it. Even at home on the weekends when she didn't have much homework, she would sit in her room for hours and create stories to share with her friends and family. Her parents always supported her and were her biggest fans.

However, there was one part about every Friday at school that Mary did not enjoy, and that was when she had to share her story in front of the class. The teacher made all of the children share on Friday afternoons, and this made Mary very nervous. She was shy, and although she knew her teacher was right, she didn't like it.

Sitting and listening to the other children, Mary heard her name called. It was her turn to share. She got out of her seat slowly, walked to the front of the room and began.

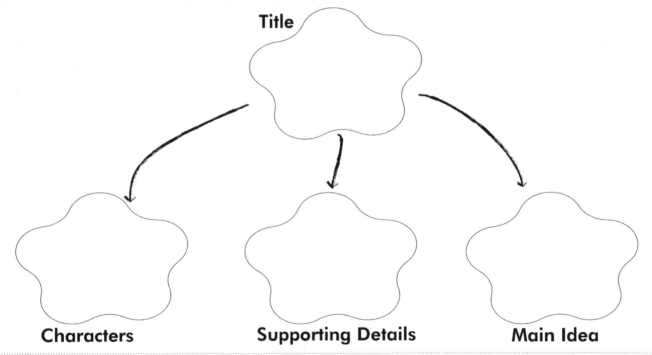

Title

Characters          Supporting Details          Main Idea

**1. What is the title of Mary's story?**

  Ⓐ  The Elephant Who Liked Candy
  Ⓑ  The Elephant Who Saw the World
  Ⓒ  The Elephant Who Wanted to See the World
  Ⓓ  The Girl who Hated Writing

**2. What didn't Mary like doing?**

  Ⓐ  Writing stories
  Ⓑ  Having her stories corrected by the teacher
  Ⓒ  Reading her stories in front of the class
  Ⓓ  Going to school

**3. Why was Mary reading her story in front of the class?**

  Ⓐ  It was something she loved to do
  Ⓑ  Her classmates asked her to
  Ⓒ  Every Friday the children had to share their creative writing stories
  Ⓓ  Her parents wanted her to

**Question 4 is based on the story below**

**After reading the story, enter the details in the map below. This will help you to answer the questions that follow.**

This year Jim and I had the most wonderful vacation compared to the one we took last year. We went to Hawaii, which is a much better place to visit than a hunting lodge in Alaska. The hotel we stayed in was a luxury suite. It included a big screen TV with all of the movie channels, a hot tub on the balcony, a small kitchen stocked with local fruits and vegetables, and a huge bed shaped like a pineapple. The weather in Hawaii could not have been any better. We enjoyed many hours on the beach sunbathing and playing volleyball. When we were not on the beach, we were in the ocean swimming or riding the waves on a surf board. Each night we enjoyed eating and dancing with all of our friends at a luau. Our week in Hawaii rushed by, making us wish we had planned a two-week vacation.

Conversely, the hunting lodge in Alaska that we stayed in had no TV, a shower with barely warm water, a small cooler for our food, and cots to sleep on each night. Furthermore, the room wasn't even the worst part of the vacation. The weather was terrible. It rained the entire time we were there. Even with the rain, our guide expected us to go on the all-day fishing trip that was part of our vacation package. All we caught on that fishing trip was a cold from the rain. After the third day in Alaska, we decided to end our nightmare, cut our trip short, and head for home. Without a doubt, we will be going back to Hawaii next year on our vacation.

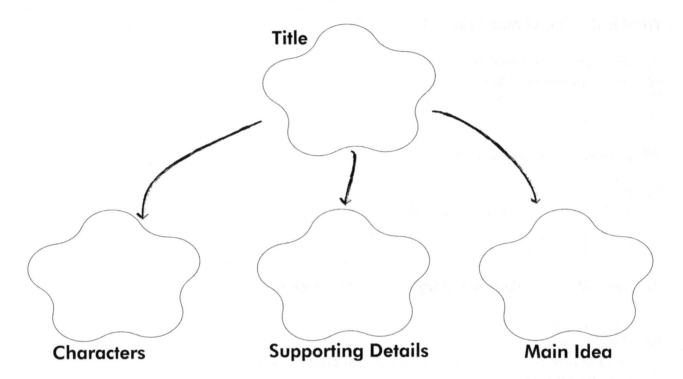

Title

Characters                    Supporting Details                    Main Idea

**4. Which statement supports the author's opinion that their Alaska vacation was miserable?**

Ⓐ  Our week in Hawaii rushed by, making us wish we had planned a two-week vacation.

Ⓑ  The weather in Hawaii could not have been better.

Ⓒ  This year Jim and I had the most wonderful vacation compared to the one we took last year in Alaska.

Ⓓ  After the third day in Alaska, we decided to end our nightmare, cut our trip short, and head for home.

**Question 5 is based on the story below**

**Disneyworld- Here We Come! Part - I**

It was a hot summer day in June. My grandmother, Mom, my brother Daniel, my cousin Valerie, and I were headed out for a long vacation. We were, first, going to Mississippi and, then, on to Florida to Disneyworld. Talk about excitement!!! I couldn't contain myself and didn't sleep much at all the night before. Valerie was visiting us because her mom had gotten sick. My wonderful mom had volunteered for her to stay with us the entire summer. It was so cool! Valerie and I were best friends already, much less best cousins. We did everything together all the time, so having her come along was just another treat for me. Of course, I had rather my little snoopy brother, Daniel, didn't come, but oh well! After all, who can complain when you are going to Disneyworld!?

We had to stop in Mississippi to leave my grandmother off at her house before the vacation. That wasn't such a bad idea either, because I loved my grandmother's house, the creek to fish and swim in, and all of her things. The night before we had packed everything we needed. I just couldn't get to sleep. Finally, I must have fallen asleep because the alarm was going off and everyone was hurrying about the house. Dad had made us breakfast. He couldn't go due to his work schedule, but insisted we go and have fun. He even told me to ride the Teacups for him and the Train! Dad is such a laugh.

The car was packed, we had double checked everything and were waving goodbye! Another reason for the stop, in Mississippi, was for rest. It was going to be a long ride to even get that far in one day. Mom turned on the a/c in the car along with the radio, and we settled in. She had it on her favorite country music, so we sang along a few songs of Merle Haggard and Johnny Cash. I must have fallen asleep right after we left the house. The next thing I knew, Mom was waking me up. We had stopped for lunch at a Whataburger restaurant. My favorite, too! She said to eat hearty as we would not stop again until we reached my grandmother's house. I ate a whole Whataburger with fries and an ice tea. Valerie did, too! Daniel had a Jr. Whataburger and so did my grandmother. Mom had a salad with chicken. Back in the car, Valerie and I decided to play, I Spy. It is loads of fun! I was spying all kinds of things from license plates from Washington to blue jays in trees. Daniel tried to join in but would get mad if we guessed his too quickly. So he got out his video game and played it. Mom had to stop for gas, one time, right before we made it to the Mississippi state line. We always honk the horn when we cross over into Mississippi, but she said she was not going to do that since it was now getting dark and it might upset other drivers. I have a very smart mom.

**5. What preparations did the author's family make to ensure that the trip was enjoyable? Write your answer in the box below using details from the story as evidence.**

**Disneyworld- Here We Come! Part - II**

Before we knew it, it was daylight again.  Mom was hustling us out of bed and into the kitchen for breakfast. She said to eat hearty as we had many more miles to go before we reached our final destination.  So thankful that my grandmother cooked her best oatmeal for us topped with cinnamon, brown sugar, strawberries, and whipped cream!  Who could ask for anything more?  Yummy!!

Then it was load back into the car and get on the road.  This time Mom found an oldies radio station and she was singing along with Patsy Cline, Tennessee Ernie Ford, and Frank Sinatra.  Talk about strange music that none of us knew except her!  Valerie and I played a game of travel trivia which was sort of fun and of course, Daniel, was back on his video games!

For lunch we stopped at a roadside park and had the sandwiches our grandmother had packed for us along with an apple and sweet iced tea. When we got back on the road, not a sound could be heard.  I figured out later that all of us kids had fallen asleep.

A loud bang woke us as Mom clapped her hands and proclaimed our arrival to the Holiday Inn at Disneyworld!  I could not tell you who was the most excited as we were all yelling sounds of glee and running around the car to get our luggage out.  Mom registered us for our room and we were giggling uncontrollably.

**6. How did the author's mom wake the kids once she arrived at the hotel? Write your answer in the box below.**

**Disneyworld- Here We Come! Part - III**

When we were settled in to our room, Mom explained the sleeping arrangements. Valerie and I would get one of the queen size beds to share, Daniel would get the fold out couch in the living area, and Mom would get the other bed. She said that is night number one, then we will switch on the second night. I love it when my mom thinks of everyone and being fair to all. We were so happy we could have slept on the floor and not minded!! Mom called Dad to let him know we made it safe and sound. Then she called our grandmother, too. She also called Valerie's mom in the hospital so Valerie could talk to her and let her know all was well. Valerie's mom's health was improving daily, too.

Mom ordered pizza for us the first night. We went to bed without any complaining, so excited to be going to Disneyworld the next day!

Mom had picked up a map of the park when she had registered us, so she was busy planning our day while we were falling asleep.

The morning came with a clap and thunder outside of our room. What was going on, we had wondered? Mom explained that it was raining and that we would have breakfast in the hotel lobby and then see what happened. She did tell us that the hotel manager had explained to her that quite often the rains would start and stop during the summers at Kissimmee, Florida. We were not too disappointed after she said that. The hotel offers a free breakfast for everyone. That was definitely a plus in Mom's opinion.

Sure enough after we had eaten the sun came out. The hotel offered a trolley bus to the theme parks, so we opted to take that rather than worrying about parking and walking. Disneyworld stays open all day and late into the evening. Mom said she had mapped out our route to take so we could get to see most everything in our two days along with purchasing us the fast passes to avoid long line delays.

**7. They were so happy, they could have slept anywhere and not minded. Write a sentence justifying this using evidence from the passage.**

**Question 8 is based on the story below**

## Disneyworld- Here We Come! Part - V

Again, on the second day, we had the free breakfast and rode the trolley. It wasn't raining this time at all. Mom got out her map, and we began our day. Daniel wanted to go back and ride the Mad Tea Party again, but thankfully Mom said no to that.

We were able to go to Splash Mountain, the Jungle Cruise, the 7 Dwarf's Mine Train and much more. Mom did make a request of her own. She wanted to meet Mickey and Minnie Mouse who were scheduled to appear outside of the Cinderella Castle. She also said she wanted to listen to the Enchanted Tales with Belle and ride the Prince Charming Regal Carrousel. What a crazy silly Mom!

What we didn't know was that she had a plan. It was right after we left the carrousel that we heard fantastic sounds coming down the main street. Yes, parade time right before our eyes. Mom told us to come and sit. There we were on the side of the castle sitting on the ledge in perfect view of the parade. We asked her how she knew to stop there. She said one of the hotel clerks had told her how to find the spot and when to be there. The parade was magnificent to say the least. The characters actually stopped in front of us and performed. Wow! We couldn't have planned it any better.

After the parade, we went to A Pirate's Adventure, Tomorrowland Speedway, and Big Thunder Mountain. Mom said we needed to head toward the front entrance as it was time for fireworks, and we needed to be ready. We got there just in time. The lights lit up the sky behind the Cinderella Castle and throughout Disneyworld. Just picture it!
What a perfect ending to our vacation!

8. **What did not happen on the second day that happened twice on the first day of their visit to Disneyworld? Enter your answer in the box below.**

   **It did not _____ on the second day.**

**Question 9 and 10 are based on the story below**

## Roses are Red

Everyone knows the poem that goes- Roses are Red, Violets are blue, Sugar is sweet and so are you! But I am not talking poetry right now. I am talking about the roses that Aunt Molly has in her yard. Yeah, you see the pictures of them! Aren't they so beautiful? How does she get them that way?

Notice the two pictures on the page. The white roses come from a huge rose bush. I call it a tree, It is so big! My aunt started that one with a branch cut off of our Great Grandma Witt's rose bush down in Centerville. She brought it home when Great Grandma was still alive. Grandma Witt told her to cut it off, wrap it in wet paper towels, put it in a bucket of red clay dirt from her front yard, and take it home. So my aunt did.

When she got home with it, she dug a deep hole in her backyard. She put the clay dirt in first, then made another hole in the middle of that. Next, she put in rose fertilizer to help it grow. Then, she put in the branch from the rose bush. After that, she pushed the dirt in real tight. When she got ready to water it, she didn't water it straight at the branch. Instead, she watered it slightly to the side of the hole at an angle. She also took a banana peel the next day and wrapped it around where the bottom of the branch was at. An old man had told her to do that whenever she planted rose bushes. I had no idea that you could grow a rose bush just from a branch. You can. The rose bush will start to make new roots under the soil. Bingo, a rose bush!

Now, look at the second red rose picture. This is a rose bush from Tyler, Texas. That town is world famous for growing the best roses. Aunt Molly bought that one about a year ago. It was on sale, she said, or she would never have paid full price for it. She put it on the side of her house near the carport. She had wanted to grow roses there for a long time. At first, she told me that it was not looking very healthy and she knew why it had been on sale. However, she kept pampering it, adding fresh clay soil around it. Of course, she had to do the banana peel thing to it, too! During the winter, Aunt Molly was afraid it was dead. But to her surprise, it came back bigger than ever. She said it produces cluster roses almost every week.

Well, apparently, she knows how to grow roses. It all seems to work just fine for Aunt Molly.

**9. Aunt Molly used a special technique when planting the rose branch from Great Grandma Witt's house. Below are the steps she followed. Enter the correct order sequence in the box given below.**

    A. She put a banana peel around the bottom of the branch.
    B. She watered the rose branch at an angle after it was planted.
    C. She added the clay dirt to the hole.
    D. She dug a deep hole.

10. **Why did Aunt Molly think that the second rose bush was going to die? Use details in the selection to support your answer.**
    **Write your answer in the box below.**

<br><br><br><br><br><br><br><br><br>

**Question 11 is based on the story below**

### THE SECRET GARDEN by Frances Hodgson Burnett - Part 1

### CHAPTER I

### THERE IS NO ONE LEFT

When Mary Lennox was sent to Misselthwaite Manor to live with her uncle everybody said she was the most disagreeable-looking child ever seen. It was true, too. She had a little thin face and a little thin body, thin light hair and a sour expression. Her hair was yellow, and her face was yellow because she had been born in India and had always been ill in one way or another. Her father had held a position under the English Government and had always been busy and ill himself, and her mother had been a great beauty who cared only to go to parties and amuse herself with gay people. She had not wanted a little girl at all, and when Mary was born she handed her over to the care of an Ayah, who was made to understand that if she wished to please the Mem Sahib she must keep the child out of sight as much as possible. So when she was a sickly, fretful, ugly baby she was kept out of the way, and when she became a sickly, fretful, toddler she was kept out of the way also. She never remembered seeing familiarly anything but the dark faces of her Ayah and the other native servants, and as they always obeyed her and gave her her own way in everything, because the Mem Sahib would be angry if she was disturbed by her crying, by the time she was six years old she was as tyrannical and a selfish little pig as ever lived. The young English governess who came to teach her to read and write disliked her so much that she gave up her place in three months, and when other governesses came to try to fill it they always went away in a shorter time than the first one. So if Mary had not chosen to really want to know how to read books she would never have learned her letters at all.

One frightfully hot morning, when she was about nine years old, she awakened feeling very cross, and she became crosser still when she saw that the servant who stood by her bedside was not her Ayah.

"Why did you come?" she said to the strange woman. "I will not let you stay. Send my Ayah to me." The woman looked frightened, but she only stammered that the Ayah could not come and when Mary threw herself into a passion and beat and kicked her, she looked only more frightened and repeated that it was not possible for the Ayah to come to Missie Sahib.

There was something mysterious in the air that morning. Nothing was done in its regular order and several of the native servants seemed missing, while those whom Mary saw slunk or hurried about with ashy and scared faces. But no one would tell her anything and her Ayah did not come. She was actually left alone as the morning went on, and at last she wandered out into the garden and began to play by herself under a tree near the veranda. She pretended that she was making a flower-bed, and she stuck big scarlet hibiscus blossoms into little heaps of earth, all the time growing more and more angry and muttering to herself the things she would say and the names she would call Saidie when she returned.

"Pig! Pig! Daughter of Pigs!" she said, because to call a native a pig is the worst insult of all.
She was grinding her teeth and saying this over and over again when she heard her mother come out on the veranda with some one. She was with a fair young man and they stood talking together in low strange voices. Mary knew the fair young man who looked like a boy. She had heard that he was a very young officer who had just come from England. The child stared at him, but she stared most at her mother. She always did this when she had a chance to see her, because the Mem Sahib—Mary used to call her that oftener than anything else—was such a tall, slim, pretty person and wore such lovely clothes. Her hair was like curly silk and she had a delicate little nose which seemed to be disdaining things, and she had large laughing eyes. All her clothes were thin and floating, and Mary said they were "full of lace." They looked fuller of lace than ever this morning, but her eyes were not laughing at all. They were large and scared and lifted imploringly to the fair boy officer's face.
"Is it so very bad? Oh, is it?" Mary heard her say.

"Awfully," the young man answered in a trembling voice. "Awfully, Mrs. Lennox. You ought to have gone to the hills two weeks ago."
The Mem Sahib wrung her hands.
"Oh, I know I ought!" she cried. "I only stayed to go to that silly dinner party. What a fool I was!"
At that very moment such a loud sound of wailing broke out from the servants' quarters that she clutched the young man's arm, and Mary stood shivering from head to foot. The wailing grew wilder and wilder. "What is it? What is it?" Mrs. Lennox gasped.

"Some one has died," answered the boy officer. "You did not say it had broken out among your servants."

"I did not know!" the Mem Sahib cried. "Come with me! Come with me!" and she turned and ran into the house.

11. **Why did Mary get upset when she woke up that morning? Write your answer in the box below using details from the passage for support of your answer.**

[empty answer box]

**Question 12 is based on the story below**

### Sandy's Soccer

Sandy Thomas enrolled in soccer when she was in first grade. She had loved to watch the soccer games on TV with her dad. Sandy's dad was a high school soccer coach. It was his passion, as well as hers. Sandy was elated when she convinced her parents to let her play soccer rather than take ballet. Her friends were astonished as they had all signed up for ballet and expected her to, as well.

The team she was on this year was called, The Blue Jets. She was playing her favorite position, goalie. She practices at home with a goal her dad made for her. He tries to make the goal and she blocks it almost every time.

**12. Which of the following shows details from the story? Select all that apply.**

Ⓐ Sandy and her dad loved soccer.
Ⓑ Sandy plays goalie.
Ⓒ She and her dad practice a lot.
Ⓓ None of the above

---

**Question 13 is based on the passage below**

## John F. Kennedy

**John Fitzgerald "Jack" Kennedy (May 29, 1917 – November 22, 1963)**

President John F. Kennedy, our 35th President of the United States, has often been referred to as simply JFK. He was President from January 1961 until he was assassinated in November 1963. He is known for his famous quote, "Ask not what your country can do for you. Ask what you can do for your country." He was the youngest US President elected and the only Roman Catholic to serve office. He is also the only US President to win the famed Pulitzer's Prize.

He is well known for his advancements in aiding the Civil Rights Movement. During his term, the Peace Corps was established, the "New Frontier" domestic program, and the Cuban Missile Crisis also occurred.

He was killed by Lee Harvey Oswald in Dallas, Texas. It is thought that there was a conspiracy to commit the murder. Jack Ruby then killed Oswald in a jail corridor. The majority of Americans alive during the time believed that it was not done simply by just one man.

**13. Which of the following apply to President Kennedy? Select all that are found as facts in the article.**

Ⓐ President Kennedy was the youngest man to be elected President to the US.
Ⓑ He did not win the Pulitzer's Prize.
Ⓒ He supported the Civil Rights Movement.
Ⓓ All of the above.

**Question 14 is based on the story below**

## THE THREE GOLDEN APPLES - By Nathaniel Hawthorne

**Part 1**

Did you ever hear of the golden apples, that grew in the garden of the Hesperides? Ah, those were such apples as would bring a great price, by the bushel, if any of them could be found growing in the orchards of nowadays! But there is not, I suppose, a graft of that wonderful fruit on a single tree in the wide world. Not so much as a seed of those apples exists any longer.

And, even in the old, old, half-forgotten times, before the garden of the Hesperides was overrun with weeds, a great many people doubted whether there could be real trees that bore apples of solid gold upon their branches. All had heard of them, but nobody remembered to have seen any. Children, nevertheless, used to listen, open-mouthed, to stories of the golden apple-tree, and resolved to discover it, when they should be big enough. Adventurous young men, who desired to do a braver thing than any of their fellows, set out in quest of this fruit. Many of them returned no more; none of them brought back the apples. No wonder that they found it impossible to gather them! It is said that there was a dragon beneath the tree, with a hundred terrible heads, fifty of which were always on the watch, while the other fifty slept.

In my opinion, it was hardly worth running so much risk for the sake of a solid golden apple. Had the apples been sweet, mellow, and juicy, indeed that would be another matter. There might then have been some sense in trying to get at them, in spite of the hundred-headed dragon.

But, as I have already told you, it was quite a common thing with young persons, when tired of too much peace and rest, to go in search of the garden of the Hesperides. And once the adventure was undertaken by a hero who had enjoyed very little peace or rest since he came into the world. At the time of which I am going to speak, he was wandering through the pleasant land of Italy, with a mighty club in his hand, and a bow and quiver slung across his shoulders. He was wrapt in the skin of the biggest and fiercest lion that ever had been seen, and which he himself had killed; and though, on the whole, he was kind, and generous, and noble, there was a good deal of the lion's fierceness in his heart. As he went on his way, he continually inquired whether that was the right road to the famous garden. But none of the country people knew anything about the matter, and many looked as if they would have laughed at the question, if the stranger had not carried so very big a club.

14. **Fill in the blanks with vocabulary from Part 1.**

   **Part A**

   The golden apples grew in the garden of _____.

   **Part B**

   Children listened _____ to the stories of the golden apples.

   **Part C**

   _____ young men set on a quest to find the apples.

   **Part D**

   He was _____ in the skin of a fierce lion.

## CHAPTER 1 → Lesson 2: Inferring

**Question 1 is based on the poem below**

I found a shell, a curly one;
Lying on the sand.
I picked it up and took it home,
Held tightly in my hand.
Mommy looked at it and then,
She held it to my ear,
And from the shell there came a song
Soft and sweet and clear.
I was surprised, I listened hard,
And it was really true:
If you can find a nice big shell,
You'll hear the singing too.
--Unknown

**1. Why was the poet surprised?**

Ⓐ  She found a curly shell on the beach.
Ⓑ  Her mother put it to her ear.
Ⓒ  She didn't expect to hear a song from the shell.
Ⓓ  She was frightened of the shell.

**Question 2 is based on the story below**

**After reading the story, enter the details in the map below. This will help you to answer the questions that follow.**

## Alexander the Great

Nearly two thousand five hundred years ago, there lived a king called Alexander the Great. He was the son of Philip II of Macedonia. When prince Alexander was a boy, a magnificent horse that was for sale was brought to the court of his father. The animal was to be sold for thirteen talents. Talents are ancient coins. Many were eager to buy the horse, but no one could get close enough to saddle the restless animal. He was wild and impossible to ride.

Alexander pleaded with his father to let him try. Realizing that the horse was terrified of its own shadow, he turned the horse towards the sun, so that its shadow fell behind it. This calmed the horse, and the prince proudly rode away. Observing this, his father said, "My son, look for a kingdom worthy of your greatness. Macedonia is too small for you."

That is exactly what Alexander tried to do when he grew up. He fought many battles and always rode Bucephalus (that was the horse's name.) Friendship and trust grew between the man and his horse. When Bucephalus died of wounds received in battle, Alexander was heartbroken and deeply mourned the loss of his horse.

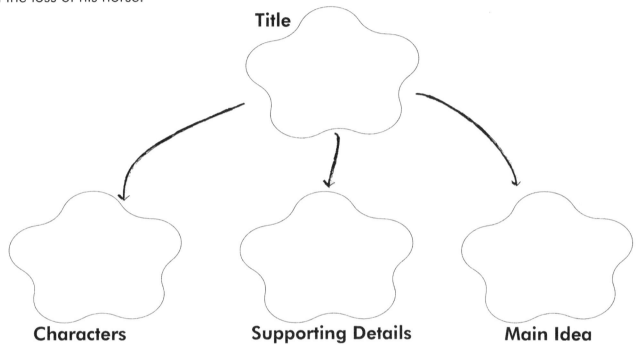

**Title**

**Characters**

**Supporting Details**

**Main Idea**

**2. According to the passage, why do you think the horse was unrideable and wild?**

    Ⓐ  because it was angry
    Ⓑ  because it was hungry
    Ⓒ  because it was scared
    Ⓓ  because it was good at riding

**3. From the passage below. What can you infer from Cindy's actions?**

    Cindy's mom called her to supper. When Cindy arrived in the kitchen, she looked at the food on the stove and made a face. She looked in the freezer and saw a frozen pizza and asked her mom if she could cook it instead.

    Ⓐ  That she was excited about what her mother had cooked
    Ⓑ  She was not very hungry for dinner.
    Ⓒ  She didn't think the meal was ready.
    Ⓓ  She didn't like what her mother cooked for dinner.

## Question 4 and 5 are based on the story below

**After reading the story, enter the details in the map below. This will help you to answer the questions that follow.**

### Mary loves writing stories

"The Elephant Who Saw the World," Mary started speaking. It was Friday, and the students had to share their creative writing stories of the week.

Mary loved writing, and this part of the week, when they were able to make up stories for creative writing, was her favorite part. She enjoyed it so much that she became really good at it. When she was home on the weekends and she didn't have much homework, she would sit in her room for hours and create stories to share with her friends and family. Her parents always supported her and were her biggest fans.

However, there was one part about every Friday at school that Mary did not enjoy, and that was when she had to share her story in front of the class. The teacher made all of the children share on Friday afternoons, and this made Mary very nervous. She was shy, and although she knew her teacher was right, she didn't like it.

After sitting and listening to the other children's share, Mary finally heard her name called. She knew it was her turn to share. She got out of her seat slowly, walked to the front of the room and began.

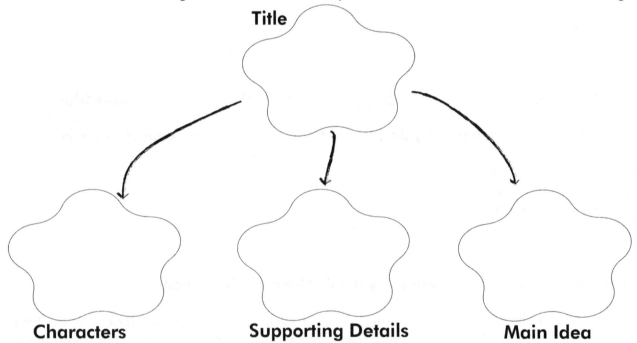

**4. What do you think Mary did next?**

&#9398; Mary began running out of the classroom.
&#9399; Mary began reading her story in front of the class.
&#9400; Mary began to cry because she was scared.
&#9401; Mary began to tell the teacher she didn't write a story.

**5. Why did Mary's parents support her love for writing stories?**

Ⓐ  so she wouldn't sit in front of the TV all day
Ⓑ  to make sure she stayed busy
Ⓒ  because she liked to write and was good at it
Ⓓ  to make sure she kept her writing skills better than everyone else's

**6. From the passage below, where do you think Ben and his dad were going?**

As Ben woke up on Sunday, he was thinking that it would be great to do something special with his dad that day, as he didn't see him very often. When he looked outside the window, he noticed that the sun was out, but a new blanket of snow had fallen during the night. He was getting dressed thinking of what they could do when all of a sudden he heard his dad say, "It is a sunny day. Grab your skis on the way down!" Ben ran to get his skis and they left.

Ⓐ  to the zoo
Ⓑ  to the mall
Ⓒ  to the mountain
Ⓓ  to school

**Question 7 and 8 are based on the passage below**

Thelma lay on the windowsill. She heard a loud noise, so she lifted her head and looked outside. The noise woke her up, and now she wasn't happy. The color of the sky was changing from dark to a light pinkish yellow,and she could hear the birds starting to chirp. Her back arched high as she stretched a deep stretch. She decided it was time to go and find some food because she was starting to get hungry.

**7. From the passage below, at what time of day do you think this is happening?**

Ⓐ  in the evening at sunset
Ⓑ  in the early afternoon
Ⓒ  in the early morning at sunrise
Ⓓ  in the middle of the day

**8. What kind of animal is Thelma?**

Ⓐ  a horse
Ⓑ  a cricket
Ⓒ  a mouse
Ⓓ  a cat

**Question 9 and 10 are based on the passage below**

Before going to bed on Friday night, Susie's parents told her that they had a surprise planned for the weekend and that she would have to wake up really early on Saturday morning. When she woke up, they left the house quickly and started driving. While in the car, Susie looked outside to see if she could figure out where they were going. She noticed that it was getting really hot out and the sun was shining brightly. Then she noticed that the surfboards were in the car. Finally, they stopped, and Susie said, "I know where we are going!"

**9. From the passage above, what season is it?**

   Ⓐ  summer
   Ⓑ  spring
   Ⓒ  winter
   Ⓓ  fall

**10. Where do Susie and her family probably live?**

   Ⓐ  in Alaska
   Ⓑ  close to the beach
   Ⓒ  in the mountains
   Ⓓ  in Arkansas

**Question 11 is based on the story below**

### DISNEYWORLD- HERE WE COME! PART - V

Again on the second day, we had the free breakfast and rode the trolley. It wasn't raining this time at all. Mom got out her map and we began our day. Daniel wanted to go back and ride the Mad Tea Party again, but thankfully Mom said no to that.

We were able to go to Splash Mountain, the Jungle Cruise, the 7 Dwarf's Mine Train and much more. Mom did make a request of her own. She wanted to meet Mickey and Minnie Mouse who were scheduled to appear outside of the Cinderella Castle. She also said she wanted to listen to the Enchanted Tales with Belle and ride the Prince Charming Regal Carrousel. What a crazy silly Mom!

What we didn't know was that she had a plan. It was right after we left the carrousel that we heard fantastic sounds coming down the main street. Yes, parade time right before our eyes. Mom told us to come and sit. There we were on the side of the castle sitting on the ledge in perfect view of the parade. We asked her how she knew to stop there. She said one of the hotel clerks had told her how to find the spot and when to be there. The parade was magnificent to say the least. The characters actually stopped in front of us and performed. Wow! We couldn't have planned it any better.

After the parade we went to A Pirate's Adventure and Tomorrowland Speedway, and Big Thunder Mountain. Mom said we needed to head toward the front entrance as it was time for fireworks and we needed to be ready. We got there just in time. The lights lit up the sky behind the Cinderella Castle and throughout Disneyworld. Just picture it! What a perfect ending to our vacation.

**11. What did the author describe and ask you as a reader to visualize near the end of the story? Write your answer below.**

---

**Question 12 and 13 are based on the story below**

### Celia Cruz

She was born in Havana, Cuba in 1925. She was told by her grandmother that she could sing before she could talk. Her grandmother used to laugh and tell the family that she practiced her singing at night. (She was thought to have cried most of the night.) Cruz' work in radio during the 1940's in Cuba led to her fame and she traveled throughout Latin America with a female band. She won her first award singing on an amateur hour TV show. Cruz sang a version of a tango song that was very popular in Cuba.

In the 1950's Celia Cruz joined the Sonora Mantancera as a lead female singer. Then she was able to go to the Tropicana, the best establishment for Cuban music. If you performed at the Tropicana, you had made it in the singing world of Cubans.

She then went to Mexico for a one year contract right before Fidel Castro took over Cuba. She and her band never returned. Cruz moved to New York in 1961. By this time she was a well- known Cuban singer and independent from her band. She became known as the "Salsa Queen" due to her style of music. During the 1990's she gained great popularity among the younger generations, as her music reappeared. Cruz has been honored by five Presidents of the United States. She died of brain cancer in 2003, but her music and legend continue to thrive throughout the world.

**12. Use vocabulary from the passage to complete the sentence.**

She was known as the _____.

**13. She did or did not return to Cuba? Write your answer in the box below as "yes" or "no"**

## Question 14 is based on the story below

### The Wolf and the Lamb

A Wolf, meeting with a Lamb astray from the fold, resolved not to lay violent hands on him, but to find some plea, which should justify to the Lamb himself his right to eat him. He then addressed him: "Sirrah, last year you grossly insulted me." "Indeed," bleated the Lamb in a mournful tone of voice, "I was not then born." Then said the Wolf: "You feed in my pasture." "No, good sir," replied the Lamb, "I have not yet tasted grass." Again said the Wolf: "You drink from my well." "No," exclaimed the Lamb, "I never yet drank water, for as yet my mother's milk is both food and drink to me." On which the Wolf seized him, and ate him up, saying: "Well! I won't remain supperless, even though you refute every one of my imputations."The tyrant will always find a pretext for his tyranny, and it is useless for the innocent to try by reasoning to get justice, when the oppressor intends to be unjust.

**14. What was the wolf trying to do when he wanted to eat the lamb?**

Ⓐ Justify his pleasure.
Ⓑ Prove he was stronger.
Ⓒ Not eat the lamb.
Ⓓ All of the above.

### The Dog, the Rooster and the Fox

A Dog and a Rooster, traveling together, took shelter at night in a thick wood. The Rooster perched himself on a high branch, while the Dog found a bed at the foot of the tree. When morning dawned, the Rooster, as usual, crowed very loudly. A Fox, hearing the sound, and wishing to make a breakfast on him, came and stood under the branches, saying how earnestly he desired to make the acquaintance of the owner of so sweet voice."If you will admit me," said he, "I should very much like to spend the day with you."The Rooster said: "Sir, do me the favor to go round and wake up my porter, that he may open the door, and let you in." On the Fox approaching the tree, the Dog sprang out and caught him and quickly tore him in pieces.Those who try to entrap others are often caught by their own schemes.

15. **What was the fox's intent? Write a sentence in the box below to explain your answer using evidence found in the fable.**

## CHAPTER 1 → Lesson 3: Finding the Theme

**Question 1 is based on the story below**

**After reading the story, enter the details in the map below. This will help you to answer the questions that follow.**

### Fred Goes to the Dentist

Fred had never been to the dentist. All of his life he had heard horror stories about the buzzing drills, the huge needles, and the scary tools that the dentist used to torture his patients. Since none of his teeth were hurting, Fred just couldn't understand why his mom was insisting on taking him to the dentist. She told him that it was important to visit the dentist each year to have his teeth checked and cleaned. This seemed silly to Fred because he cleaned his teeth everyday by brushing and flossing them, but nothing would change his mother's mind. He found it hard to believe that she would think it was a good idea to take him somewhere to be tortured. However, he had no choice but to go.

On the way to the dentist, Fred's imagination went wild. He pictured walking into a room with a huge chair that the dentist would strap him to. He could just see the dentist pulling out a huge drill and drilling his tooth while his mother and several others held him in the chair. By the time he got to the dentist's office, he was shaking all over.

Surprisingly, the office was nothing like he expected. The dentist was friendly, and the chair was comfortable. It didn't have any straps. He looked around the room and didn't see any huge drills or torture devices. He was relieved when all the dentist did was look in his mouth, show him how to properly brush and floss his teeth, and give him a balloon. His mom made another appointment to have his teeth cleaned in six months. Maybe this wouldn't be as bad as he had thought it would be.

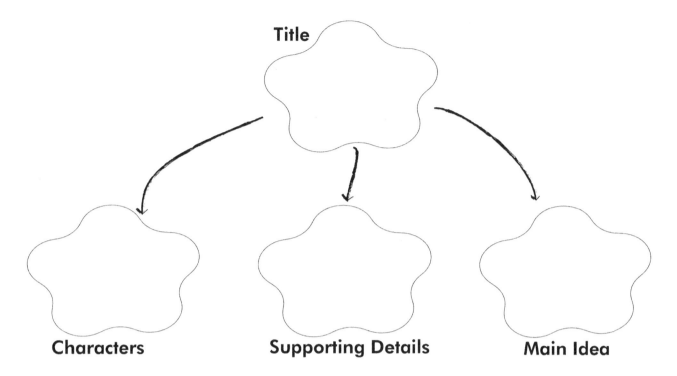

**Title**

**Characters**          **Supporting Details**          **Main Idea**

## 1. What is the theme of the passage?

Ⓐ Dentists are good people so don't worry about visiting them.
Ⓑ Moms usually know best so trust them.
Ⓒ Things are usually not as bad as you think they will be.
Ⓓ An imagination is good but it can make things seem scary sometimes.

## 2. What is the theme of the below passage?

Opal walked into the store not wanting to do what she had planned. She knew when she took the makeup without paying for it that it was wrong. She felt so guilty. She knew she couldn't keep the makeup. So, gathering up all of her courage, she walked over to the security officer and confessed what she had done. He admonished her for shoplifting but let her off with a warning because she had been honest. She felt very relieved.

Ⓐ The unknown can be scary
Ⓑ It is best to be honest
Ⓒ Don't cry over spilled milk
Ⓓ Mom knows best

## 3. What is the theme of the below passage?

Libby's grandmother didn't have much money, so she couldn't buy Libby an expensive present for Christmas like her other grandmother could. She didn't want to buy her a cheap toy that wouldn't last long, but she just couldn't afford the things that were on Libby's wish list. She decided to make Libby a quilt. She was concerned that her granddaughter wouldn't like the gift, but it was the best that she could do.

When Christmas day arrived, Grandmother went to Libby's house. She saw all of the nice gifts that her granddaughter had received. She was worried as Libby began to open her present. Libby squealed with delight when she saw the handmade quilt. She ran and hugged her grandmother and thanked her. She ran and put the new quilt on her bed. The rest of the day she talked about how much she loved the quilt, especially since her grandmother had made it all by hand.

Ⓐ  It is not the cost of the gift that matters but the thought and love put into it.
Ⓑ  Expensive gifts are better than hand-made ones.
Ⓒ  Hand-made gifts are as good as expensive toys.
Ⓓ  Good manners have positive results.

## 4. Which of the following is NOT the theme of this passage?

Ⓐ  It's not the cost of the gift that matters.
Ⓑ  Expensive gifts are better than homemade ones.
Ⓒ  A gift from the heart is valuable.
Ⓓ  A gift made with love is the best gift of all.

## 5. What is the theme of the below passage?

Today was Rhonda's first day at her new school. She was very nervous and wished that she was going back to her old school; but, that was impossible since her family had moved. Although she didn't have many friends at her old school, she would still prefer being back there because she knew the teachers, the routines, and the rules.

The first day, Rhonda met three girls that she really liked. They had all of their classes together, so she spent much of the day with them. But Rhonda's favorite discovery was that this school offered art and music classes; her old school had neither. Rhonda and her new friends had a great time in art that first day. She couldn't wait to go to music tomorrow. Maybe this new school would work out well after all.

Ⓐ  Friends help each other
Ⓑ  Bullying hurts everyone
Ⓒ  Change can be good
Ⓓ  It's OK to be different

## 6. What can you learn from the below passage?

Polly's little brother begged her to read him a story. She told him to go away, that she didn't have time to bother with him. But, a few minutes later, he came back and asked her again. This time, she yelled at him to go away, and she heard him crying as he ran down the hallway. Later, when she went to the family room, her mother told her that she had hurt her brother's feelings. Polly looked over at him and told him that she was sorry. Although she apologized, her little brother's feelings were still hurt; he felt like Polly didn't like to spend time with him. Polly's mom told her that sometimes words were not enough. So, when Polly got his favorite book and asked him to read with her, her little brother smiled and ran to sit by Polly. He hugged her and told her that she was the best big sister a brother could have.

- Ⓐ  Knowledge is power
- Ⓑ  Never give up
- Ⓒ  Face your fears
- Ⓓ  Actions speak louder than words

## Question 7 is based on the story below

**After reading the story, enter the details in the map below. This will help you to answer the questions that follow.**

Karen and Steve were both in Ms. Taylor's math class. Ms. Taylor wasn't very strict about when they had to turn their work in, and Steve took full advantage of that. He always did his homework for his other classes, but he would put off the math assignments thinking he could do them later. However, Karen finished each assignment that Ms. Taylor assigned right away. She had to work a little longer each night, but she didn't want to get marked down for turning in her math homework late. At the end of the semester, Karen and Steve both wanted to go to the amusement park. Ms. Taylor called Steve's mother to let her know about Steve not turning the work in on time, and Steve's mother put Steve on restriction until all of his work was turned in. What a horrible weekend for Steve! Even though he stayed up really late each night, he still couldn't finish everything. The whole time Steve was working, Karen had a great time eating hot dogs at the amusement park, watching movies, and having a great weekend. When they got their report cards, Steve was lucky to get by with a "C" minus in math while Karen got an "A."

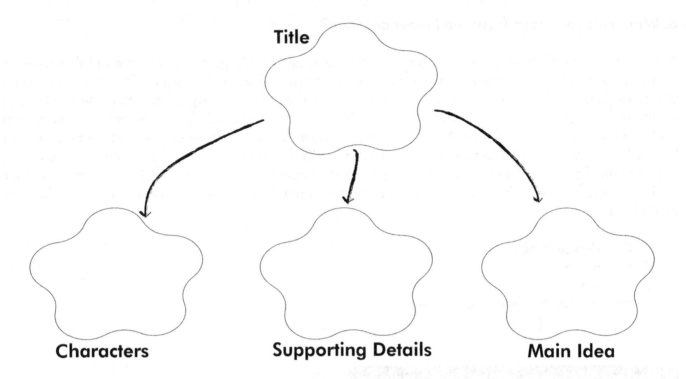

## Title

**Characters**        **Supporting Details**        **Main Idea**

**7. What did Karen and Steve learn from this?**

Ⓐ It doesn't matter when you do it as long as it gets done.
Ⓑ Lazy people are sometimes rewarded with good things.
Ⓒ It's better to do things on time instead of putting them off for later.
Ⓓ Doing things early doesn't help you earn rewards in life.

**Question 8 is based on the story below**

Mr. Toad and Mr. Rabbit were eating at the food court in the shopping mall. Mr. Toad was eating many slices of pizza and drinking a huge soda, and Mr. Rabbit was watching him.

"Hey, Mr. Toad. If you give me some of your pizza, I'll let you have the next fly I find," called out Mr. Rabbit.

Mr. Toad said no, even though he was very full. "I'm sorry, Mr. Rabbit," Mr. Toad said, "but this pizza cost a lot of more so I won't be able to share."

Mr. Rabbit was sad and waited for Mr. Toad to finish. Then they left the mall together. On their way out the door, a hunter saw them and started to chase them. Mr. Toad normally could have escaped, but since he had eaten so much, he was moving quite slowly. The hunter caught Mr. Toad. Mr. Rabbit was able to escape easily.

## 8. What is the theme of the story?

&#9398; It's better to share.
&#9399; If you paid for it, it's all yours.
&#9400; Better late than never
&#9401; Racing can be difficult.

**Question 9 is based on the story below**

Frank studied all of the time, and felt that he was very smart. One day at school, a student from Frank's class asked him if he wanted to play baseball, but Frank said, "I've read all about baseball in books, and it sounds boring. No, thanks."

Another day, a different student asked Frank if he wanted to go for a burger after school. Frank responded, "I've read that burgers are made with beef heart and organ meat. No, thank you."

Frank's classmates were hesitant to ask Frank to hang out. As a result, Frank decided to study about the importance of having friends.

## 9. What would be an appropriate theme for the above passage?

&#9398; It's not nice to be mean to your friends.
&#9399; Friends are always getting in the way.
&#9400; Learning from books is no substitute for real life experience.
&#9401; Friendship gets in the way of learning important things.

## 10. What would be an appropriate theme for the below passage?

A monkey put his hand into a jar of cookies and grasped as many as he could possibly hold. But, when he tried to pull out, his hand wouldn't fit! Unwilling to lose the cookies, and yet unable to pull out his hand, he burst into tears and cried about his situation.

&#9398; The grass is always greener on the other side.
&#9399; Always ask before taking.
&#9400; Don't be greedy.
&#9401; Work now and play later.

## YOUNG NIGHT THOUGHT

All night long and every night,
When my mama puts out the light
I see the people marching by,
As plain as day, before my eye.
Armies and emperors and kings,
All carrying different kinds of things,
And marching in so grand a way,
You never saw the like by day.
So fine a show was never seen
At the great circus on the green;
For every kind of beast and man
Is marching in that caravan.
At first they move a little slow,
But still the faster on they go,
And still beside them close I keep
Until we reach the Town of Sleep.

By Robert Louis Stevenson

**11. What is the poet trying to do with his visions? Write your answer in the box below.**

**Question 12 is based on the poem below**

I found a shell, a curly one;
Lying on the sand.
I picked it up and took it home,
Held tightly in my hand.

Mommy looked at it and then,
She held it to my ear,
And from the shell there came a song
Soft and sweet and clear.

I was surprised, I listened hard,
And it was really true:
If you can find a nice big shell,
You'll hear the singing too.

--Unknown

**12. Choose the most appropriate title for this poem.**

Ⓐ The Singing Shell
Ⓑ The Song
Ⓒ Sea Shells
Ⓓ Sea Shell Song

# CHAPTER 1 → Lesson 4: Summarizing the Text

**1. Choose the best summary of the below text.**

Mary walked quietly through the house so that she would not wake her parents. Before entering the kitchen, she stood and listened. She wanted to make sure that no one had heard her and woken up. She slowly opened the cabinet door, trying to make sure that it didn't squeak. As Mary reached into the cabinet, something warm and furry touched her hand. Mary ran from the kitchen screaming loudly. Her father ran in to see what had happened. He started laughing when he saw their cat Purr Purr sitting quietly in the kitchen cabinet wagging her tail.

Ⓐ  Mary went to the kitchen. She stopped and listened. She opened the cabinet. She screamed. Her dad laughed.

Ⓑ  Mary snuck quietly into the kitchen. When she opened the cabinet, something touched her hand and made her scream. Her dad came to help and discovered it was their cat in the cabinet.

Ⓒ  The cat hid in the cabinet and scared Mary when she reached into it.

Ⓓ  Mary walked into the kitchen after listening to make sure that no one body heard her. She opened the cabinet slowly and felt something touch her. She ran away screaming. She didn't know that it was her cat Purr Purr.

**2. Choose the best summary of the below text.**

I was so scared when I first learned that I would be having my tooth pulled. I didn't sleep at all the night before the procedure. I was terrified that it would hurt more than I could tolerate. I was shaking when I sat in the dentist's chair. He promised me that it would not hurt, but I certainly had my doubts. The dentist gave me some medicine. When I awoke, my tooth was gone, and I didn't remember a thing.

Ⓐ  The writer was scared about having to have a tooth pulled and thought it would hurt. The dentist gave her medicine, and she didn't feel it when her tooth was pulled.

Ⓑ  The writer was scared. She got her tooth pulled. The dentist gave her medicine.

Ⓒ  The dentist gave the writer some medicine so that it wouldn't hurt when her tooth was pulled.

Ⓓ  The writer was scared about having her tooth pulled. She didn't sleep the night before. She was terrified. She was shaking. The dentist gave her medicine. She didn't feel a thing when he pulled her tooth.

### 3. Choose the best summary of the below text.

Huckleberry Hound ran through the yard and into the field next to his house. Suddenly, he put his nose to the ground and started sniffing as he walked. Yep, he definitely smelled a rabbit. He raised his head and howled loudly to let the other dogs know what he had found. Then, he shot after the rabbit like a bolt of lightning. He chased the rabbit for what seemed like hours, but he never caught it. He returned to his yard with his head hanging and his tail tucked between his legs.

 Ⓐ  Huckleberry Hound smelled a rabbit. He chased it for a long time, but never caught it.
 Ⓑ  Huckleberry Hound smelled a rabbit. He ran across the yard to the field. He howled so the other dogs would know he found a rabbit. He shot after the rabbit and chased it for a long time. He didn't catch the rabbit. He went home with his head hung down.
 Ⓒ  Huckleberry Hound chased a rabbit.
 Ⓓ  Huckleberry Hound smelled a rabbit. He put his nose to the ground and followed its trail. He definitely smelled a rabbit. He chased it for a long time. He let the other dogs know he had found a rabbit. He didn't catch the rabbit.

### 4. Summarize the below text using one sentence.

I had been craving chocolate ice cream all day. Finally, the school was over and I could get a huge chocolate ice cream cone. The line was long, but it was worth the wait. The first taste of my ice cream cone was delicious. Then, the worst thing imaginable happened. I bumped into the person behind me and dropped my ice cream cone and it fell on the floor.

 Ⓐ  I craved ice cream all day, but when I finally got a cone I dropped it and it fell on the floor.
 Ⓑ  I craved ice cream all day, but I dropped it.
 Ⓒ  I bought chocolate ice cream, and I bumped into someone and dropped it.
 Ⓓ  The first taste of ice cream was great because I had been craving it all day.

### 5. Summarize the below text using only one sentence.

Opal walked into the store not wanting to do what she had planned. She knew when she took the makeup without paying for it that it was wrong. She felt so guilty. She knew she couldn't keep the makeup. So, gathering up all her courage, she walked over to the security officer and confessed what she had done.

 Ⓐ  Opal was ashamed of what she did, so she returned it.
 Ⓑ  Opal stole some makeup; however, she returned it because she felt guilty.
 Ⓒ  Opal walked to the store, and she returned the make-up.
 Ⓓ  Opal walked to the store, and gathered up her courage because she had stolen some make-up.

## Mary loves writing stories

"The Elephant Who Saw the World," Mary started speaking. It was Friday, and the students had to share their creative writing stories of the week.

Mary loved writing, and this part of the week, when they were able to make up stories for creative writing, was her favorite part. She enjoyed it so much that she became really good at it. When she was home on the weekends and she didn't have much homework, she would sit in her room for hours and create stories to share with her friends and family. Her parents always supported her and were her biggest fans.

However, there was one part about every Friday at school that Mary did not enjoy, and that was when she had to share her story in front of the class. The teacher made all of the children share on Friday afternoons, and this made Mary very nervous. She was shy, and although she knew her teacher was right, she didn't like it.

After sitting and listening to the other children's share, Mary finally heard her name called. She knew it was her turn to share. She got out of her seat slowly, walked to the front of the room and began.

**6. Choose the sentence that best summarizes the passage.**

Ⓐ  The teacher required each student to read their story out loud.
Ⓑ  They were presenting creative short stories as part of their Friday share time.
Ⓒ  Although Mary loved creative writing, she did not enjoy reading her stories out loud.
Ⓓ  Mary agreed that it would be good experience, but she still didn't like it.

**7. Which information is NOT necessary for the summary?**

Ⓐ  Mary enjoyed creating the stories, but when it came to presenting them, she got really nervous.
Ⓑ  She enjoyed writing.
Ⓒ  Writing was a strong point of Mary's.
Ⓓ  Mary wrote at home during her free time.

## 8. What would be the best summary for the passage above?

Ⓐ Mary wrote a story about an elephant who traveled the world. She loved writing stories and was excited when they had to do one for class. The teacher always asked the students to present their stories to the class during Friday share time. This was the part that Mary didn't like. She got really nervous speaking in front of the class although she knew it would be a good experience. When it was her turn, she took a deep breath and started sharing her story.

Ⓑ Mary wrote a story called "The Elephant Who Saw the World." Her family supported her passion for writing stories because she was so good at it. She was excited when the teacher assigned this for class one day.

Ⓒ "The Elephant Who Saw the World," Mary started speaking. It was Friday, and the students had to share their creative writing stories of the week. Mary loved writing, and this part of the week, when they were able to make up stories for creative writing, was her favorite part. She enjoyed it so much that she became really good at it. When she was home on the weekends and she didn't have much homework, she would sit in her room for hours and create stories to share with her friends and family. Her parents always supported her and were her biggest fans. However, there was one part about every Friday at school that Mary did not enjoy, and that was when she had to share her story in front of the class. The teacher made all of the children share on Friday afternoons, and this made Mary very nervous. She was shy, and although she knew her teacher was right, she didn't like it. After sitting and listening to the other children's share, Mary finally heard her name called. She knew it was her turn to share. She got out of her seat slowly, walked to the front of the room and began.

Ⓓ Mary loved writing stories. She wrote one about a donkey traveling the world and had to present it in front of the class. She was nervous about this.

**Question 9 and 10 are based on the passage below**

It was a beautiful day outside. A group of children were playing in the yard. They noticed a bees' nest on the roof, so they started throwing rocks, sticks, and other items to try to knock it down. The nest moved a little, but it didn't fall to the ground. Instead, hundreds of bees flew out going in many directions.

Robert turned and ran away as fast as he could while yelling, "Get down! Get down!" He could hear Louise screaming. Robert dove to the ground as many bees flew over him. He could hear all of the other kids responding in the same way.

The bees' nest was still hanging. John looked around the yard for something really long to use. He noticed his dad's rake sitting by the porch, so he took the rake and ran over to the porch. He swung it as hard as he could, hitting the nest. The nest was dislodged, went flying through the air, and landed near Robert. With a shriek, Robert jumped to his feet and ran to the other side of the yard. The others were also yelping and trying to run away.

**9. What is the best summary for the above passage?**

Ⓐ  John continued throwing things at the nest even after his friends were lying on the ground.

Ⓑ  John wanted to destroy a bees' nest with his friends. They destroyed it and had to try and escape when the bees came flying out of it. Everyone was scared.

Ⓒ  John and his friends were planning to destroy a bees' nest. They started throwing rocks and sticks at the nest. The bees swarmed from the nest, the kids started to run to escape the bees. The nest was still hanging so John knocked it off with a rake. It landed near Robert who jumped up and ran to the other side of the yard.

Ⓓ  John and his friends prepared to destroy a bees' nest. They threw sticks and stones at the nest to knock it off the porch. It didn't work, so John had to do it again. The nest went flying towards Robert who got scared and ran to the other side of the yard.

**10. Which sentence is not necessary for the summary?**

Ⓐ  It was a beautiful day outside.
Ⓑ  The kids wanted to destroy a bees' nest.
Ⓒ  John and his friends tried to run from the bees that came flying out of their nest when the kids hit it.
Ⓓ  Robert yelled, "Get down! Get down!"

### The United States National Parks System

George Catlin, an artist who traveled throughout North America in the 1800's, was one of the first people to be concerned about the westward expansion impact on the beauty of the land being destroyed. He felt that only the government could protect the land and Native Americans by creating a national park.

The popularity of this belief gained national recognition and in 1872 Congress established Yellowstone National Park. This designated public lands to be authorized by the federal government for all to enjoy. The foundation of the system began with President Woodrow Wilson creating the National Parks Service in 1916.

In 1933 by Executive Order, the National Park Service was established to maintain the lands. This transferred the 63 national monuments and military sites from the Forest Service and the War Department to the new service that included areas of beautification, historical, scientific and cultural importance.

Finally in 1970, under the General Authorities Act, Congress made known that all units have legal standing in the national system.

"though distinct in character, are united through their inter-related purposes and resources into one national park system as cumulative expressions of a single national heritage; that, individually and collectively, these areas derive increased national dignity and recognition of their superb environmental quality through their inclusion jointly with each other in one national park system preserved and managed for the benefit and inspiration of all people of the United States..."

Congress now generally makes additions to the National Parks System to add any national parks. Currently there are 376 areas covered by the National Parks System throughout the United States and its holdings. All areas are protected in accordance with the acts of Congress.

**11. Explain in your own words why the artist, George Catlin wanted to preserve the land. Write your answer in the box below.**

## Question 12 is based on the passage below

**Sam Walton**

**Sam Walton (1918-1992)** founded Walmart and Sam's Club.  He opened the first Wal-Mart Discount City in 1962 after having several franchise Ben Franklin stores. His main effort was to market American made products. Although after his death, this practice was not continued. He placed his stores close to distribution centers, thereby having stores in multiple areas, not just in major cities.

He was listed as the richest man in the US from 1982 to 1988. Walmart and Sam's Club stores operate in the US and in 15 other countries including, Canada, Japan, Mexico, and the UK.

## 12. Sam Walton tried to do which of the following with his stores?

Ⓐ  He tried to offer US made products in his chain of stores to help promote US made products and to help the country thrive.

Ⓑ  Walton tried to have more stores than any other chain of discount stores.

Ⓒ  Sam Walton offered his employees many days off and was never open on a holiday.

Ⓓ  Sam Walton made sure that all of his stores were in major cities.

### Question 13 is based on the poem below

**I think that I shall never see**

I think that I shall never see
A poem lovely as a tree.

A tree whose hungry mouth is prest
Against the earth's sweet flowing breast;

A tree that looks at God all day,
And lifts her leafy arms to pray;

A tree that may in summer wear
A nest of robins in her hair;

Upon whose bosom snow has lain;
Who intimately lives with rain.

Poems are made by fools like me,
But only God can make a tree.

Joyce Kilmer

Public domain

13. Who do you think that the poet is comparing a tree to in this poem? Write your answer in the box below.

> (empty answer box)

## Question 14 is based on the story below

### THE THREE GOLDEN APPLES, Part - 2

So he journeyed on and on, still making the same inquiry, until, at last, he came to the brink of a river where some beautiful young women sat twining wreaths of flowers.

"Can you tell me, pretty maidens," asked the stranger, "whether this is the right way to the garden of the Hesperides?"

The young women had been having a fine time together, weaving the flowers into wreaths, and crowning one another's heads. And there seemed to be a kind of magic in the touch of their fingers that made the flowers more fresh and dewy, and of brighter lines, and sweeter fragrance while they played with them than even when they had been growing on their native stems. But, on hearing the stranger's question, they dropped all their flowers on the grass, and gazed at him with astonishment.

"The garden of the Hesperides!" cried one. "We thought mortals had been weary of seeking it, after so many disappointments. And pray, adventurous traveler, what do you want there?"

"A certain king, who is my cousin," replied he, "has ordered me to get him three of the golden apples.

"Most of the young men who go in quest of these apples," observed another of the damsels, "desire to obtain them for themselves, or to present them to some fair maiden whom they love. Do you, then, love this king, your cousin, so very much?"

"Perhaps not," replied the stranger, sighing. "He has often been severe and cruel to me. But it is my destiny to obey him."

"And do you know," asked the damsel who had first spoken, "that a terrible dragon, with a hundred heads, keeps watch under the golden apple-tree?"

"I know it well," answered the stranger, calmly. "But, from my cradle upwards, it has been my business, and almost my pastime, to deal with serpents and dragons."

The young women looked at his massive club, and at the shaggy lion's skin which he wore, and likewise at his heroic limbs and figure; and they whispered to each other that the stranger appeared to be one who might reasonably expect to perform deeds far beyond the might of other men. But, then, the dragon with a hundred heads! What mortal, even if he possessed a hundred lives, could hope to escape the fangs of such a monster? So kind-hearted were the maidens, that they could not bear to see this brave and, handsome traveler attempt what was so very dangerous, and devote himself, most probably, to become a meal for the dragon's hundred ravenous mouths.

"Go back," cried they all,—"go back to your own home! Your mother, beholding you safe and sound, will shed tears of joy; and what can she do more, should you win ever so great a victory? No matter for the golden apples! No matter for the king, your cruel cousin! We do not wish the dragon with the hundred heads to eat you up!"

The stranger seemed to grow impatient at these remonstrances. He carelessly lifted his mighty club, and let it fall upon a rock that lay half buried in the earth, near by. With the force of that idle blow, the great rock was shattered all to pieces. It cost the stranger no more effort to achieve this feat of a giant's strength than for one of the young maidens to touch her sister's rosy cheek with a flower.

## 14. Why did the young women want him to go back home?

**Question 15 is based on the story below**

## THE THREE GOLDEN APPLES, Part - 11
## THE THREE GOLDEN APPLES, By Nathaniel Hawthorne

### Part 11

I know not how long it was before, to his unspeakable joy, he beheld the huge shape of the giant, like a cloud, on the far-off edge of the sea. At his nearer approach, Atlas held up his hand, in which Hercules could perceive three magnificent golden apples, as big as pumpkins, all banging from one branch.

"I am glad to see you again," shouted Hercules, when the giant was within hearing. "So you have got the golden apples?"

"Certainly, certainly," answered Atlas; "and very fair apples they are. I took the finest that grew on the tree, I assure you. Ah! it is a beautiful spot, that garden of the Hesperides. Yes; and the dragon with a hundred heads is a sight worth any man's seeing. After all, you had better have gone for the apples yourself."

"No matter," replied Hercules. "You have had a pleasant ramble, and have done the business as well as I could. I heartily thank you for your trouble. And now, as I have a long way to go, and am rather in haste,—and as the king, my cousin, is anxious to receive the golden apples,—will you be kind enough to take the sky off my shoulders again?"

"Why, as to that," said the giant, chucking the golden apples into the air, twenty miles high, or there-abouts, and catching them as they came down,—"as to that, my good friend, I consider you a little unreasonable. Cannot I carry the golden apples to the king, your cousin, much quicker than you could? As his majesty is in such a hurry to get them, I promise you to take my longest strides. And, besides, I have no fancy for burdening myself with the sky, just now."

Here Hercules grew impatient, and gave a great shrug of his shoulders. It being now twilight, you might have seen two or three stars tumble out of their places. Everybody on earth looked upward in affright, thinking that the sky might be going to fall next.

"O, that will never do!" cried Giant Atlas, with a great roar of laughter. "I have not let fall so many stars within the last five centuries. By the time you have stood there as long as I did, you will begin to learn patience!"

"What!" shouted Hercules, very wrathfully, "do you intend to make me bear this burden forever?"

"We will see about that, one of these days," answered the giant. "At all events, you ought not to complain, if you have to bear it the next hundred years, or perhaps the next thousand. I bore it a good while longer, in spite of the back-ache. Well, then, after a thousand years, if I happen to feel in the mood, we may possibly shift about again. You are certainly a very strong man, and can never have a better opportunity to prove it. Posterity will talk of you, I warrant it!"

"Pish! a fig for its talk!" cried Hercules, with another hitch of his shoulders. "Just take the sky upon your head one instant, will you? I want to make a cushion of my lion's skin, for the weight to rest upon. It really chafes me, and will cause unnecessary inconvenience in so many centuries as I am to stand here."

"That's no more than fair, and I'll do it!" quoth the giant; for he had no unkind feeling towards Hercules, and was merely acting with a too selfish consideration of his own ease. "For just five minutes, then, I'll take back the sky. Only for five minutes, recollect! I have no idea of spending another thousand years as I spent the last. Variety is the spice of life, say I."

Ah, the thick-witted old rogue of a giant! He threw down the golden apples, and received back the sky, from the head and shoulders of Hercules, upon his own, where it rightly belonged. And Hercules picked up the three golden apples, that were as big or bigger than pumpkins, and straightway set out on his journey homeward, without paying the slightest heed to the thundering tones of the giant, who bellowed after him to come back. Another forest sprang up around his feet, and grew ancient there; and again might be seen oak-trees, of six or seven centuries old, that had waxed thus again betwixt his enormous toes.

And there stands the giant, to this day; or, at any rate, there stands a mountain as tall as he, and which bears his name; and when the thunder rumbles about its summit, we may imagine it to be the voice of Giant Atlas, bellowing after Hercules!

## 15. How does the myth end? Mark all that apply.

Ⓐ Hercules held the sky up until Atlas returned.
Ⓑ Atlas agreed to take back the sky for a while.
Ⓒ Hercules was able to get the golden apples that Atlas brought and take them back to the king.
Ⓓ Atlas tricked Hercules and did not return with the golden apples.

# CHAPTER 1 → Lesson 5: Describing Characters

**Question 1 and 2 are based on the story below**

## Timothy

Timothy is a student at my school. He is well-liked by all of the teachers and students. We all know that we can count on Timothy to keep our secrets, to help us if we ask, and to always be on time. We know that he is always honest and expects others to be honest as well.

Last summer, Timothy got a job walking dogs each morning. When school started this year, everyone encouraged him to quit his job, but he decided to keep it. He knew it would be hard to get up every morning at 5 a.m. in order to get all of the dogs walked and then go to school all day. Additionally, he planned to sing in the chorus, play basketball, and be a mentor in the tutoring program this year. He knows it will not be easy, but he thinks his hard work will be worth it. He is trying to save enough money to go to a youth camp next summer.

1. **According to the above passage, which set of adjectives would you choose to describe Timothy?**

    Ⓐ  responsible and depressed
    Ⓑ  trustworthy and thoughtless
    Ⓒ  responsible and ambitious
    Ⓓ  arrogant and unfriendly

2. **Based on the above passage, what do you think Timothy would do if someone asked him to help them cheat on a test?**

    Ⓐ  He would help them cheat but ask them not to tell anyone.
    Ⓑ  He would tell them that cheating is dishonest and encourage them not to do it.
    Ⓒ  He might help them cheat because he doesn't want them to make a bad grade.
    Ⓓ  He might tell them to ask someone else to help them cheat.

## Fred Goes to the Dentist

Fred had never been to the dentist. All of his life he had heard horror stories about the buzzing drills, the huge needles, and the scary tools that the dentist used to torture his patients. Since none of his teeth were hurting, Fred just couldn't understand why his mom was insisting on taking him to the dentist. She told him that it was important to visit the dentist each year to have his teeth checked and cleaned. This seemed silly to Fred because he cleaned his teeth everyday by brushing and flossing them, but nothing would change his mother's mind. He found it hard to believe that she would think it was a good idea to take him somewhere to be tortured. However, he had no choice but to go.

On the way to the dentist, Fred's imagination went wild. He pictured walking into a room with a huge chair that the dentist would strap him to. He could just see the dentist pulling out a huge drill and drilling his tooth while his mother and several others held him in the chair. By the time he got to the dentist's office, he was shaking all over.

Surprisingly, the office was nothing like he expected. The dentist was friendly, and the chair was comfortable. It didn't have any straps. He looked around the room and didn't see any huge drills or torture devices. He was relieved when all the dentist did was look in his mouth, show him how to properly brush and floss his teeth, and give him a balloon. His mom made another appointment to have his teeth cleaned in six months. Maybe this wouldn't be as bad as he had thought it would be.

3. **Based on the passage, how do you think Fred felt about going to his first visit to the dentist?**

   Ⓐ   He was excited and looked forward to it.
   Ⓑ   He was afraid and didn't understand the reason he had to go.
   Ⓒ   He was afraid but wanted to go and see the drills.
   Ⓓ   He felt shy about meeting the dentist.

4. **How do you think Fred felt after seeing the dentist office and meeting the dentist?**

   Ⓐ   scared
   Ⓑ   intimidated
   Ⓒ   relieved
   Ⓓ   joyful

Adam lives with his dad and his older brother Stanley. Adam and Stanley share a room. Most of the time Adam enjoys sharing a room with his brother, but there are times that he wishes he had his own room. Being brothers, they have a lot in common; however, they are different in many ways.

Adam likes to spend time with his friends. If he is not with them, he is texting them or playing games with them online. Adam is always busy. He cannot stand to sit around and do nothing. In fact, the only time he is still is when he is sleeping. Adam plays football, basketball, soccer, and baseball. He loves to be involved in school activities or at the town's youth volunteering center. He spends a lot of his time encouraging people to recycle. Although he loves spending time with his friends, he is willing to give up time with them to help others.

Stanley, on the other hand, loves to stay at home. He enjoys activities that can be done alone such as reading, drawing, and spending time with his dogs. Most days after school he can be found at home enjoying one of his favorite activities. He thinks recycling is important and makes sure his family does it. Although he likes being alone, he enjoys volunteering at the youth center with his brother. He thinks it is important to make a difference in the lives of others, which is the reason that he thinks he would like to be a doctor. Adam and Stanley have some differences, but they do join together to make an impact in their community.

**5. Choose the set of words that best describes Stanley.**

- Ⓐ solitary and caring
- Ⓑ rude and outgoing
- Ⓒ selfish and quiet
- Ⓓ solitary and rude

**6. Based on the passage, how do you think Adam and Stanley feel about one another?**

- Ⓐ They like and respect one another.
- Ⓑ They do not like to spend time together.
- Ⓒ They do not enjoy one another's company.
- Ⓓ They are jealous of each other.

**7. Choose the set of words that best describes Adam.**

- Ⓐ friendly and greedy
- Ⓑ thoughtful and outgoing
- Ⓒ unhappy and mean
- Ⓓ outgoing and greedy

## 8. Which adjective describes how Beau was feeling?

It was the last round of the school spelling bee and only two students were left. Beau's heart was pounding and he was sweating. He began fidgeting with the button on one of his shirt sleeves.

Ⓐ  anxious
Ⓑ  proud
Ⓒ  depressed
Ⓓ  envious

### Question 9 and 10 are based on the story below

Libby's grandmother didn't have much money, so she couldn't buy Libby an expensive present for Christmas like her other grandmother could. She didn't want to buy her a cheap toy that wouldn't last long, but she just couldn't afford the things that were on Libby's wish list. She decided to make Libby a quilt. She was concerned that her granddaughter wouldn't like the gift, but it was the best that she could do.

When Christmas day arrived, Grandmother went to Libby's house. She saw all of the nice gifts that her granddaughter had received. She was worried as Libby began to open her present. Libby squealed with delight when she saw the handmade quilt. She ran and hugged her grandmother and thanked her. She ran and put the new quilt on her bed. The rest of the day she talked about how much she loved the quilt, especially since her grandmother had made it all by hand.

## 9. How would you describe the way Libby's grandmother felt before Libby opened her gift?

Ⓐ  nervous
Ⓑ  kind
Ⓒ  lazy
Ⓓ  angry

## 10. How do you think Libby's grandmother felt after Libby opened the gift?

Ⓐ  sad
Ⓑ  hungry
Ⓒ  angry
Ⓓ  happy

Question 11 is based on the story below

## A Chosen Child

Mary Ann Woods was a bright and happy 10 year old.  She loved playing with her friends outside and working on arts and craft projects with her mother.  Mary Ann even helped her dad out in the yard with the garden, weed eating, mowing, and clipping hedges.  Mary Ann was an only child and often longed to have a baby brother or sister. She truly envied her neighborhood friends that had many siblings.

Her house was just as large as most of the other houses, but several bedrooms were empty.  Not that they didn't have furniture in them, it was that no one lived or slept in the rooms unless guests came for a visit.  Mary Ann liked to go in the rooms and pretend that her make-believe sister lived there.  She would sit on the bed and pretend to be talking to her, smiling and even laughing out loud at times.

While she was doing just that one day, her mom walked down the hall.  She heard talking and laughing, but it wasn't coming from Mary Ann's bedroom.  Puzzled, her mom peered around the corner to one of the guest bedrooms and spotted Mary Ann on the bed looking up to the ceiling.

"Child, what on Earth are you doing?" questioned her mother.

"Oh, sorry, Mom, didn't mean to scare you or mess up the bed." She replied.
"I was talking to Josephine."

"And WHO is Josephine, might I ask?"

"My imaginary sister!"  And with that reply, Mary Ann hopped off the bed and scurried out of the room.

Her mother was in a quandary, as she wondered why Mary Ann would need an imaginary sister, when she had friends galore.  That evening after dinner, Mary Ann's mother told her dad about what had occurred earlier in the day.  "Sam, I am quite concerned about her behaving in this manner. What do you think we should do?"

"Do?  Why do anything, Sheila?  It is normal for kiddos to have pretend friends." Replied Sam, Mary Ann's dad.

"Do you think we need to tell her now? You know we said we would when she got old enough to understand."

Mary Ann's dad breathed a deep sigh and agreed it was time for the dreaded talk.  You see Sheila and Sam couldn't have children and they had adopted Mary Ann when she was only a few days old. The adoption had cost them quite a bit of money. In fact, it was all of their savings at the time.  They were so thrilled to be able to have Mary Ann as their baby, they did not care about the expense. It was only later as Mary Ann grew up when they wanted to adopt another child that they realized it was not feasible with the costs. They had moved into the large house so that Mary Ann could be in a neighborhood full of other children to be her playmates.

How to break the news was on both of their minds as they tried to prepare for bed. As always, Mary Ann had helped with the dishes and was about to make her way upstairs. Her dad asked her to come sit in the living room with him and her mom. Thinking nothing of it, Mary Ann skipped into the room.

"What's up, Dad?"

Her dad began to tell the story of her adoption. Mary Ann sat quietly, face wrinkled, and listened intently to every word. Her mom held one hand and her dad the other. They were both in tears as they explained that due to health reasons, they could not have children of their own. They grinned as they told of how excited they were to be able to adopt her. Words of love and commitment flowed from their mouths. When they had finished, they looked Mary Ann in the eyes and said, "You are our chosen child!"

Mary Ann hugged them both fiercely and exclaimed with her own sigh of relief, "No wonder I do not have brown eyes like either of you! I love being chosen! My turn to choose! So now I choose you, too, forever to be my chosen parents!"

## 11. Part A

**After reading the passage, what type of characteristic traits do you think Mary Ann has? Select all that apply.**

Ⓐ She is a helpful child.
Ⓑ She is a troubled child.
Ⓒ She is a loving child.
Ⓓ She bullies everyone.
Ⓔ She is bright and helpful.

## Part B

**Write a sentence that supports your answer based on the evidence in the story. Write your answer in the box below.**

[ empty answer box ]

**Question 12 is based on the story below**

### THE SECRET GARDEN by Frances Hodgson Burnett - Part 1

### CHAPTER I

### THERE IS NO ONE LEFT

When Mary Lennox was sent to Misselthwaite Manor to live with her uncle everybody said she was the most disagreeable-looking child ever seen. It was true, too. She had a little thin face and a little thin body, thin light hair and a sour expression. Her hair was yellow, and her face was yellow because she had been born in India and had always been ill in one way or another. Her father had held a position under the English Government and had always been busy and ill himself, and her mother had been a great beauty who cared only to go to parties and amuse herself with gay people.

She had not wanted a little girl at all, and when Mary was born she handed her over to the care of an Ayah, who was made to understand that if she wished to please the Mem Sahib she must keep the child out of sight as much as possible. So when she was a sickly, fretful, ugly baby she was kept out of the way, and when she became a sickly, fretful, toddler she was kept out of the way also. She never remembered seeing familiarly anything but the dark faces of her Ayah and the other native servants, and as they always obeyed her and gave her her own way in everything, because the Mem Sahib would be angry if she was disturbed by her crying, by the time she was six years old she was as tyrannical and a selfish little pig as ever lived. The young English governess who came to teach her to read and write disliked her so much that she gave up her place in three months, and when other governesses came to try to fill it they always went away in a shorter time than the first one. So if Mary had not chosen to really want to know how to read books she would never have learned her letters at all.

One frightfully hot morning, when she was about nine years old, she awakened feeling very cross, and she became crosser still when she saw that the servant who stood by her bedside was not her Ayah.

"Why did you come?" she said to the strange woman. "I will not let you stay. Send my Ayah to me." The woman looked frightened, but she only stammered that the Ayah could not come and when Mary threw herself into a passion and beat and kicked her, she looked only more frightened and repeated that it was not possible for the Ayah to come to Missie Sahib.

There was something mysterious in the air that morning. Nothing was done in its regular order and several of the native servants seemed missing, while those whom Mary saw slunk or hurried about with ashy and scared faces. But no one would tell her anything and her Ayah did not come. She was actually left alone as the morning went on, and at last she wandered out into the garden and began to play by herself under a tree near the veranda. She pretended that she was making a flower-bed, and she stuck big scarlet hibiscus blossoms into little heaps of earth, all the time growing more and more angry and muttering to herself the things she would say and the names she would call Saidie when she returned.

"Pig! Pig! Daughter of Pigs!" she said, because to call a native a pig is the worst insult of all.

She was grinding her teeth and saying this over and over again when she heard her mother come out on the veranda with some one. She was with a fair young man and they stood talking together in low strange voices. Mary knew the fair young man who looked like a boy. She had heard that he was a very young officer who had just come from England. The child stared at him, but she stared most at her mother. She always did this when she had a chance to see her, because the Mem Sahib— Mary used to call her that oftener than anything else—was such a tall, slim, pretty person and wore such lovely clothes. Her hair was like curly silk and she had a delicate little nose which seemed to be disdaining things, and she had large laughing eyes. All her clothes were thin and floating, and Mary said they were "full of lace." They looked fuller of lace than ever this morning, but her eyes were not laughing at all. They were large and scared and lifted imploringly to the fair boy officer's face.

"Is it so very bad? Oh, is it?" Mary heard her say. "Awfully," the young man answered in a trembling voice. "Awfully, Mrs. Lennox. You ought to have gone to the hills two weeks ago."

The Mem Sahib wrung her hands.

"Oh, I know I ought!" she cried. "I only stayed to go to that silly dinner party. What a fool I was!" At that very moment such a loud sound of wailing broke out from the servants' quarters that she clutched the young man's arm, and Mary stood shivering from head to foot. The wailing grew wilder and wilder. "What is it? What is it?" Mrs. Lennox gasped.

"Some one has died," answered the boy officer. "You did not say it had broken out among your servants."

"I did not know!" the Mem Sahib cried. "Come with me! Come with me!" and she turned and ran into the house.

**12. The passage describes Mary's characteristics and behavior. Mark all that apply.**

Ⓐ Mary was a sweet quiet child and quite agreeable.
Ⓑ Mary was very spoiled by the servants and selfish.
Ⓒ Mary was ill-tempered and tyrannical.
Ⓓ All of the above.

**Question 13 is based on the fables below**

### The Stag, The Wolf and The Dog

**The Stag at the Pool**

A stag saw his shadow reflected in the water, and greatly admired the size of his horns, but felt angry with himself for having such weak feet. While he was thus contemplating himself, a Lion appeared at the pool. The Stag betook himself to flight, and kept himself with ease at a safe distance from the Lion, until he entered a wood and became entangled with his horns. The Lion quickly came up with him and caught him. When too late he thus reproached himself: "Woe is me! How have I deceived myself! These feet which would have saved me I despised, and I gloried in these antlers which have proved my destruction."

What is most truly valuable is often underrated.

**The Wolf and the Lamb**

A Wolf, meeting with a Lamb astray from the fold, resolved not to lay violent hands on him, but to find some plea, which should justify to the Lamb himself his right to eat him. He then addressed him: "Sirrah, last year you grossly insulted me." "Indeed," bleated the Lamb in a mournful tone of voice, "I was not then born." Then said the Wolf: "You feed in my pasture." "No, good sir," replied the Lamb,

"I have not yet tasted grass." Again said the Wolf: "You drink of my well." "No," exclaimed the Lamb, "I never yet drank water, for as yet my mother's milk is both food and drink to me." On which the Wolf seized him, and ate him up, saying: "Well! I won't remain supperless, even though you refute every one of my imputations."

The tyrant will always find a pretext for his tyranny, and it is useless for the innocent to try by reasoning to get justice, when the oppressor intends to be unjust.

**The Dog, the Rooster and the Fox**

A Dog and a Rooster, traveling together, took shelter at night in a thick wood. The Rooster perched himself on a high branch, while the Dog found a bed at the foot of the tree. When morning dawned, the Rooster, as usual, crowed very loudly. A Fox, hearing the sound, and wishing to make a breakfast on him, came and stood under the branches, saying how earnestly he desired to make the acquaintance of the owner of so sweet voice.

"If you will admit me," said he, "I should very much like to spend the day with you."

The Rooster said: "Sir, do me the favor to go round and wake up my porter, that he may open the door, and let you in." On the Fox approaching the tree, the Dog sprang out and caught him and quickly tore him in pieces.

Those who try to entrap others are often caught by their own schemes.

13. **Now compare all three fables and analyze each character and give an adjective or two to describe them. Write your answer in the box below.**

1. The Stag          2. The Lion          3. The Wolf          4. The Lamb
5. The Rooster       6. The Dog           7. The Fox

## 14. Who are the main characters in the below story? Circle the names.

The Haunted House on Rio Vista Drive

The neighborhood of Rio Vista Drive had two parts to it. On one side of Riverside Avenue were about 14 houses. Each house had approximately three bedrooms, two baths, an extremely grand living area, kitchen, washroom, and most often a small office area. The backyards were all chain linked hurricane fences of around 1.2 acres with a covered garage, back driveway and security locked gate. Most of the front yards were unique to themselves and had a theme which was painted on a plaque on the outside of the house itself. The realtors said that the architect had named each house as he had built it and decorated the fronts to match the names.

However, on the other side of Rio Vista Drive at the end of the block- a dead end, stood a rickety two story house assumed to be about 50-75 years old. This was dubbed the Haunted House. There was an old woman, Widow Crankston, who lived there. The kids say she would come out in the evening and sit on her porch. Several thought they saw her carrying a black cat and presumed she was a witch of sorts. Briars grew up along the fence line and sidewalks. The windows were covered in cobwebs and the like. It had been years and years since the house had been painted or anything in the yard taken care of either. Many a dare had been made among the neighborhood kids to go and ring the doorbell or knock on the door. Most dares were made on Halloween or around that time.

So it was on the night before Halloween that Howard, Ernie and Edward were riding their bikes down Rio Vista Drive. Up one side and down the other, quickly turning around before they reached Widow Crankston's Haunted House! Suddenly, Howard came to a screeching stop right in front of the house.

"Ok, dare ya' to do it!" He hollered at Ernie.
"No, dare you!" Ernie screamed back.
"Scaredy Cats!" Laughed Edward!! "I will do it!"

So off he went, straight up to the front door. He rang the doorbell, but no one answered. Hurriedly he turned around and was running down the steps when he heard a tiny voice behind him.

"Yes, young man, may I help you?" Inquired , as she peeped out the massive door. "Is today Halloween, I thought it was tomorrow. Let me get you some chocolate brownies and a caramel apple. Do your friends want some, too? Haven't had young- ins come here in ages. Please sit on the porch while I get y'all treats and some cold milk."

Edward stopped in his tracks. She wasn't an old witch, but just a kind hearted little old lady. He motioned for Howard and Ernie. Both came running up the sidewalk just in time to eat the goodies!

Now the other kids in the neighborhood aren't sure yet what to think. There are no more briars, no more cobwebs, and the fresh paint on the house looks wonderful. The boys have a part-time job cleaning and painting while enjoying good company and great snacks!

**Question 15 is based on the story below**

### THE THREE GOLDEN APPLES, Part - 5
### THE THREE GOLDEN APPLES, By Nathaniel Hawthorne

Meanwhile, Hercules travelled constantly onward, over hill and dale, and through the solitary woods. Sometimes he swung his club aloft, and splintered a mighty oak with a downright blow. His mind was so full of the giants and monsters with whom it was the business of his life to fight, that perhaps he mistook the great tree for a giant or a monster. And so eager was Hercules to achieve what he had undertaken, that he almost regretted to have spent so much time with the damsels, wasting idle breath upon the story of his adventures. But thus it always is with persons who are destined to perform great things. What they have already done seems less than nothing. What they have taken in hand to do seems worth toil, danger, and life itself.

Persons who happened to be passing through the forest must have been affrighted to see him smite the trees with his great club. With but a single blow, the trunk was riven as by the stroke of lightning, and the broad boughs came rustling and crashing down.

Hastening forward, without ever pausing or looking behind, he by and by heard the sea roaring at a distance. At this sound, he increased his speed, and soon came to a beach, where the great surf-waves tumbled themselves upon the hard sand, in a long line of snowy foam. At one end of the beach, however, there was a pleasant spot, where some green shrubbery clambered up a cliff, making its rocky face look soft and beautiful. A carpet of verdant grass, largely intermixed with sweet-smelling clover, covered the narrow space between the bottom of the cliff and the sea. And what should Hercules espy there, but an old man, fast asleep!

But was it really and truly an old man? Certainly, at first sight, it looked very like one; but, on closer inspection, it rather seemed to be some kind of a creature that lived in the sea. For, on his legs and arms there were scales, such as fishes have; he was web-footed and web-fingered, after the fashion of a duck; and his long beard, being of a greenish tinge, had more the appearance of a tuft of sea-weed than of an ordinary beard. Have you never seen a stick of timber, that has been long tossed about by the waves, and has got all overgrown with barnacles, and, at last drifting ashore, seems to have been thrown up from the very deepest bottom of the sea? Well, the old man would have put you in mind of just such a wave-tost spar! But Hercules, the instant he set eyes on this strange figure, was convinced that it could be no other than the Old One, who was to direct him on his way.

**15. Hercules was a very strong man. Choose from the list below all the details that help support this characteristic.**

Ⓐ  He was destined to perform great things.
Ⓑ  With a single blow he could down trees.
Ⓒ  He should not have wasted his time talking to the maidens.
Ⓓ  All of the above.

# CHAPTER 1 → Lesson 6: Describing the Setting

**Question 1 is based on the story below**

## Alexander the Great

Nearly two thousand five hundred years ago, there lived a king called Alexander the Great. He was the son of Philip II of Macedonia. When Prince Alexander was a boy, a magnificent horse that was for sale was brought to the court of his father. The animal was to be sold for thirteen talents. Talents are ancient coins. Many were eager to buy the horse, but no one could get close enough to saddle the restless animal. He was wild and impossible to ride.

Alexander pleaded with his father to let him try. Realizing that the horse was terrified of its own shadow, he turned the horse towards the sun, so that its shadow fell behind it. This calmed the horse, and the prince proudly rode away. Observing this, his father said, "My son, look for a kingdom worthy of your greatness. Macedonia is too small for you."

That is exactly what Alexander tried to do when he grew up. He fought many battles and always rode Bucephalus (that was the horse's name.) Friendship and trust grew between the man and his horse. When Bucephalus died of wounds received in battle, Alexander was heartbroken and deeply mourned the loss of his horse.

**1. When did this story take place?**

- Ⓐ two thousand five hundred years ago
- Ⓑ two hundred and fifty years ago
- Ⓒ twenty five hundred years ago
- Ⓓ It is happening now

**Question 2 is based on the story below**

## Fred Goes to the Dentist

Fred had never been to the dentist. All of his life he had heard horror stories about the buzzing drills, the huge needles, and the scary tools that the dentist used to torture his patients. Since none of his teeth were hurting, Fred just couldn't understand why his mom was insisting on taking him to the dentist. She told him that it was important to visit the dentist each year to have his teeth checked and cleaned. This seemed silly to Fred because he cleaned his teeth everyday by brushing and flossing them, but nothing would change his mother's mind. He found it hard to believe that she would think it was a good idea to take him somewhere to be tortured. However, he had no choice but to go.

On the way to the dentist, Fred's imagination went wild. He pictured walking into a room with a huge chair that the dentist would strap him to. He could just see the dentist pulling out a huge drill and drilling his tooth while his mother and several others held him in the chair. By the time he got to the dentist's office, he was shaking all over.

Surprisingly, the office was nothing like he expected. The dentist was friendly, and the chair was comfortable. It didn't have any straps. He looked around the room and didn't see any huge drills or torture devices. He was relieved when all the dentist did was look in his mouth, show him how to properly brush and floss his teeth, and give him a balloon. His mom made another appointment to have his teeth cleaned in six months. Maybe this wouldn't be as bad as he had thought it would be.

**2. The setting for the second paragraph of the above passage is probably:**

&#9398; the dentist's office
&#9399; an automobile
&#9400; Fred's home
&#9401; school

### Question 3-5 are based on the story below

Huckleberry Hound ran through the yard and into the field next to his house. Suddenly, he put his nose to the ground and started sniffing as he walked. Yep, he definitely smelled a rabbit. He raised his head and howled loudly to let the other dogs know what he had found. Then, he shot after the rabbit like a bolt of lightning. He chased the rabbit for what seemed like hours, but he never caught it. He returned to his yard with his head hanging and his tail tucked between his legs.

**3. At the beginning of the story, where was Huckleberry Hound?**

&#9398; in the yard
&#9399; in a field
&#9400; on the porch
&#9401; in his kennel

**4. Where did Huckleberry Hound chase the rabbit?**

&#9398; in the yard
&#9399; in a field
&#9400; on the porch
&#9401; in his kennel

**5. Where was Huckleberry Hound at the end of the story?**

Ⓐ in the yard
Ⓑ in a field
Ⓒ on the porch
Ⓓ in his kennel

---

**Question 6 and 7 are based on the story below**

I had been craving chocolate ice cream all day. Finally, the school was over and I could get a huge chocolate ice cream cone. The line was long, but it was worth the wait. The first taste of my ice cream cone was delicious. Then, the worst thing imaginable happened. I bumped into the person behind me and dropped my ice cream cone and it fell on the floor.

**6. Where was the writer of the above passage while she was craving chocolate ice cream?**

Ⓐ at home
Ⓑ at school
Ⓒ at work
Ⓓ at the mall

**7. Where was the writer when she dropped her ice cream on the floor?**

Ⓐ at the ice cream shop
Ⓑ in the park
Ⓒ in her car
Ⓓ at home

---

**Question 8 is based on the story below**

"Dad and I need to go out of town this weekend," said Mom. "We'll be back on Monday, so the three of you are going to spend the weekend with your two aunts. "

Lindsay, Scarlet, and Austin loved their aunts and were really excited. They ran upstairs and started getting their things together to take with them. They put everything in one bag that they would need for school. They were going to stay with Aunt Margaret for two nights and the last night with their Auntie Josephine.

At the end of the school day, the children came running out of classroom doors from all different directions. Aunt Margaret was waiting for her nieces and nephew at the entrance of the school. She was wearing a bright red suit with a sparkly cat pin on it. She also had on a proper wool hat to match. She noticed a scuff on her shoes when her nieces and nephew ran up to her.

She cried, "Oh, my goodness! I am so happy you are here. The children at your school are just a bunch of toughies. I was nearly trampled while I was standing here! Let's get into the car." Aunt Margaret pointed to a large, green, four-door station wagon that was parked in the lot.

The next day, a funny-sounding honk came from the front of the house. The children ran outside and saw Auntie Jo sitting in her convertible. She was wearing a big cowboy hat. She wore a pair of polka dot shorts with a too large shirt.

**8. Where does the end of the story take place?**

    Ⓐ  outside in the yard
    Ⓑ  in the children's bedroom
    Ⓒ  at the children's school
    Ⓓ  at Aunt Margaret's house

**Question 9 is based on the story below**

### Mary loves writing stories

"The Elephant Who Saw the World," Mary started speaking. It was Friday, and the students had to share their creative writing stories of the week.

Mary loved writing, and this part of the week, when they were able to make up stories for creative writing, was her favorite part. She enjoyed it so much that she became really good at it. When she was home on the weekends and she didn't have much homework, she would sit in her room for hours and create stories to share with her friends and family. Her parents always supported her and were her biggest fans.

However, there was one part about every Friday at school that Mary did not enjoy, and that was when she had to share her story in front of the class. The teacher made all of the children share on Friday afternoons, and this made Mary very nervous. She was shy, and although she knew her teacher was right, she didn't like it.

After sitting and listening to the other children's share, Mary finally heard her name called. She knew it was her turn to share. She got out of her seat slowly, walked to the front of the room and began.

**9. Where does the story take place?**

    Ⓐ  Mary's house
    Ⓑ  Mary's school playground
    Ⓒ  Mary's classroom
    Ⓓ  Mary's neighborhood library

It was a beautiful day outside. A group of children were playing in the yard. They noticed a bees' nest on the roof, so they started throwing rocks, sticks, and other items to try to knock it down. The nest moved a little, but it didn't fall to the ground. Instead, hundreds of bees flew out going in many directions.

Robert turned and ran away as fast as he could while yelling, "Get down! Get down!" He could hear Louise screaming. Robert dove to the ground as many bees flew over him. He could hear all of the other kids responding in the same way.

The bees' nest was still hanging. John looked around the yard for something really long to use. He noticed his dad's rake sitting by the porch, so he took the rake and ran over to the porch. He swung it as hard as he could, hitting the nest. The nest was dislodged, went flying through the air, and landed near Robert. With a shriek, Robert jumped to his feet and ran to the other side of the yard. The others were also yelping and trying to run away.

**10. Where does the story take place?**

Ⓐ near a lake
Ⓑ outside in the yard
Ⓒ in the basement of the house
Ⓓ at the school

### The Haunted House on Rio Vista Drive

The neighborhood of Rio Vista Drive had two parts to it. On one side of Riverside Avenue were about 14 houses. Each house had approximately three bedrooms, two baths, an extremely grand living area, kitchen, washroom, and most often a small office area. The backyards were all chain linked hurricane fences of around 1.2 acres with a covered garage, back driveway and security locked gate. Most of the front yards were unique to themselves and had a theme which was painted on a plaque on the outside of the house itself. The realtors said that the architect had named each house as he had built it and decorated the fronts to match the names.

However, on the other side of Rio Vista Drive at the end of the block- a dead end, stood a rickety two story house assumed to be about 50-75 years old. This was dubbed the Haunted House. There was an old woman, Widow Crankston, who lived there. The kids say she would come out in the evening and sit on her porch. Several thought they saw her carrying a black cat and presumed she was a witch of sorts. Briars grew up along the fence line and sidewalks. The windows were covered in cobwebs and the like. It had been years and years since the house had been painted or anything in the yard taken care of either. Many a dare had been made among the neighborhood kids to go and ring the doorbell or knock on the door. Most dares were made on Halloween or around that time.

So it was on the night before Halloween that Howard, Ernie and Edward were riding their bikes down Rio Vista Drive. Up one side and down the other, quickly turning around before they reached Widow Crankston's Haunted House! Suddenly, Howard came to a screeching stop right in front of the house.

"Ok, dare ya' to do it!" He hollered at Ernie.
"No, dare you!" Ernie screamed back.
"Scaredy Cats!" Laughed Edward!! "I will do it!"

So off he went, straight up to the front door. He rang the doorbell, but no one answered. Hurriedly he turned around and was running down the steps when he heard a tiny voice behind him.

"Yes, young man, may I help you?" Inquired Widow Crankston, as she peeped out the massive door. "Is today Halloween, I thought it was tomorrow. Let me get you some chocolate brownies and a caramel apple. Do your friends want some, too? Haven't had young-ins come here in ages. Please sit on the porch while I get y'all treats and some cold milk."

Edward stopped in his tracks. She wasn't an old witch, but just a kind hearted little old lady. He motioned for Howard and Ernie. Both came running up the sidewalk just in time to eat the goodies!

Now the other kids in the neighborhood aren't sure yet what to think. There are no more briars, no more cobwebs, and the fresh paint on the house looks wonderful. The boys have a part-time job cleaning and painting while enjoying good company and great snacks!

**11. What is the setting of the story? Write your answer in the box below.**

### Going Mudding with Dad

Jeff and his dad love to go mudding on their four wheelers. Mudding is great fun, but can be dangerous! Jeff has his own four wheeler, too. It is not as massive as his dad's but can go fast and sling mud everywhere. Mudding has become a sort of sports in the swamp country in Louisiana where they live. So picture this in your mind. A four wheeler with a kid on it going through muddy paths covered in moss and vines. The mud is thick and water is everywhere. Get the picture, if you like mud like they do, it is a blast. The object of mudding is to see who can go the fastest, beat the other "mudders" while getting the most mud and filth on them as well.

There are several things to remember and keep in mind when preparing to drive and while driving four wheelers through mud. First, never go out alone. Buddy up is the best policy. Always wear plenty of clothing. Jeff and his dad wear long sleeve shirts, jeans, and high top hunting boots.

Never go on a four wheeler without wearing a helmet for protection. Most of them have seat belts, so buckle up. Take water or a vitamin sports drink and a healthy snack with you. Keep a first aid kit in your four wheeler, too. If you are going out on a path that has several trails, take strips of cloth and tie on branches along the way to find your way back. Be sure to inspect your vehicle before going out. Check the basic like oil, gas, clean off any mud left before hand and make sure that your vehicle starts and stops when needed. While driving do not turn your four wheeler too sharp at any time as this could cause it to flip over. If the curve ahead of you looks sharp, slow down before you approach, or you might have an accident, as well. Safety is more important than winning or being the muddiest one out there!

Then hit the trails, have fun and enjoy the mud!

**12. Review the list of tips on mudding and mark all that apply.**

Ⓐ Do not worry about going out alone.
Ⓑ Buddy up, buckle up, and wear plenty of clothing.
Ⓒ Take a first aid kit, take water and snacks, mark your path and inspect your vehicle before going out.
Ⓓ Wear a helmet, slow down on sharp curves, and do not turn sharp.
     Do not take snacks or drinks with you.

**Question 13 is based on the story below**

### Disneyworld- Here We Come

It was a hot summer day in June. My grandmother, Mom, my brother Daniel, my cousin Valerie, and I were headed out for a long vacation. We were first going to Mississippi and then on to Florida to Disneyworld. Talk about excitement!!! I couldn't contain myself and didn't sleep much at all the night before. Valerie was visiting us because her mom had gotten sick. My wonderful mom had volunteered for her to stay with us the entire summer. It was so cool. Valerie and I were best friends already, much less best cousins. We did everything together all the time. So having her come along was just another treat for me. Of course, I had rather my little snoopy brother, Daniel, didn't come, but oh well! After all, who can complain when you are going to Disneyworld!

We had to stop in Mississippi to leave my grandmother off at her house before the vacation. That wasn't such a bad idea either, because I loved my grandmother's house, the creek to fish and swim in and all of her things. The night before we had packed everything we needed. I just couldn't get to sleep. Finally I must have fallen asleep because the alarm was going off and everyone was hurrying about the house. Dad had made us breakfast. He couldn't go due to his work schedule, but insisted we go and have fun. He even told me to ride the Teacups for him and the Train!  Dad is such a laugh.

The car was packed, we had double checked everything and were waving goodbye! Another reason for the stop in Mississippi was for rest. It was going to be a long ride to even get that far in one day. Mom turned on the a/c in the car along with the radio and we settled in. She had it on her favorite country music, so we sang along a few songs of Merle Haggard and Johnny Cash.

I must have fallen asleep right after we left the house. The next thing I knew, Mom was waking me up. We had stopped for lunch at a Whataburger restaurant. My favorite, too!  She said to eat hearty as we would not stop again until we reached my grandmother's house. I ate a whole Whataburger with fries and an ice tea. Valerie did, too!  Daniel had a Jr. Whataburger and so did my grandmother. Mom had a salad with chicken. Back in the car, Valerie and I decided to play, I spy. It is loads of fun! I was spying all kinds of things from license plates from Washington to blue jays in trees. Daniel tried to join in but would get mad if we guessed his too quickly. So he got out his video game and played it. Mom had to stop for gas one time right before we made it to the Mississippi state line. We always honk the horn when we cross over into Mississippi, but she said she was not going to do that since it was now getting dark and it might upset other drivers. I have a very smart mom.

### Part 2

Soon enough we were at my grandmother's. Mom had made us pack one light bag with just enough for each of us our night clothes, and a clean outfit for the next day. That way we didn't have to take so much out at my grandmother's house. We were ready for a light soup supper and off to bed.

Before we knew it, it was daylight again. Mom was hustling us out of bed and into the kitchen for breakfast. She said to eat hearty as we had many more miles to go before we reached our final destination. So thankful that my grandmother cooked her best oatmeal for us topped with cinnamon, brown sugar, strawberries, and whipped cream! Who could ask for anything more? Yummy!!

Then it was load back into the car and get on the road. This time Mom found an oldies radio station and she was singing along with Patsy Cline, Tennessee Ernie Ford, and Frank Sinatra. Talk about strange music that none of us knew except her! Valerie and I played a game of travel trivia which was sort of fun and of course, Daniel, was back on his video games!

For lunch we stopped at a roadside park and had the sandwiches our grandmother had packed for us along with an apple and sweet iced tea. When we got back on the road, not a sound could be heard. I figured out later that all of us kids had fallen asleep.

A loud bang woke us as Mom clapped her hands and proclaimed our arrival to the Holiday Inn at Disneyworld! I could not tell you who was the most excited as we were all yelling sounds of glee and running around the car to get our luggage out. Mom registered us for our room and we were giggling uncontrollably.

## Part 3

When we were settled in to our room, Mom explained the sleeping arrangements. Valerie and I would get one of the queen size beds to share, Daniel would get the fold out couch in the living area, and Mom would get the other bed. She said that is night number one, then we will switch on the second night. I love it when my mom thinks of everyone and being fair to all. We were so happy we could have slept on the floor and not minded!! Mom called Dad to let him know we made it safe and sound. Then she called our grandmother, too. She also called Valerie's mom in the hospital so Valerie could talk to her and let her know all was well. Valerie's mom's health was improving daily, too.

Mom ordered pizza for us the first night. We went to bed without any complaining, so excited to be going to Disneyworld the next day!

Mom had picked up a map of the park when she had registered us, so she was busy planning our day while we were falling asleep.

The morning came with a clap and thunder outside of our room. What was going on, we had wondered? Mom explained that it was raining and that we would have breakfast in the hotel lobby and then see what happened. She did tell us that the hotel manager had explained to her that quite often the rains would start and stop during the summers at Kissimmee, Florida. We were not too disappointed after she said that. The hotel offers a free breakfast for everyone. That was definitely a plus in Mom's opinion.

Sure enough after we had eaten the sun came out. The hotel offered a trolley bus to the theme parks, so we opted to take that rather than worrying about parking and walking. Disneyworld stays open all day and late into the evening. Mom said she had mapped out our route to take so we could get to see most everything in our two days along with purchasing us the fast passes to avoid long line delays.

What a cool Mom, right?

## Part 4

The awesome view, the rides, the larger than life Disney characters, people laughing and having fun everywhere. Yes, Welcome to Disneyworld!  First we started following the crowds that were going down the main street with shops galore. Then Mom got out her map and starting us on our route. By lunchtime, we had already seen more than imaginable. We had ridden the Liberty Square Riverboat, gone to the Swiss Family Treehouse, enjoyed the birds at the Enchanted Tiki Room, and countless of stops to listen to theatrical groups perform. Mom had thought of packing a lunch, but had decided against that. We had hot dogs, chips and a soda. Mom said the prices might be a bit high, but it was well worth it!

In the afternoon, the rain began to return, so we went inside a western style dance hall and listened to a group of singers dance and perform. It was really quite entertaining. Then it was time for more rides. Space Mountain was indeed worth it! Scary, and adventurous and well, mostly scary! My little brother couldn't go it and he pouted about that. So we switched directions and went to a kind of petty zoo afterwards, and to ride the Mad Tea Party (Dad's Teacups) to keep him happy. Valerie and I did not mind a bit. Mom steadily had her phone out taking pictures to post and to make copies for us. Needless to say, by the end of the day, we were all exhausted and a little sun burned, too.

Mom said we would stay the second night for the parade and fireworks. She said it was time to call it a day. We all moaned, but happily boarded the trolley back to our hotel. Once at the hotel, we settled for the buffet dinner. They let kids eat free at this hotel if you choose the buffet.

That night we all chatted about the rides and all of the attractions we saw. Mom didn't even have to tell us to go to bed. We bathed and took to the sheets! The morning was just around the corner.

## Part 5

Again on the second day, we had the free breakfast and rode the trolley. It wasn't raining this time at all. Mom got out her map and we began our day. Daniel wanted to go back and ride the Mad Tea Party again, but thankfully Mom said no to that.

We were able to go to Splash Mountain, the Jungle Cruise, the 7 Dwarf's Mine Train and much more. Mom did make a request of her own. She wanted to meet Mickey and Minnie Mouse who were scheduled to appear outside of the Cinderella Castle. She also said she wanted to listen to the Enchanted

Tales with Belle and ride the Prince Charming Regal Carrousel. What a crazy silly Mom!

What we didn't know was that she had a plan. It was right after we left the carrousel that we heard fantastic sounds coming down the main street. Yes, parade time right before our eyes. Mom told us to come and sit. There we were on the side of the castle sitting on the ledge in perfect view of the parade. We asked her how she knew to stop there. She said one of the hotel clerks had told her how to find the spot and when to be there. The parade was magnificent to say the least. The characters actually stopped in front of us and performed. Wow! We couldn't have planned it any better.

After the parade we went to A Pirate's Adventure and Tomorrowland Speedway, andBig Thunder Mountain. Mom said we needed to head toward the front entrance as it was time for fireworks and we needed to be ready. We got there just in time. The lights lit up the sky behind the Cinderella Castle and throughout Disneyworld. Just picture it!

What a perfect ending to our vacation.

**13. In thinking about the entire vacation story, answer the following questions. Arrange the events in order as they happened in the story and write it in the boxes given below.**

A. They were able to see the parade and fireworks.
B. It rained as soon as they got up on their first day at Disneyworld.
C. They stopped off in Mississippi before going to Disneyworld.
D. They had the car packed the night before they left on their vacation.
E. They rode the Liberty Square Riverboat.
F. Mom assigned sleeping arrangements.
G. Mom had to wake the kids when they arrived at the hotel.

1. _____

2. _____

3. _____

4. _____

5. _____

6. _____

7. _____

**Question 14 is based on the story below**

## THE THREE GOLDEN APPLES, Part - 2

So he journeyed on and on, still making the same inquiry, until, at last, he came to the brink of a river where some beautiful young women sat twining wreaths of flowers.

"Can you tell me, pretty maidens," asked the stranger, "whether this is the right way to the garden of the Hesperides?"

The young women had been having a fine time together, weaving the flowers into wreaths, and crowning one another's heads. And there seemed to be a kind of magic in the touch of their fingers that made the flowers more fresh and dewy, and of brighter lines, and sweeter fragrance while they played with them than even when they had been growing on their native stems. But, on hearing the stranger's question, they dropped all their flowers on the grass, and gazed at him with astonishment.

"The garden of the Hesperides!" cried one. "We thought mortals had been weary of seeking it, after so many disappointments. And pray, adventurous traveler, what do you want there?"

"A certain king, who is my cousin," replied he, "has ordered me to get him three of the golden apples."

"Most of the young men who go in quest of these apples," observed another of the damsels, "desire to obtain them for themselves, or to present them to some fair maiden whom they love. Do you, then, love this king, your cousin, so very much?"

"Perhaps not," replied the stranger, sighing. "He has often been severe and cruel to me. But it is my destiny to obey him."

"And do you know," asked the damsel who had first spoken, "that a terrible dragon, with a hundred heads, keeps watch under the golden apple-tree?"

"I know it well," answered the stranger, calmly. "But, from my cradle upwards, it has been my business, and almost my pastime, to deal with serpents and dragons."

The young women looked at his massive club, and at the shaggy lion's skin which he wore, and likewise at his heroic limbs and figure; and they whispered to each other that the stranger appeared to be one who might reasonably expect to perform deeds far beyond the might of other men. But, then, the dragon with a hundred heads! What mortal, even if he possessed a hundred lives, could hope to escape the fangs of such a monster? So kind-hearted were the maidens, that they could not bear to see this brave and, handsome traveler attempt what was so very dangerous, and devote himself, most probably, to become a meal for the dragon's hundred ravenous mouths.

"Go back," cried they all,—"go back to your own home! Your mother, beholding you safe and sound, will shed tears of joy; and what can she do more, should you win ever so great a victory? No matter for the golden apples! No matter for the king, your cruel cousin! We do not wish the dragon with the hundred heads to eat you up!"

The stranger seemed to grow impatient at these remonstrances. He carelessly lifted his mighty club, and let it fall upon a rock that lay half buried in the earth, near by. With the force of that idle blow, the great rock was shattered all to pieces. It cost the stranger no more effort to achieve this feat of a giant's strength than for one of the young maidens to touch her sister's rosy cheek with a flower.

"Do you not believe," said he, looking at the damsels with a smile, "that such a blow would have crushed one of the dragon's hundred heads?"

**14. What were the young women doing when the stranger came upon them? Write your answer in the box below.**

## THE THREE GOLDEN APPLES, Part - 4

Going on with his wonderful narrative, he informed the maidens that as strange an adventure as ever happened was when he fought with Geryon, the six-legged man. This was a very odd and frightful sort of figure, as you may well believe. Any person, looking at his tracks in the sand or snow, would suppose that three sociable companions had been walking along together. On hearing his footsteps at, a little distance, it was no more than reasonable to judge that several people must be coming. But it was only the strange man Geryon clattering onward, with his six legs!

Six legs, and one gigantic body! Certainly, he must have been a very queer monster to look at; and, my stars, what a waste of shoe-leather!

When the stranger had finished the story of his adventures, he looked around at the attentive faces of the maidens.

"Perhaps you may have heard of me before," said he, modestly. "My name is Hercules!"

"We had already guessed it," replied the maidens; "for your wonderful deeds are known all over the world. We do not think it strange, any longer, that you should set out in quest of the golden apples of the Hesperides. Come, sisters, let us crown the hero with flowers!"

Then they flung beautiful wreaths over his stately head and mighty shoulders, so that the lion's skin was almost entirely covered with roses. They took possession of his ponderous club, and so entwined it about with the brightest, softest, and most fragrant blossoms, that not a finger's breadth of its oaken substance could be seen. It looked all like a huge bunch of flowers. Lastly, they joined hands, and danced around him, chanting words which became poetry of their own accord, and grew into a choral song, in honor of the illustrious Hercules.

And Hercules was rejoiced, as any other hero would have been, to know that these fair young girls had heard of the valiant deeds which it had cost him so much toil and danger to achieve. But, still, he was not satisfied. He could not think that what he had already done was worthy of so much honor, while there remained any bold or difficult adventure to be undertaken.

"Dear maidens," said he, when they paused to take breath, "now that you know my name, will you not tell me how I am to reach the garden of the Hesperides?"

"Ah! Must you go so soon?" they exclaimed. "You—that have performed so many wonders, and spent such a toilsome life—cannot you content yourself to repose a little while on the margin of this peaceful river?"

Hercules shook his head.

"I must depart now," said he.

"We will then give you the best directions we can," replied the damsels. "You must go to the sea-shore, and find out the Old One, and compel him to inform you where the golden apples are to be found."

"The Old One!" repeated Hercules, laughing at this odd name. "And, pray, who may the Old One be?"

"Why, the Old Man of the Sea, to be sure!" answered one of the damsels. "He has fifty daughters, whom some people call very beautiful; but we do not think it proper to be acquainted with them, because they have sea-green hair, and taper away like fishes. You must talk with this Old Man of the Sea. He is a sea-faring person, and knows all about the garden of the Hesperides; for it is situated in an island which he is often in the habit of visiting."

Hercules then asked whereabouts the Old One was most likely to be met with. When the damsels had informed him, he thanked them for all their kindness,—for the bread and grapes with which they had fed him, the lovely flowers with which they had crowned him, and the songs and dances wherewith they had done him honor,—and he thanked them, most of all, for telling him the right way,—and immediately set forth upon his Journey.

But, before he was out of hearing, one of the maidens called after him.

"Keep fast hold of the Old-One, when you catch him!" cried she, smiling, and lifting her finger to make the caution more impressive. "Do not be astonished at anything that may happen. Only hold him fast, and he will tell you what you wish to know."

Hercules again thanked her, and pursued his way, while the maidens resumed their pleasant labor of making flower-wreaths. They talked about the hero, long after he was gone.

"We will crown him with the loveliest of our garlands," said they, "when he returns hither with the three golden apples, after slaying the dragon with a hundred heads."

**15. What can you infer that the Old Man of the Sea was known to do when approached? Write your answer in the box below.**

# CHAPTER 1 → Lesson 7: Describing Events

## Question 1 and 2 based on the story below

### Timothy

Timothy is a student at my school. He is well-liked by all of the teachers and students. We all know that we can count on Timothy to keep our secrets, to help us if we ask, and to always be on time. We know that he is always honest and expects others to be honest as well.

Last summer, Timothy got a job walking dogs each morning. When school started this year, everyone encouraged him to quit his job, but he decided to keep it. He knew it would be hard to get up every morning at 5 a.m. in order to get all of the dogs walked and then go to school all day. Additionally, he planned to sing in the chorus, play basketball, and be a mentor in the tutoring program this year. He knows it will not be easy, but he thinks his hard work will be worth it. He is trying to save enough money to go to a youth camp next summer.

1. According to the above passage, Timothy is saving his money for what upcoming event?

   Ⓐ  a football game
   Ⓑ  a chorus trip
   Ⓒ  youth camp
   Ⓓ  a basketball game

2. Timothy gets up at 5 a.m. every morning to:

   Ⓐ  practice basketball
   Ⓑ  walk dogs
   Ⓒ  do his homework
   Ⓓ  tutor a classmate

## Question 3-5 are based on the story below

After reading the story, enter the details in the map below. This will help you to answer the questions that follow.

### Fred Goes to the Dentist

Fred had never been to the dentist. All of his life he had heard horror stories about the buzzing drills, the huge needles, and the scary tools that the dentist used to torture his patients. Since none of his teeth were hurting, Fred just couldn't understand why his mom was insisting on taking him to the dentist. She told him that it was important to visit the dentist each year to have his teeth checked and cleaned. This seemed silly to Fred because he cleaned his teeth everyday by brushing and flossing them, but nothing would change his mother's mind. He found it hard to believe that she would think it was a good idea to take him somewhere to be tortured. However, he had no choice but to go.

On the way to the dentist, Fred's imagination went wild. He pictured walking into a room with a huge chair that the dentist would strap him to. He could just see the dentist pulling out a huge drill and drilling his tooth while his mother and several others held him in the chair. By the time he got to the dentist's office, he was shaking all over.

Surprisingly, the office was nothing like he expected. The dentist was friendly, and the chair was comfortable. It didn't have any straps. He looked around the room and didn't see any huge drills or torture devices. He was relieved when all the dentist did was look in his mouth, show him how to properly brush and floss his teeth, and give him a balloon. His mom made another appointment to have his teeth cleaned in six months. Maybe this wouldn't be as bad as he had thought it would be.

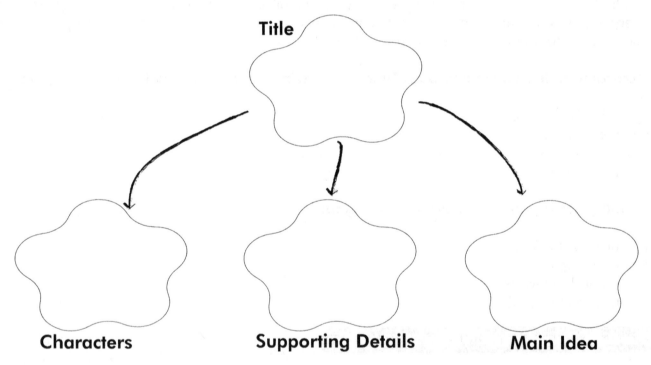

**3. Which detail shows that Fred is worried about going to the dentist?**

    Ⓐ  "To his surprise, the office was nothing like he expected."
    Ⓑ  "Since none of his teeth were hurting, Fred just couldn't understand the reason that his mom was insisting on taking him to a dentist."
    Ⓒ  "By the time he got to the dentist he was shaking all over."
    Ⓓ  "Maybe this wouldn't be as bad as he thought it would be."

**4. What did Fred imagine was going to happen to him at the dentist office?**

Ⓐ The dentist would pull a tooth and then give him a balloon.
Ⓑ The dentist would tie him to the chair and use a huge drill on him.
Ⓒ His mother would hold him down, and the dentist would clean his teeth.
Ⓓ The dentist would tie him down and floss his teeth.

**5. What actually happened at the dentist office?**

Ⓐ The dentist showed him how to brush and floss his teeth.
Ⓑ The dentist pulled a tooth.
Ⓒ The dentist drilled his tooth.
Ⓓ The dentist pulled a tooth and gave him a balloon.

## Question 6 is based on the story below

Adam lives with his dad and his older brother Stanley. Adam and Stanley share a room. Most of the time Adam enjoys sharing a room with his brother, but there are times that he wishes he had his own room. Being brothers, they have a lot in common; however, they are different in many ways.

Adam likes to spend time with his friends. If he is not with them, he is texting them or playing games with them online. Adam is always busy. He cannot stand to sit around and do nothing. In fact, the only time he is still is when he is sleeping. Adam plays football, basketball, soccer, and baseball. He loves to be involved in school activities or at the town's youth volunteering center. He spends a lot of his time encouraging people to recycle. Although he loves spending time with his friends, he is willing to give up time with them to help others.

Stanley, on the other hand, loves to stay at home. He enjoys activities that can be done alone such as reading, drawing, and spending time with his dogs. Most days after school he can be found at home enjoying one of his favorite activities. He thinks recycling is important and makes sure his family does it. Although he likes being alone, he enjoys volunteering at the youth center with his brother. He thinks it is important to make a difference in the lives of others, which is the reason that he thinks he would like to be a doctor. Adam and Stanley have some differences, but they do join together to make an impact in their community.

**6. According to the passage, what do Adam and Stanley enjoy doing together?**

Ⓐ Playing football
Ⓑ Drawing cartoons
Ⓒ Playing video games
Ⓓ Volunteering at the youth center

### Mary loves writing stories

"The Elephant Who Saw the World," Mary started speaking. It was Friday, and the students had to share their creative writing stories of the week.

Mary loved writing, and this part of the week, when they were able to make up stories for creative writing, was her favorite part. She enjoyed it so much that she became really good at it. When she was home on the weekends and she didn't have much homework, she would sit in her room for hours and create stories to share with her friends and family. Her parents always supported her and were her biggest fans.

However, there was one part about every Friday at school that Mary did not enjoy, and that was when she had to share her story in front of the class. The teacher made all of the children share on Friday afternoons, and this made Mary very nervous. She was shy, and although she knew her teacher was right, she didn't like it.

After sitting and listening to the other children's share, Mary finally heard her name called. She knew it was her turn to share. She got out of her seat slowly, walked to the front of the room and began.

**7. Which event in the above passage made Mary nervous?**

Ⓐ   writing a story
Ⓑ   talking to the teacher
Ⓒ   sharing her work in front of the class
Ⓓ   showing her family what she had done

"Dad and I need to go out of town this weekend," said Mom. "We'll be back on Monday, so the three of you are going to spend the weekend with your two aunts. "

Lindsay, Scarlet, and Austin loved their aunts and were really excited. They ran upstairs and started getting their things together to take with them. They put everything in one bag that they would need for school. They were going to stay with Aunt Margaret for two nights and the last night with their Auntie Josephine.

At the end of the school day, the children came running out of classroom doors from all different directions. Aunt Margaret was waiting for her nieces and nephew at the entrance of the school. She was wearing a bright red suit with a sparkly cat pin on it. She also had on a proper wool hat to match. She noticed a scuff on her shoes when her nieces and nephew ran up to her.

She cried, "Oh, my goodness! I am so happy you are here. The children at your school are just a bunch of toughies. I was nearly trampled while I was standing here! Let's get into the car." Aunt Margaret pointed to a large, green, four-door station wagon that was parked in the lot.

The next day, a funny-sounding honk came from the front of the house. The children ran outside and saw Auntie Jo sitting in her convertible. She was wearing a big cowboy hat. She wore a pair of polka dot shorts with a too large shirt.

## 8. What most likely happened to Aunt Margaret while she was waiting for her nieces and nephew?

Ⓐ The children ambushed her while she was waiting in the parking lot.
Ⓑ She was in a bad mood already and called the children "toughies" for no reason.
Ⓒ Mean spirited children knocked her down because she was a stranger.
Ⓓ The school children were excited that school was out and they bumped into her in their hurry to get home and to after school activities.

## 9. Why did the children need to stay with their two aunts?

Ⓐ Their parents needed to hang decorations around the house.
Ⓑ Their parents were celebrating their anniversary.
Ⓒ Their parents needed to go out of town.
Ⓓ Their parents needed to help their little brother Austin go shopping for school.

## Question 10 is based on the passage below

This year Jim and I had the most wonderful vacation compared to the one we took last year. This year Jim and I went to Hawaii, which is a much better place to visit than a hunting lodge in Alaska. The hotel we stayed in was a luxury suite. It included a big screen TV with all of the movie channels, a hot tub on the balcony, a small kitchen stocked with local fruits and vegetables, and a huge bed shaped like a pineapple. The weather in Hawaii could not have been any better. We enjoyed many hours on the beach sunbathing and playing volleyball. When we were not on the beach, we were in the ocean swimming or riding the waves on a surf board. Each night we enjoyed eating and dancing with all of our friends at a luau. Our week in Hawaii rushed by, making us wish we had planned a two-week vacation.

On the other hand, the hunting lodge we stayed in Alaska had no TV, a shower with barely warm water, a small cooler for our food, and cots to sleep on each night. The room wasn't even the worst part of the vacation. The weather was terrible. It rained the entire time we were there. Even with the rain, our guide expected us to go on the all-day fishing trip that was part of our vacation package. All we caught on that fishing trip was a cold from the rain. After the third day, we decided to cut our trip short and head for home. Without a doubt, we will be going back to Hawaii next year on our vacation.

**10.** **What event in the above passage caused the writer to catch a cold?**

Ⓐ A day of surfing
Ⓑ Attending a luau
Ⓒ Swimming
Ⓓ Fishing in the rain

**Question 11 is based on the story below**

## The Mall - What Fun

Santiago and Felix wanted to go to the mall on Saturday. They had both saved up their money from lawn mowing and yard work. Each had been working for 3 weeks on Saturdays and Sunday afternoons to earn money. Their favorite place in the mall was around the food court and video arcade.

Santiago's older sister, Felicia, offered to drive them since she was going to get her hair done at Pro-Cuts there anyway. Felicia told them to be ready by her car at 9:45 Saturday morning. The mall opened at 10:00 and it would take them about 15 minutes or so to get there. Felix had a tendency to be late all the time, so Santiago was a little worried that he wouldn't show up on time. Santiago had a plan to make sure that didn't happen this time.

He asked his mother on Friday after school, if Felix could spend the night. Luckily she agreed if they didn't stay up late and if he cleaned his room before Felix came over. So Santiago quickly called Felix to see if he could come over and spend the night. Felix was elated! "Sure thing, buddy! I will be there in a jiffy!"

"Don't come too soon, I have to clean my room! Mama made me promise to do it!" Santiago said. "No worries, dude, I can help." Felix replied.

So it was set. Santiago did ask his mama if Felix could help him clean his room. His mama just laughed and said, "Sure, you boys are so silly."

As soon as Felix got there, the boys started on their room cleaning project. This gave Felicia an idea, too.

"Guys, if I am giving you a ride to the mall tomorrow, how about cleaning my room, too?"
"No way! Not a girl's room!!" They both exclaimed at the same exact time.
"Oh, well, can't blame a girl for trying!" Laughed Felicia. "Don't worry, I will still take you."

That night the boys played video games and watched a combat movie. About 10:30pm, Santiago remembered what his mama said about not staying up late. He told Felix, "We better get to bed, Mama said not to stay up late if you came over."

"No problem, let's hit the sack," Said Felix.

The next morning, they were up, bathed, dressed, and had eaten breakfast by the time Felicia was ready to go.

"Wow, on time both of you and ready. This must be a special mall day for y'all!" She said.

When they got to the mall, Felicia told them to be sure to keep an eye on their watches. She also told them to meet her back at the door they came in exactly at 12:30.  Her hair appointment would take one hour and then she wanted to meet friends to shop, as well.  The boys agreed.

Their first stop was the video arcade where they met up with other friends and started playing games. It wasn't long before Felix wanted to go get a snack at the food court. You could say Felix liked food. He wasn't over weight or anything, he just liked to eat. Santiago was in the middle of a game and said he would be there shortly.  Well, you guessed it, shortly didn't happen.  Felix had his snack and waited for about 30 minutes for Santiago to show up. He didn't know what to do.  So he headed back to the video arcade. He did notice that his watch showed it to be 12:10.  They only had 20 minutes left and they had not even gone to any shops.  Felix felt a sick feeling that he better find Santiago fast or Felicia would not be happy. She might not ever take them again if they did not make it back on time. Felix started almost running around a corner and splat!  He ran right into Santiago!

"What took you so long, dude?  I had my snack and waited on you forever!" Felix said in a bit of a disgruntled voice.

"My fault, all my fault!  I was beating the game and didn't want to stop!  Sorry. You are my best friend and I feel bad for letting you down." Replied Santiago.

"No worries, we better get going back to the door we came in at and meet Felicia." Said Felix.

When they got to the meeting place, Felicia was just walking up.

"Hey guys, y'all want to stay longer?" She said.

The guys grinned and nodded yes.

"Great, meet me here at 2:30.  I am going to the movies with my friends. I already called Mama to let her know we would be staying longer."

Happily the boys went to shop with their money, bought new sneakers, ate lunch and even got to play video games again.

11. **Sequence the events in order as they happened. Write the steps in the correct sequence in the boxes given below.**

    **A.** Santiago and Felix get to go to the shops and eat lunch.
    **B.** Felicia tells the boys to meet her back at 12:30.
    **C.** Mama allows Santiago to have Felix over to spend the night.
    **D.** The boys clean Santiago's bedroom and do not stay up late.
    **E.** Santiago forgets to meet Felix at the food court and Felix waits for him.

1.

2.

3.

4.

5.

**Question 12 is based on the story below**

### The Haunted House on Rio Vista Drive

The neighborhood of Rio Vista Drive had two parts to it. On one side of Riverside Avenue were about 14 houses. Each house had approximately three bedrooms, two baths, an extremely grand living area, kitchen, washroom, and most often a small office area. The backyards were all chain linked hurricane fences of around 1.2 acres with a covered garage, back driveway and security locked gate. Most of the front yards were unique to themselves and had a theme which was painted on a plaque on the outside of the house itself. The realtors said that the architect had named each house as he had built it and decorated the fronts to match the names.

However, on the other side of Rio Vista Drive at the end of the block- a dead end, stood a rickety two story house assumed to be about 50-75 years old. This was dubbed the Haunted House. There was an old woman, Widow Crankston, who lived there. The kids say she would come out in the evening and sit on her porch. Several thought they saw her carrying a black cat and presumed she was a witch of sorts. Briars grew up along the fence line and sidewalks. The windows were covered in cobwebs and the like. It had been years and years since the house had been painted or anything in the yard taken care of either. Many a dare had been made among the neighborhood kids to go and ring the doorbell or knock on the door.  Most dares were made on Halloween or around that time.

So it was on the night before Halloween that Howard, Ernie and Edward were riding their bikes down Rio Vista Drive.  Up one side and down the other, quickly turning around before they reached Widow Crankston's Haunted House!  Suddenly, Howard came to a screeching stop right in front of the house.

"Ok, dare ya' to do it!"  He hollered at Ernie.

"No, dare you!"  Ernie screamed back.

"Scaredy Cats!"  Laughed Edward!!  "I will do it!"

So off he went, straight up to the front door. He rang the doorbell, but no one answered.  Hurriedly he turned around and was running down the steps when he heard a tiny voice behind him.

"Yes, young man, may I help you?" Inquired Widow Crankston, as she peeped out the massive door.  "Is today Halloween, I thought it was tomorrow.  Let me get you some chocolate brownies and a car-amel apple.  Do your friends want some, too?  Haven't had young- ins come here in ages.  Please sit on the porch while I get y'all treats and some cold milk."

Edward stopped in his tracks.  She wasn't an old witch, but just a kind hearted little old lady.  He motioned for Howard and Ernie.  Both came running up the sidewalk just in time to eat the goodies!

Now the other kids in the neighborhood aren't sure yet what to think.  There are no more briars, no more cobwebs, and the fresh paint on the house looks wonderful. The boys have a part-time job cleaning and painting while enjoying good company and great snacks!

**12. Write the sequence of events in the story in the correct order in the boxes given below.**

    **A**. The boys help paint the house and fix it up.
    **B**. Edward decides to take the dare.
    **C**. The house is in bad shape with briars, cobwebs, and needs painting.
    **D**. It is the night before Halloween.
    **E**. Widow Crankston offers them treats to eat and cold milk to drink.
    **F**. There are two parts of Rio Vista Drive.
    **G**. Some kids believe Widow Crankston is a witch because of her black cat.

**1.** (                                                              )

**2.** (                                                              )

**3.** (                                                              )

4. 

5. 

6. 

7. 

Question 13 is based on the story below

### The Case of the Missing Lasagna

It was a bright and sunny afternoon at Everton Middle School. Fourth-grade students were returning from lunch. The tardy bell was about to ring. Mr. Hart sat at his teacher's desk with a smudged red stain on the sleeve of his shirt, while Mrs. Waterton told students to find their seats.

"Best lunch I can remember eating in a long time!" Mr. Hart exclaimed. "What was it like for the cafeteria lunch today?" He didn't get a reply from the students. Instead they all just looked at him rather puzzled by that comment.

Out of the blue, Mr. Smith, the Principal, called on the intercom system. He asked Mrs. Waterton to come to the office. When she returned, she asked Mr. Hart to step outside of the classroom. She then told him that Ms. Abernathy's lunch had gone missing, had he seen anything since he had been in her room right before lunch.

Mr. Hart had an astonished look on his face as he quickly returned to the classroom. It was then that he went to his desk and picked up his lunch bag. Splat on the floor went the contents of his bag, 2 lettuce wraps and a banana. "Hmmm," he said to the class while laughing, "Got any ideas about where a missing plate of lasagna for Ms. Abernathy could have gone?"

13. Part A

Consider all of the evidence in the story and determine who you think might have taken Ms. Abernathy's lunch.

List the pieces of evidence from the story that make you think that. Write your answer in the box below.

Part B

Why do these pieces of evidence make you think that this person took Ms. Abernathy's lunch? Explain and Write your answer in the box below.

## Question 14 is based on the story below

### A Chosen Child

Mary Ann Woods was a bright and happy 10 year old.  She loved playing with her friends outside and working on arts and craft projects with her mother.  Mary Ann even helped her dad out in the yard with the garden, weed eating, mowing, and clipping hedges.  Mary Ann was an only child and often longed to have a baby brother or sister. She truly envied her neighborhood friends that had many siblings.

Her house was just as large as most of the other houses, but several bedrooms were empty.  Not that they didn't have furniture in them, it was that no one lived or slept in the rooms unless guests came for a visit.  Mary Ann liked to go in the rooms and pretend that her make-believe sister lived there.  She would sit on the bed and pretend to be talking to her, smiling and even laughing out loud at times.

While she was doing just that one day, her mom walked down the hall.  She heard talking and laughing, but it wasn't coming from Mary Ann's bedroom.  Puzzled, her mom peered around the corner to one of the guest bedrooms and spotted Mary Ann on the bed looking up to the ceiling.

"Child, what on Earth are you doing?" questioned her mother.
"Oh, sorry, Mom, didn't mean to scare you or mess up the bed." She replied.
"I was talking to Josephine."
"And WHO is Josephine, might I ask?"

"My imaginary sister!"  And with that reply, Mary Ann hopped off the bed and scurried out of the room.

Her mother was in a quandary, as she wondered why Mary Ann would need an imaginary sister, when she had friends galore.  That evening after dinner, Mary Ann's mother told her dad about what had occurred earlier in the day.  "Sam, I am quite concerned about her behaving in this manner. What do you think we should do?"

"Do?  Why do anything, Sheila?  It is normal for kiddos to have pretend friends." Replied Sam, Mary Ann's dad.

"Do you think we need to tell her now?  You know we said we would when she got old enough to understand."

Mary Ann's dad breathed a deep sigh and agreed it was time for the dreaded talk.  You see Sheila and Sam couldn't have children and they had adopted Mary Ann when she was only a few days old. The adoption had cost them quite a bit of money. In fact, it was all of their savings at the time.  They were so thrilled to be able to have Mary Ann as their baby, they did not care about the expense.  It was only later as Mary Ann grew up when they wanted to adopt another child that they realized it was not feasible with the costs. They had moved into the large house so that Mary Ann could be in a neighborhood full of other children to be her playmates.

How to break the news was on both of their minds as they tried to prepare for bed. As always, Mary Ann had helped with the dishes and was about to make her way upstairs. Her dad asked her to come sit in the living room with him and her mom. Thinking nothing of it, Mary Ann skipped into the room.

"What's up, Dad?"

Her dad began to tell the story of her adoption. Mary Ann sat quietly, face wrinkled, and listened intently to every word. Her mom held one hand and her dad the other. They were both in tears as they explained that due to health reasons, they could not have children of their own. They grinned as they told of how excited they were to be able to adopt her. Words of love and commitment flowed from their mouths. When they had finished, they looked Mary Ann in the eyes and said, "You are our chosen child!"

Mary Ann hugged them both fiercely and exclaimed with her own sigh of relief, "No wonder I do not have brown eyes like either of you! I love being chosen! My turn to choose! So now I choose you, too, forever to be my chosen parents!"

**14. Sequence arrange the events of the story in order in the boxes given below.**

    A. Mary Ann is an only child.
    B. Mary Ann's parents tell her she is adopted.
    C. Mary Ann likes to go into the empty bedrooms, and pretend her make believe sister lives there.
    D. Mary Ann's mother is worried about her behavior.
    E. Mary Ann skipped into the living room.

1. (    )

2. (    )

3. (    )

4. (    )

5. (    )

**Question 15 is based on the story below**

**Disneyworld- Here We Come! Part - V**

Again on the second day, we had the free breakfast and rode the trolley. It wasn't raining this time at all. Mom got out her map and we began our day.  Daniel wanted to go back and ride the Mad Tea Party again, but thankfully Mom said no to that.

We were able to go to Splash Mountain, the Jungle Cruise, the 7 Dwarf's Mine Train and much more. Mom did make a request of her own. She wanted to meet Mickey and Minnie Mouse who were scheduled to appear outside of the Cinderella Castle. She also said she wanted to listen to the Enchanted Tales with Belle and ride the Prince Charming Regal Carrousel.   What a crazy silly Mom!

What we didn't know was that she had a plan. It was right after we left the carrousel that we heard fantastic sounds coming down the main street.  Yes, parade time right before our eyes. Mom told us to come and sit. There we were on the side of the castle sitting on the ledge in perfect view of the parade.  We asked her how she knew to stop there.  She said one of the hotel clerks had told her how to find the spot and when to be there. The parade was magnificent to say the least.  The characters actually stopped in front of us and performed.  Wow!  We couldn't have planned it any better.

After the parade we went to A Pirate's Adventure and Tomorrowland Speedway, and Big Thunder Mountain.  Mom said we needed to head toward the front entrance as it was time for fireworks and we needed to be ready.  We got there just in time. The lights lit up the sky behind the Cinderella Castle and throughout Disneyworld.  Just picture it!

What a perfect ending to our vacation

15. **Explain the events that led up to them being able to see the parade from a wonderful view. Be sure to use details from the story to support your evidence. Write your answer in the box below.**

## CHAPTER 1 → Lesson 8: Figurative Language

**1. Identify the simile used in the below sentence.**

Her eyes twinkled like diamonds as she looked lovingly at her new kitten.

Ⓐ her eyes twinkled
Ⓑ as she looked lovingly
Ⓒ at her new kitten
Ⓓ twinkled like diamonds

**2. Identify the metaphor in the below sentence.**

Elaine has no sympathy for others. You know she has a heart of stone.

Ⓐ no sympathy for others
Ⓑ a heart of stone
Ⓒ no sympathy
Ⓓ she has a heart

**3. Identify the sentence that contains a metaphor.**

Ⓐ She is as sweet as sugar.
Ⓑ She is as blind as a bat.
Ⓒ The sound of the chirping birds is music to my ears.
Ⓓ Billy is as stubborn as a mule.

**4. Suzy eats like a bird.**

**This simile means that Suzy:**

Ⓐ eats nuts and seeds
Ⓑ eats many large meals
Ⓒ eats while flying
Ⓓ eats very little

## 5. The metaphor in the below sentence compares his wife to:

My wife is my compass that guides me to the correct paths in life.

Ⓐ  a passage
Ⓑ  compass
Ⓒ  a guide
Ⓓ  life

## 6. The metaphor in this sentence is used to let you know that the car:

I really got a bad deal on the used car I bought. That <u>car was a real lemon</u>.

Ⓐ  was a good buy
Ⓑ  had a very low price
Ⓒ  was yellow
Ⓓ  didn't run well

## 7. Choose the answer that contains a simile.

Ⓐ  Your room is a pig pen. How do you even find your bed?
Ⓑ  It has rained cats and dogs all day long. I wish the rain would stop.
Ⓒ  Our math home work was a breeze.
Ⓓ  I could not eat Susan's biscuits because they were as hard as a rock.

## 8. Janice is such an angel means that Janice:

Ⓐ  is mean
Ⓑ  is annoying
Ⓒ  is kind
Ⓓ  has wings

## 9. Jimmy is an ox.

### The metaphor 'is an ox' means what?

Ⓐ  He is weak.
Ⓑ  He is blind.
Ⓒ  He is strong.
Ⓓ  He is deaf.

**10. What is the metaphor in the sentence below?**

Linda is a road hog. She drives too fast.

Ⓐ She drives too fast.
Ⓑ Linda is a road hog.
Ⓒ Linda is.
Ⓓ She drives.

Question 11 is based on the story below

### Disneyworld Here We Come! Part -II

Soon enough we were at my grandmother's. Mom had made us pack one light bag with just enough for each of us our night clothes, and a clean outfit for the next day. That way we didn't have to take so much out at my grandmother's house. We were ready for a light soup supper and off to bed.
Before we knew it, it was daylight again. Mom was hustling us out of bed and into the kitchen for breakfast. She said to eat hearty as we had many more miles to go before we reached our final destination. So thankful that my grandmother cooked her best oatmeal for us topped with cinnamon, brown sugar, strawberries, and whipped cream! Who could ask for anything more? Yummy!!
Then it was load back into the car and get on the road. This time Mom found an oldies radio station and she was singing along with Patsy Cline, Tennessee Ernie Ford, and Frank Sinatra. Talk about strange music that none of us knew except her! Valerie and I played a game of travel trivia which was sort of fun and of course, Daniel, was back on his video games!

For lunch we stopped at a roadside park and had the sandwiches our grandmother had packed for us along with an apple and sweet iced tea. When we got back on the road, not a sound could be heard. I figured out later that all of us kids had fallen asleep.

A loud bang woke us as Mom clapped her hands and proclaimed our arrival to the Holiday Inn at Disneyworld! I could not tell you who was the most excited as we were all yelling sounds of glee and running around the car to get our luggage out. Mom registered us for our room and we were giggling uncontrollably.

92

LumosLearning.com

## 11. Select and write from the following list of words.

out of control/unable to stop
strong/healthy
hurrying
something to wear

### Part A

**What do you think the following words mean based on the story?**

hustling means _____

### Part B
outfit means _____

### Part C
uncontrollably means _____

### Part D
hearty means _____

## GRAINS, GRAINS, GRAINS

Everyone knows that grains are an important healthy part of a good diet.  It is important to make sure that you are eating the right amount of grains daily.

To make sure this happens include grains in half of your diet each day. Whole grain and wheat help to keep your digestive system in order and run smoothly as well.

Did you know that whole grains and whole grain foods are made up of all three layers of the grain seed or kernel?

Here are the layers and explanations that will help you to understand.

1. The bran (outer layer): give you all of the fiber as well as B vitamins; minerals such as magnesium, iron and zinc, and some protein.

2. The endosperm (middle layer): makes up for most of the weight of the grain and is made up mainly of carbohydrate and protein.

3. The germ (inner layer): has B vitamins, unsaturated fats, vitamin E, and minerals.

Most whole grains are quite tasty such as brown rice, barley, whole oats or oatmeal, wheat and rye breads.

When you go shopping with your parents, do the healthy choice thing and read labels.

Whole grain foods will have the words 'whole' or 'whole grain' followed by the name of the grain as one of the first ingredients.

## 12. Match the term with its definition

|  | germ (inner layer) | endosperm (middle layer) | bran (outer layer) |
| --- | --- | --- | --- |
| the weight of the grain |  |  |  |
| the fiber |  |  |  |
| unsaturated fats |  |  |  |

**Question 13 is based on the story below**

## THE THREE GOLDEN APPLES
### By Nathaniel Hawthorne

### Part - 3

Then he sat down on the grass, and told them the story of his life, or as much of it as he could remember, from the day when he was first cradled in a warrior's brazen shield. While he lay there, two immense serpents came gliding over the floor, and opened their hideous jaws to devour him; and he, a baby of a few months old, had griped one of the fierce snakes in each of his little fists, and strangled them to death. When he was but a stripling, he had killed a huge lion, almost as big as the one whose vast and shaggy hide he now wore upon his shoulders. The next thing that he had done was to fight a battle with an ugly sort of monster, called a hydra, which had no less than nine heads, and exceedingly sharp teeth in every one of them.

"But the dragon of the Hesperides, you know," observed one of the damsels, "has a hundred heads!"

"Nevertheless," replied the stranger, "I would rather fight two such dragons than a single hydra. For, as fast as I cut off a head, two others grew in its place; and, besides, there was one of the heads that could not possibly be killed, but kept biting as fiercely as ever, long after it was cut off. So I was forced to bury it under a stone, where it is doubtless alive, to this vary day. But the hydra's body, and its eight other heads, will never do any further mischief."

The damsels, judging that the story was likely to last a good while, had been preparing a repast of bread and grapes, that the stranger might refresh himself in the intervals of his talk. They took pleasure in helping him to this simple food; and, now and then, one of them would put a sweet grape between her rosy lips, lest it should make him bashful to eat alone.

The traveler proceeded to tell how he had chased a very swift stag, for a twelve-month together, without ever stopping to take breath, and had at last caught it by the antlers, and carried it home alive. And he had fought with a very odd race of people, half horses and half men, and had put them all to death, from a sense of duty, in order that their ugly figures might never be seen any more. Besides all this, he took to himself great credit for having cleaned out a stable.

"Do you call that a wonderful exploit?" asked one of the young maidens, with a smile. "Any clown in the country has done as much!"

"Had it been an ordinary stable," replied the stranger, "I should not have mentioned it. But this was so gigantic a task that it would have taken me all my life to perform it, if I had not luckily thought of turning the channel of a river through the stable-door. That did the business in a very short time!"

Seeing how earnestly his fair auditors listened, he next told them how he had shot some monstrous birds, and had caught a wild bull alive, and let him go again, and had tamed a number of very wild horses, and had conquered Hippolyta, the warlike queen of the Amazons. He mentioned, likewise, that he had taken off Hippolyta's enchanted girdle, and had given it to the daughter of his cousin, the king.

"Was it the girdle of Venus," inquired the prettiest of the damsels, "which makes women beautiful?" "No," answered the stranger. "It had formerly been the sword-belt of Mars; and it can only make the wearer valiant and courageous."

"An old sword-belt!" cried the damsel, tossing her head. "Then I should not care about having it!" "You are right," said the stranger.

**13. The stranger told the damsels (young women) many things about his life and his strength. Mark all answers that apply to his story.**

   Ⓐ  He killed snakes as a baby.
   Ⓑ  He killed a lion as a young child.
   Ⓒ  He killed a monster with many heads.
   Ⓓ  He had been to the garden but forgot how to get back there.

**Question 14 is based on the story below**

### THE THREE GOLDEN APPLES, Part - 4

Going on with his wonderful narrative, he informed the maidens that as strange an adventure as ever happened was when he fought with Geryon, the six-legged man. This was a very odd and frightful sort of figure, as you may well believe. Any person, looking at his tracks in the sand or snow, would suppose that three sociable companions had been walking along together. On hearing his footsteps at, a little distance, it was no more than reasonable to judge that several people must be coming. But it was only the strange man Geryon clattering onward, with his six legs!

Six legs, and one gigantic body! Certainly, he must have been a very queer monster to look at; and, my stars, what a waste of shoe-leather!

When the stranger had finished the story of his adventures, he looked around at the attentive faces of the maidens.

"Perhaps you may have heard of me before," said he, modestly. "My name is Hercules!"

"We had already guessed it," replied the maidens; "for your wonderful deeds are known all over the world. We do not think it strange, any longer, that you should set out in quest of the golden apples of the Hesperides. Come, sisters, let us crown the hero with flowers!"

Then they flung beautiful wreaths over his stately head and mighty shoulders, so that the lion's skin was almost entirely covered with roses. They took possession of his ponderous club, and so entwined it about with the brightest, softest, and most fragrant blossoms, that not a finger's breadth of its oaken substance could be seen. It looked all like a huge bunch of flowers. Lastly, they joined hands, and danced around him, chanting words which became poetry of their own accord, and grew into a choral song, in honor of the illustrious Hercules.

And Hercules was rejoiced, as any other hero would have been, to know that these fair young girls had heard of the valiant deeds which it had cost him so much toil and danger to achieve. But, still, he was not satisfied. He could not think that what he had already done was worthy of so much honor, while there remained any bold or difficult adventure to be undertaken.

"Dear maidens," said he, when they paused to take breath, "now that you know my name, will you not tell me how I am to reach the garden of the Hesperides?"

"Ah! Must you go so soon?" they exclaimed. "You—that have performed so many wonders, and spent such a toilsome life—cannot you content yourself to repose a little while on the margin of this peaceful river?"

Hercules shook his head.

"I must depart now," said he.

"We will then give you the best directions we can," replied the damsels. "You must go to the sea-shore, and find out the Old One, and compel him to inform you where the golden apples are to  be found."

"The Old One!" repeated Hercules, laughing at this odd name. "And, pray, who may the Old One be?"

"Why, the Old Man of the Sea, to be sure!" answered one of the damsels. "He has fifty daughters, whom some people call very beautiful; but we do not think it proper to be acquainted with them, because they have sea-green hair, and taper away like fishes. You must talk with this Old Man of the Sea. He is a sea-faring person, and knows all about the garden of the Hesperides; for it is situated in an island which he is often in the habit of visiting."

Hercules then asked whereabouts the Old One was most likely to be met with. When the damsels had informed him, he thanked them for all their kindness,—for the bread and grapes with which they had fed him, the lovely flowers with which they had crowned him, and the songs and dances wherewith they had done him honor,—and he thanked them, most of all, for telling him the right way,—and immediately set forth upon his Journey.

But, before he was out of hearing, one of the maidens called after him.

"Keep fast hold of the Old-One, when you catch him!" cried she, smiling, and lifting her finger to make the caution more impressive. "Do not be astonished at anything that may happen. Only hold him fast, and he will tell you what you wish to know."

Hercules again thanked her, and pursued his way, while the maidens resumed their pleasant labor of making flower-wreaths. They talked about the hero, long after he was gone.

"We will crown him with the loveliest of our garlands," said they, "when he returns hither with the three golden apples, after slaying the dragon with a hundred heads."

**14. Who was this stranger?**

---

**Question 15 is based on the story below**

### THE THREE GOLDEN APPLES, Part - 7

It was in this journey, if I mistake not, that he encountered a prodigious giant, who was so wonderfully contrived by nature, that, every time he touched the earth, he became ten times as strong as ever he had been before. His name was Antreus. You may see, plainly enough, that it was a very difficult business to fight with such a fellow; for, as often as he got a knock-down blow, up he started again, stronger, fiercer, and abler to use his weapons, than if his enemy had let him alone, Thus, the harder Hercules pounded the giant with his club, the further be seemed from winning the victory. I have sometimes argued with such people, but never fought with one. The only way in which Hercules found it possible to finish the battle, was by lifting Antreus off his feet into the air, and squeezing, and squeezing, and squeezing him, until, finally, the strength was quite squeezed out of his enormous body.

When this affair was finished, Hercules continued his travels, and went to the land of Egypt, where he was taken prisoner, and would have been put to death, if he had not slain the king of the country, and made his escape. Passing through the deserts of Africa, and going as fast as he could, he arrived at last on the shore of the great ocean. And here, unless he could walk on the crests of the billows, it seemed as if his journey must needs be at an end.

Nothing was before him, save the foaming, dashing, measureless ocean. But, suddenly, as he looked towards the horizon, he saw something, a great way off, which he had not seen the moment before. It gleamed very brightly, almost as you may have beheld the round, golden disk of the sun, when it rises or sets over the edge of the world.

It evidently drew nearer; for, at every instant, this wonderful object became larger and more lustrous. At length, it had come so nigh that Hercules discovered it to be an immense cup or bowl, made either of gold or burnished brass. How it had got afloat upon the sea, is more than I can tell you. There it was, at all events, rolling on the tumultuous billows, which tossed it up and down, and heaved their foamy tops against its sides, but without ever throwing their spray over the brim.

"I have seen many giants, in my time," thought Hercules, "but never one that would need to drink his wine out of a cup like this!"

And, true enough, what a cup it must have been! It was as large—as large—but, in short, I am afraid to say how immeasurably large it was. To speak within bounds, it was ten times larger than a great mill-wheel; and, all of metal as it was, it floated over the heaving surges more lightly than an acorn-cup adown the brook. The waves tumbled it onward, until it grazed against the shore, within a short distance of the spot where Hercules was standing.

As soon as this happened, he knew what was to be done; for he had not gone through so many re-markable adventures without learning pretty well how to conduct himself, whenever anything came to pass a little out of the common rule. It was just as clear as daylight that this marvellous cup had been set adrift by some unseen power, and guided hitherward, in order to carry Hercules across the sea, on his way to the garden of the Hesperides. Accordingly, without a moment's delay, he clambered over the brim, and slid down on the inside, where, spreading out his lion's skin, he proceeded to take a little repose. He had scarcely rested, until now, since he bade farewell to the damsels on the margin of the river. The waves dashed, with a pleasant and ringing sound, against the circumference of the hollow cup; it rocked lightly to and fro, and the motion was so soothing that, it speedily rocked Hercules into an agreeable slumber.

**15. Use vocabulary from the story to complete the following sentences.**

   **The cup had been set _____ by some unseen power and guided _____, in order to carry Hercules across the sea, on his way to the garden of the _____.**

## CHAPTER 1 → Lesson 9: Text Structure

**1. Which text structure is used in the classic story "The Three Little Pigs?"**

- Ⓐ  Cause and effect
- Ⓑ  Compare and contrast
- Ⓒ  Problem and solution
- Ⓓ  Sequence

**2. What is the structure of the below text?**

I saw the most unusual chair in a furniture store today while walking around the mall. The chair was shaped like a high-heeled shoe. The seat was created from the toe of the shoe, and the high heel and back of the shoe created the chair's back. Hot pink velvet covered the top portion of the chair. Black velvet covered the bottom and heel of the chair. Along the sides of the toes and heel, huge rhinestones were glued to the velvet. I wonder who would want this type of chair.

- Ⓐ  Cause and effect
- Ⓑ  Compare and contrast
- Ⓒ  Problem and solution
- Ⓓ  Description

### Question 3 is based on the story below

"Dad and I need to go out of town this weekend," said Mom. "We'll be back on Monday, so the three of you are going to spend the weekend with your two aunts. "

Lindsay, Scarlet, and Austin loved their aunts and were really excited. They ran upstairs and started getting their things together to take with them. They put everything in one bag that they would need for school. They were going to stay with Aunt Margaret for two nights and the last night with their Auntie Josephine.

At the end of the school day, the children came running out of classroom doors from all different directions. Aunt Margaret was waiting for her nieces and nephew at the entrance of the school. She was wearing a bright red suit with a sparkly cat pin on it. She also had on a proper wool hat to match. She noticed a scuff on her shoes when her nieces and nephew ran up to her.

She cried, "Oh, my goodness! I am so happy you are here. The children at your school are just a bunch of toughies. I was nearly trampled while I was standing here! Let's get into the car." Aunt Margaret pointed to a large, green, four-door station wagon that was parked in the lot.

LumosLearning.com

The next day, a funny-sounding honk came from the front of the house. The children ran outside and saw Auntie Jo sitting in her convertible. She was wearing a big cowboy hat. She wore a pair of polka dot shorts with a too large shirt.

## 3. What is the structure of the text?

Ⓐ  a play
Ⓑ  a comedy
Ⓒ  a poem
Ⓓ  a narrative

## 4. What is the structure of the below text?

Before going to bed on Friday night, Susie's parents told her that they had a surprise planned for the weekend and that she would have to wake up really early on Saturday morning. When she woke up, they left the house quickly and started driving. While in the car, Susie looked outside to see if she could figure out where they were going. She noticed that it was getting really hot out and the sun was shining brightly. Then she noticed that the surfboards were in the car. Finally, they stopped, and Susie said, "I know where we are going!"

Ⓐ  Cause and effect
Ⓑ  Problem and solution
Ⓒ  Sequence
Ⓓ  Description

## 5. What is the structure of the below text?

One day James went to town to buy new clothes. First, he tried on a pair of trousers. He didn't like the trousers, so he gave them back to the shopkeeper. Then, he tried on a robe which was the same price as the trousers. James was pleased with the robe, and he left the shop. Before he climbed on his donkey to ride home, the shopkeeper and the shop-assistant ran out.

Ⓐ  Descriptive
Ⓑ  Problem and solution
Ⓒ  Cause and effect
Ⓓ  Sequence

## 6. What is the text structure of this passage?

Beau was a nine-year-old boy who wanted a pet dog very badly. Every day, he asked his parents for a dog. They always told him no, because they didn't think he was responsible enough to take care of a dog. One day, Beau negotiated with his parents. He told them that he would keep his room clean and do other household chores for an entire month to prove he was responsible enough to have a pet. Beau did exactly as he promised, and his parents got him a fluffy, white puppy that he named Snow White.

   Ⓐ  Description
   Ⓑ  Cause and effect
   Ⓒ  Compare and contrast
   Ⓓ  Problem and solution

### Question 7 is based on the passage below

The blue whale is quite an extraordinary creature. To begin with, it is a mammal that lives its entire life in the ocean. The size of its body is amazing. This whale can grow up to 98 feet long and weigh as much as 200 tons, making it the largest known animal to have ever existed. Its body is long and elegantly tapered, unlike other whales which have a rounder, stockier build. Their build, along with their extreme size, gives them a unique appearance and the ability to move more gracefully and at greater speeds than one might imagine. They can reach speeds up to 31 mph for short periods. Their normal traveling speed is around 12 mph, but they slow to 3.1 mph when feeding. Although they are extremely large animals, they eat small shrimp-like creatures called krill. Since the krill are so small, the blue whale eats about four tons daily as they swim deep in the ocean.

Unlike other whales that live in small, close-knit groups called pods, blue whales live and travel alone or with one other whale. While traveling through the ocean, they surface to breathe air into their lungs through blowholes. They emerge from the ocean, spewing water out of their blowhole, roll, and re-enter the water with a grand splash of their large tail. They make loud, deep, and rumbling low-frequency sounds that travel great distances, which allow them to communicate with other whales as far as 100 miles away. Their cries can be felt as much as heard. Their resonating call makes them the loudest animal on Earth. If you ever have the opportunity to see or hear a blue whale, it will be an experience you will not soon forget.

## 7. What is the structure of the text in the first paragraph of this passage?

   Ⓐ  Descriptive
   Ⓑ  Compare and contrast
   Ⓒ  Problem and solution
   Ⓓ  Sequence or chronological

## 8. What is the structure of the below text?

When I was little my mom gave me a diary. She told me that it was something really personal and special and I could use it to write down all of my thoughts and ideas. She said that some famous people kept diaries and when they died, their diary was published into a book. Anne Frank is someone who did this. She was originally from Germany. During the time of World War II, the Nazi soldiers were in power in Germany; they did not like Jews. Anne and her family were Jewish so they had to hide. They went to Amsterdam in the Netherlands. Her diary tells the story of the time when they lived in hiding in concealed rooms in Amsterdam.

- Ⓐ Chronological
- Ⓑ Cause and Effect
- Ⓒ Descriptive
- Ⓓ Problem and Solution

### Question 9 is based on the passage below

This year Jim and I had the most wonderful vacation. Especially, compared to the one we took last year. We went to Hawaii, which was a better place to visit than last year's hunting lodge in Alaska. The hotel we stayed in was a luxury suite; it included a big screen TV with all of the movie channels, a hot tub on the balcony, a small kitchen stocked with local fruits and vegetables, and a huge bed shaped like a pineapple. The weather in Hawaii was superb. We enjoyed many hours on the beach sunbathing and playing volleyball. When we were not on the beach, we were in the ocean swimming or riding the waves on a surf board. Each night we enjoyed eating and dancing with all of our friends at a luau. Our week in Hawaii rushed by, making us wish we had planned a two-week vacation. Without a doubt, we will be going back to Hawaii next year for our vacation.

The hunting lodge in Alaska had a shower with hardly any warm water, a small cooler for our food, and cots to sleep on each night. But, the room wasn't even the worst part of the vacation. The weather was terrible; it rained the entire time we were there.  Even with the rain, our guide expected us to go on an all-day fishing trip that was part of our vacation package. All we caught on that fishing trip was a cold from the rain.  After the third day in Alaska, we decided to end our nightmare, cut our trip short, and head for home.

## 9. Choose the text structure used in this passage.

- Ⓐ Cause and effect
- Ⓑ Compare and contrast
- Ⓒ Problem and solution
- Ⓓ Sequence

## 10. What is the structure of the below text?

A science book might have a lesson about a child who catches an illness from germs that are spread. The child has to see a doctor who cures the illness. Then the Physician tells the child how to prevent the illness in the future. The child learns about hand-washing as one way to prevent disease.

Ⓐ Cause and effect
Ⓑ Compare and contrast
Ⓒ Problem and solution
Ⓓ Sequence or chronological

### Question 11 is based on the story below

### The Mall - What Fun

Santiago and Felix wanted to go to the mall on Saturday. They had both saved up their money from lawn mowing and yard work. Each had been working for 3 weeks on Saturdays and Sunday afternoons to earn money. Their favorite place in the mall was around the food court and video arcade.

Santiago's older sister, Felicia, offered to drive them since she was going to get her hair done at Pro-Cuts there anyway. Felicia told them to be ready by her car at 9:45 Saturday morning. The mall opened at 10:00 and it would take them about 15 minutes or so to get there. Felix had a tendency to be late all the time, so Santiago was a little worried that he wouldn't show up on time. Santiago had a plan to make sure that didn't happen this time.

He asked his mother on Friday after school, if Felix could spend the night. Luckily she agreed if they didn't stay up late and if he cleaned his room before Felix came over. So Santiago quickly called Felix to see if he could come over and spend the night. Felix was elated! "Sure thing, buddy! I will be there in a jiffy!"

"Don't come too soon, I have to clean my room! Mama made me promise to do it!" Santiago said. "No worries, dude, I can help." Felix replied.

So it was set. Santiago did ask his mama if Felix could help him clean his room. His mama just laughed and said, "Sure, you boys are so silly."

As soon as Felix got there, the boys started on their room cleaning project. This gave Felicia an idea, too.

"Guys, if I am giving you a ride to the mall tomorrow, how about cleaning my room, too?"

"No way! Not a girl's room!!" They both exclaimed at the same exact time.

"Oh, well, can't blame a girl for trying!" Laughed Felicia. "Don't worry, I will still take you."

That night the boys played video games and watched a combat movie. About 10:30pm, Santiago remembered what his mama said about not staying up late. He told Felix, "We better get to bed, Mama said not to stay up late if you came over."

"No problem, let's hit the sack," Said Felix.

The next morning, they were up, bathed, dressed, and had eaten breakfast by the time Felicia was ready to go.

"Wow, on time both of you and ready. This must be a special mall day for y'all!" She said.

When they got to the mall, Felicia told them to be sure to keep an eye on their watches. She also told them to meet her back at the door they came in exactly at 12:30. Her hair appointment would take one hour and then she wanted to meet friends to shop, as well. The boys agreed.

Their first stop was the video arcade where they met up with other friends and started playing games. It wasn't long before Felix wanted to go get a snack at the food court. You could say Felix liked food. He wasn't over weight or anything, he just liked to eat. Santiago was in the middle of a game and said he would be there shortly. Well, you guessed it, shortly didn't happen. Felix had his snack and waited for about 30 minutes for Santiago to show up. He didn't know what to do. So he headed back to the video arcade. He did notice that his watch showed it to be 12:10. They only had 20 minutes left and they had not even gone to any shops. Felix felt a sick feeling that he better find Santiago fast or Felicia would not be happy. She might not ever take them again if they did not make it back on time. Felix started almost running around a corner and splat! He ran right into Santiago!

"What took you so long, dude? I had my snack and waited on you forever!" Felix said in a bit of a disgruntled voice.

"My fault, all my fault! I was beating the game and didn't want to stop! Sorry. You are my best friend and I feel bad for letting you down." Replied Santiago.

"No worries, we better get going back to the door we came in at and meet Felicia." Said Felix.

When they got to the meeting place, Felicia was just walking up.

"Hey guys, y'all want to stay longer?" She said.

The guys grinned and nodded yes.

"Great, meet me here at 2:30. I am going to the movies with my friends. I already called Mama to let her know we would be staying longer."

Happily the boys went to shop with their money, bought new sneakers, ate lunch and even got to play video games again.

**11. How did Felicia save the day for the boys?**

  **Write a sentence in the box below using evidence from the story to support your answer.**

---

**Question 12 is based on the story below**

### Disneyworld- Here We Come! Part - I

It was a hot summer day in June. My grandmother, Mom, my brother Daniel, my cousin Valerie, and I were headed out for a long vacation. We were first going to Mississippi and then on to Florida to Disneyworld. Talk about excitement!!! I couldn't contain myself and didn't sleep much at all the night before. Valerie was visiting us because her mom had gotten sick. My wonderful mom had volunteered for her to stay with us the entire summer. It was so cool. Valerie and I were best friends already, much less best cousins. We did everything together all the time. So having her come along was just another treat for me. Of course, I had rather my little snoopy brother, Daniel, didn't come, but oh well! After all, who can complain when you are going to Disneyworld!

We had to stop in Mississippi to leave my grandmother off at her house before the vacation. That wasn't such a bad idea either, because I loved my grandmother's house, the creek to fish and swim in and all of her things. The night before we had packed everything we needed. I just couldn't get to sleep. Finally I must have fallen asleep because the alarm was going off and everyone was hurrying about the house. Dad had made us breakfast. He couldn't go due to his work schedule, but insisted we go and have fun. He even told me to ride the Teacups for him and the Train! Dad is such a laugh.

The car was packed, we had double checked everything and were waving goodbye! Another reason for the stop in Mississippi was for rest. It was going to be a long ride to even get that far in one day. Mom turned on the a/c in the car along with the radio and we settled in. She had it on her favorite country music, so we sang along a few songs of Merle Haggard and Johnny Cash. I must have fallen asleep right after we left the house. The next thing I knew, Mom was waking me up. We had stopped for lunch at a Whataburger restaurant. My favorite, too! She said to eat hearty as we would not stop again until we reached my grandmother's house. I ate a whole Whataburger with fries and an ice tea. Valerie did, too! Daniel had a Jr. Whataburger and so did my grandmother. Mom had a salad with chicken. Back in the car, Valerie and I decided to play, I spy. It is loads of fun! I was spying all kinds of things from license plates from Washington to blue jays in trees. Daniel tried to join in but would get mad if we guessed his too quickly. So he got out his video game and played it. Mom had to stop for gas one time right before we made it to the Mississippi state line. We always honk the horn when we cross over into Mississippi, but she said she was not going to do that since it was now getting dark and it might upset other drivers. I have a very smart mom.

**12. Write a sentence that tells why the author is not too upset about her little brother going on vacation. Write your answer in the box below.**

**Question 13 is based on the story below**

## THE THREE GOLDEN APPLES, Part - 2

So he journeyed on and on, still making the same inquiry, until, at last, he came to the brink of a river where some beautiful young women sat twining wreaths of flowers.

"Can you tell me, pretty maidens," asked the stranger, "whether this is the right way to the garden of the Hesperides?"

The young women had been having a fine time together, weaving the flowers into wreaths, and crowning one another's heads. And there seemed to be a kind of magic in the touch of their fingers that made the flowers more fresh and dewy, and of brighter lines, and sweeter fragrance while they played with them than even when they had been growing on their native stems. But, on hearing the stranger's question, they dropped all their flowers on the grass, and gazed at him with astonishment.

"The garden of the Hesperides!" cried one. "We thought mortals had been weary of seeking it, after so many disappointments. And pray, adventurous traveler, what do you want there?"

"A certain king, who is my cousin," replied he, "has ordered me to get him three of the golden apples."

"Most of the young men who go in quest of these apples," observed another of the damsels, "desire to obtain them for themselves, or to present them to some fair maiden whom they love. Do you, then, love this king, your cousin, so very much?"

"Perhaps not," replied the stranger, sighing. "He has often been severe and cruel to me. But it is my destiny to obey him."

"And do you know," asked the damsel who had first spoken, "that a terrible dragon, with a hundred heads, keeps watch under the golden apple-tree?"

"I know it well," answered the stranger, calmly. "But, from my cradle upwards, it has been my business, and almost my pastime, to deal with serpents and dragons."

The young women looked at his massive club, and at the shaggy lion's skin which he wore, and likewise at his heroic limbs and figure; and they whispered to each other that the stranger appeared to be one who might reasonably expect to perform deeds far beyond the might of other men. But, then, the dragon with a hundred heads! What mortal, even if he possessed a hundred lives, could hope to escape the fangs of such a monster? So kind-hearted were the maidens, that they could not bear to see this brave and, handsome traveler attempt what was so very dangerous, and devote himself, most probably, to become a meal for the dragon's hundred ravenous mouths.

"Go back," cried they all,—"go back to your own home! Your mother, beholding you safe and sound, will shed tears of joy; and what can she do more, should you win ever so great a victory? No matter for the golden apples! No matter for the king, your cruel cousin! We do not wish the dragon with the hundred heads to eat you up!"

The stranger seemed to grow impatient at these remonstrances. He carelessly lifted his mighty club, and let it fall upon a rock that lay half buried in the earth, near by. With the force of that idle blow, the great rock was shattered all to pieces. It cost the stranger no more effort to achieve this feat of a giant's strength than for one of the young maidens to touch her sister's rosy cheek with a flower.

"Do you not believe," said he, looking at the damsels with a smile, "that such a blow would have crushed one of the dragon's hundred heads?"

**13.** What would you have told the stranger if he had asked you directions? Explain why. Write your answer in the box below.

Question 14 is based on the story below

**THE THREE GOLDEN APPLES, Part - 5**
**THE THREE GOLDEN APPLES, By Nathaniel Hawthorne**

**Part 5**

Meanwhile, Hercules travelled constantly onward, over hill and dale, and through the solitary woods. Sometimes he swung his club aloft, and splintered a mighty oak with a downright blow. His mind was so full of the giants and monsters with whom it was the business of his life to fight, that perhaps he mistook the great tree for a giant or a monster. And so eager was Hercules to achieve what he had undertaken, that he almost regretted to have spent so much time with the damsels, wasting idle breath upon the story of his adventures. But thus it always is with persons who are destined to perform great things. What they have already done seems less than nothing. What they have taken in hand to do seems worth toil, danger, and life itself.

Persons who happened to be passing through the forest must have been affrighted to see him smite the trees with his great club. With but a single blow, the trunk was riven as by the stroke of lightning, and the broad boughs came rustling and crashing down.

Hastening forward, without ever pausing or looking behind, he by and by heard the sea roaring at a distance. At this sound, he increased his speed, and soon came to a beach, where the great surf-waves tumbled themselves upon the hard sand, in a long line of snowy foam. At one end of the beach, however, there was a pleasant spot, where some green shrubbery clambered up a cliff, making its rocky face look soft and beautiful. A carpet of verdant grass, largely intermixed with sweet-smelling clover, covered the narrow space between the bottom of the cliff and the sea. And what should Hercules espy there, but an old man, fast asleep!

But was it really and truly an old man? Certainly, at first sight, it looked very like one; but, on closer inspection, it rather seemed to be some kind of a creature that lived in the sea. For, on his legs and arms there were scales, such as fishes have; he was web-footed and web-fingered, after the fashion of a duck; and his long beard, being of a greenish tinge, had more the appearance of a tuft of sea-weed than of an ordinary beard. Have you never seen a stick of timber, that has been long tossed about by the waves, and has got all overgrown with barnacles, and, at last drifting ashore, seems to have been thrown up from the very deepest bottom of the sea? Well, the old man would have put you in mind of just such a wave-tost spar! But Hercules, the instant he set eyes on this strange figure, was convinced that it could be no other than the Old One, who was to direct him on his way.

14. **Describe in your own words, what the Old Man in the Sea looked like to Hercules. Use details from the selection and write your answer in the box below.**

## THE THREE GOLDEN APPLES, Part - 8

His nap had probably lasted a good while, when the cup chanced to graze against a rock, and, in consequence, immediately resounded and reverberated through its golden or brazen substance, a hundred times as loudly as ever you heard a church-bell. The noise awoke Hercules, who instantly started up and gazed around him, wondering whereabouts he was. He was not long in discovering that the cup had floated across a great part of the sea, and was approaching the shore of what seemed to be an island. And, on that island, what do you think he saw?

No; you will never guess it, not if you were to try fifty thousand times! It positively appears to me that this was the most marvelous spectacle that had ever been seen by Hercules, in the whole course of his wonderful travels and adventures. It was a greater marvel than the hydra with nine heads, which kept growing twice as fast as they were cut off; greater than the six-legged man-monster; greater than Antreus; greater than anything that was ever beheld by anybody, before or since the days of Hercules, or than anything that remains to be beheld, by travelers in all time to come. It was a giant!

But such an intolerably big giant! A giant as tall as a mountain; so vast a giant, that the clouds rested about his midst, like a girdle, and hung like a hoary beard from his chin, and flitted before his huge eyes, so that he could neither see Hercules nor the golden cup in which he was voyaging. And, most wonderful of all, the giant held up his great hands and appeared to support the sky, which, so far as Hercules could discern through the clouds, was resting upon his head! This does really seem almost too much to believe.

Meanwhile, the bright cup continued to float onward, and finally touched the strand. Just then a breeze wafted away the clouds from before the giant's visage, and Hercules beheld it, with all its enormous features; eyes each of them as big as yonder lake, a nose a mile Long, and a mouth of the same width. It was a countenance terrible from its enormity of size, but disconsolate and weary, even as you may see the faces of many people, nowadays, who are compelled to sustain burdens above their strength. What the sky was to the giant, such are the cares of earth to those who let themselves be weighed down by them. And whenever men undertake what is beyond the just measure of their abilities, they encounter precisely such a doom as had befallen this poor giant.

Poor fellow! He had evidently stood there a long while. An ancient forest had been growing and de-caying around his feet; and oak-trees, of six or seven centuries old, had sprung from the acorn, and forced themselves between his toes.

15. **The narrator uses two sentences to intrigue and motivate the reader to go on. Choose the two sentences below from the passage that are evidence of this.**

Ⓐ  And, on that island, what do you think he saw?
Ⓑ  Poor fellow!
Ⓒ  No; you will never guess it, not if you were to try fifty thousand times!
Ⓓ  None of the above

# CHAPTER 1 → Lesson 10: Point of View

## 1. The below passage uses which style of narration?

*You are not the kind of guy who would be at a place like this at this time of the morning. But here you are, and you cannot say that the terrain is entirely unfamiliar, although the details are fuzzy. —Opening lines of Jay McInerney's Bright Lights, Big City (1984)*

- Ⓐ First person
- Ⓑ Second person
- Ⓒ Third person
- Ⓓ Fourth person

## 2. The below passage uses which style of narration?

I was so scared when I first learned that I would be having my tooth pulled. I didn't sleep at all the night before the procedure. I was terrified that it would hurt more than I could tolerate. I was shaking when I sat in the dentist's chair. He promised me that it would not hurt, but I certainly had my doubts. The dentist gave me some medicine. When I awoke, my tooth was gone, and I didn't remember a thing.

- Ⓐ First person
- Ⓑ Second person
- Ⓒ Third person
- Ⓓ Fourth person

## 3. The below passage uses which style of narration?

Huckleberry Hound ran through the yard and into the field next to his house. Suddenly, he put his nose to the ground and started sniffing as he walked. Yep, he definitely smelled a rabbit. He raised his head and howled loudly to let the other dogs know what he had found. Then, he shot after the rabbit like a bolt of lightning. He chased the rabbit for what seemed like hours, but he never caught it. He returned to his yard with his head hanging and his tail tucked between his legs.

- Ⓐ First person
- Ⓑ Second person
- Ⓒ Third person
- Ⓓ Fourth person

## 4. The below passage uses which style of narration?

You didn't want to ask for a loan, but you had no choice. You spent all of your allowance at the ball-game, and now you don't have the money to buy your mom a birthday present.

   Ⓐ First person
   Ⓑ Second person
   Ⓒ Third person
   Ⓓ Fourth person

## 5. The below passage uses which style of narration?

Max went for a bike ride in the park. While on the ride, he saw his best friend, Sammy. They decided to go to the movies instead of bike riding in the park. Max called his mom and asked if it would be alright to go to the movie with his friend. She said yes, so Max and Sammy jumped on their bikes and went to see The Emoji Movie.

   Ⓐ First person
   Ⓑ Second person
   Ⓒ Third person
   Ⓓ Fourth person

## 6. The below passage uses which style of narration?

I had been craving chocolate ice cream all day. Finally, school was over and I could get a huge chocolate ice cream cone. The line was long, but it was worth the wait. The first taste of my ice cream cone was delicious. Then, the worst thing imaginable happened. I bumped into the person behind me and dropped my ice cream cone and it fell on the floor.

   Ⓐ First person
   Ⓑ Second person
   Ⓒ Third person
   Ⓓ Fourth person

**7. The below passage uses which style of narration?**

I wanted to learn how to knit, so I asked my grandmother to teach me. She agreed, so I went to the store and bought yarn and knitting needles. I had my first lesson last week. I quickly learned that knitting is much harder than I thought it would be. I don't think I want to learn to knit anymore.

Ⓐ First person
Ⓑ Second person
Ⓒ Third person
Ⓓ Fourth person

**8. The below passage uses which style of narration?**

I wonder why Mindy didn't come to the meeting. Did I forget to tell her about it? Did she forget about it? I think I will call her and see why she isn't here.

Ⓐ First person
Ⓑ Second person
Ⓒ Third person
Ⓓ Fourth person

**9. The below passage uses which style of narration?**

Opal walked into the store not wanting to do what she had planned. She knew when she took the makeup without paying for it that it was wrong. She felt so guilty. She knew she couldn't keep the makeup. So, gathering up all her courage, she walked over to the security officer and confessed what she had done.

Ⓐ First person
Ⓑ Second person
Ⓒ Third person
Ⓓ Fourth person

## 10. What style of narration is the below text?

One day James went to town to buy new clothes. First, he tried on a pair of trousers. He didn't like the trousers, so he gave them back to the shopkeeper. Then, he tried on a robe which was the same price as the trousers. James was pleased with the robe, and he left the shop. Before he climbed on his donkey to ride home, the shopkeeper and the shop-assistant ran out.

- (A) First person
- (B) Second person
- (C) Third person
- (D) Fourth person

**Question 11 is based on the story below**

### The Mall - What Fun

Santiago and Felix wanted to go to the mall on Saturday. They had both saved up their money from lawn mowing and yard work. Each had been working for 3 weeks on Saturdays and Sunday afternoons to earn money. Their favorite place in the mall was around the food court and video arcade.

Santiago's older sister, Felicia, offered to drive them since she was going to get her hair done at Pro-Cuts there anyway. Felicia told them to be ready by her car at 9:45 Saturday morning. The mall opened at 10:00 and it would take them about 15 minutes or so to get there. Felix had a tendency to be late all the time, so Santiago was a little worried that he wouldn't show up on time. Santiago had a plan to make sure that didn't happen this time.

He asked his mother on Friday after school, if Felix could spend the night. Luckily she agreed if they didn't stay up late and if he cleaned his room before Felix came over. So Santiago quickly called Felix to see if he could come over and spend the night. Felix was elated! "Sure thing, buddy!  I will be there in a jiffy!"

"Don't come too soon, I have to clean my room!  Mama made me promise to do it!" Santiago said. "No worries, dude, I can help."  Felix replied.

So it was set.  Santiago did ask his mama if Felix could help him clean his room.  His mama just laughed and said, "Sure, you boys are so silly."

As soon as Felix got there, the boys started on their room cleaning project.  This gave Felicia an idea, too.
"Guys, if I am giving you a ride to the mall tomorrow, how about cleaning my room, too?"
"No way! Not a girl's room!!" They both exclaimed at the same exact time.

"Oh, well, can't blame a girl for trying!" Laughed Felicia.  "Don't worry, I will still take you."

That night the boys played video games and watched a combat movie. About 10:30pm, Santiago remembered what his mama said about not staying up late. He told Felix, "We better get to bed, Mama said not to stay up late if you came over."

"No problem, let's hit the sack," Said Felix.

The next morning, they were up, bathed, dressed, and had eaten breakfast by the time Felicia was ready to go.

"Wow, on time both of you and ready. This must be a special mall day for y'all!" She said.

When they got to the mall, Felicia told them to be sure to keep an eye on their watches. She also told them to meet her back at the door they came in exactly at 12:30. Her hair appointment would take one hour and then she wanted to meet friends to shop, as well. The boys agreed.

Their first stop was the video arcade where they met up with other friends and started playing games. It wasn't long before Felix wanted to go get a snack at the food court. You could say Felix liked food. He wasn't over weight or anything, he just liked to eat. Santiago was in the middle of a game and said he would be there shortly. Well, you guessed it, shortly didn't happen. Felix had his snack and waited for about 30 minutes for Santiago to show up. He didn't know what to do. So he headed back to the video arcade. He did notice that his watch showed it to be 12:10. They only had 20 minutes left and they had not even gone to any shops. Felix felt a sick feeling that he better find Santiago fast or Felicia would not be happy. She might not ever take them again if they did not make it back on time. Felix started almost running around a corner and splat! He ran right into Santiago!

"What took you so long, dude? I had my snack and waited on you forever!" Felix said in a bit of a disgruntled voice.

"My fault, all my fault! I was beating the game and didn't want to stop! Sorry. You are my best friend and I feel bad for letting you down." Replied Santiago.

"No worries, we better get going back to the door we came in at and meet Felicia." Said Felix.

When they got to the meeting place, Felicia was just walking up.

"Hey guys, y'all want to stay longer?" She said.

The guys grinned and nodded yes.

"Great, meet me here at 2:30. I am going to the movies with my friends. I already called Mama to let her know we would be staying longer."

Happily the boys went to shop with their money, bought new sneakers, ate lunch and even got to play video games again.

**11. If you could change the ending of the story, what would have happen? Write your answer in the box below.**

<br>

## Question 12 is based on the story below

### The Haunted House on Rio Vista Drive

The neighborhood of Rio Vista Drive had two parts to it.  On one side of Riverside Avenue were about 14 houses.  Each house had approximately three bedrooms, two baths, an extremely grand living area, kitchen, washroom, and most often a small office area.   The backyards were all chain linked hurricane fences of around 1.2 acres with a covered garage, back driveway and security locked gate. Most of the front yards were unique to themselves and had a theme which was painted on a plaque on the outside of the house itself.   The realtors said that the architect had named each house as he had built it and decorated the fronts to match the names.

However, on the other side of Rio Vista Drive at the end of the block- a dead end, stood a rickety two story house assumed to be about 50-75 years old.  This was dubbed the Haunted House. There was an old woman, Widow Crankston, who lived there.  The kids all say she would come out in the evening and sit on her porch.  Several thought they saw her carrying a black cat and presumed she was a witch of sorts.   Briars grew up along the fence line and sidewalks.  The windows were covered in cobwebs and the like.  It had been years and years since the house had been painted or anything in the yard taken care of either.   Many a dare had been made among the neighborhood kids to go and ring the doorbell or knock on the door.  Most dares were made on Halloween or around that time.

So it was on the night before Halloween that Howard, Ernie and Edward were riding their bikes down Rio Vista Drive. Up one side and down the other, quickly turning around before they reached Widow Crankston's Haunted House! Suddenly, Howard came to a screeching stop right in front of the house.

"Ok, dare ya' to do it!" He hollered at Ernie.
"No, dare you!" Ernie screamed back.
"Scaredy Cats!" Laughed Edward!! "I will do it!"

So off he went, straight up to the front door. He rang the doorbell, but no one answered. Hurriedly he turned around and was running down the steps when he heard a tiny voice behind him.

"Yes, young man, may I help you?" Inquired Widow Crankston, as she peeped out the massive door. "Is today Halloween, I thought it was tomorrow. Let me get you some chocolate brownies and a caramel apple. Do your friends want some, too? Haven't had young- ins come here in ages. Please sit on the porch while I get y'all treats and some cold milk."

Edward stopped in his tracks. She wasn't an old witch, but just a kind hearted little old lady. He motioned for Howard and Ernie. Both came running up the sidewalk just in time to eat the goodies!

Now the other kids in the neighborhood aren't sure yet what to think. There are no more briars, no more cobwebs, and the fresh paint on the house looks wonderful. The boys have a part-time job cleaning and painting while enjoying good company and great snacks!

**12. What do you think the author's purpose is in this story?**

Write a sentence or two to explain your answer using evidence supported in the passage. Write your answer in the box below.

## Disneyworld- Here We Come

It was a hot summer day in June.  My grandmother, Mom, my brother Daniel, my cousin Valerie, and I were headed out for a long vacation.  We were first going to Mississippi and then on to Florida to Disneyworld.  Talk about excitement!!!  I couldn't contain myself and didn't sleep much at all the night before.  Valerie was visiting us because her mom had gotten sick.  My wonderful mom had volunteered for her to stay with us the entire summer.  It was so cool. Valerie and I were best friends already, much less best cousins.  We did everything together all the time.  So having her come along was just another treat for me.  Of course, I had rather my little snoopy brother, Daniel, didn't come, but oh well!  After all, who can complain when you are going to Disneyworld!

We had to stop in Mississippi to leave my grandmother off at her house before the vacation.  That wasn't such a bad idea either, because I loved my grandmother's house, the creek to fish and swim in and all of her things.  The night before we had packed everything we needed.  I just couldn't get to sleep.  Finally I must have fallen asleep because the alarm was going off and everyone was hurrying about the house.  Dad had made us breakfast.  He couldn't go due to his work schedule, but insisted we go and have fun.  He even told me to ride the Teacups for him and the Train!  Dad is such a laugh.

The car was packed, we had double checked everything and were waving goodbye! Another reason for the stop in Mississippi was for rest.  It was going to be a long ride to even get that far in one day.  Mom turned on the a/c in the car along with the radio and we settled in.  She had it on her favorite country music, so we sang along a few songs of Merle Haggard and Johnny Cash.  I must have fallen asleep right after we left the house.  The next thing I knew, Mom was waking me up.  We had stopped for lunch at a Whataburger restaurant.  My favorite, too!  She said to eat hearty as we would not stop again until we reached my grandmother's house.  I ate a whole Whataburger with fries and an ice tea.  Valerie did, too!  Daniel had a Jr. Whataburger and so did my grandmother.  Mom had a salad with chicken.  Back in the car, Valerie and I decided to play, I spy.  It is loads of fun!  I was spying all kinds of things from license plates from Washington to blue jays in trees.  Daniel tried to join in but would get mad if we guessed his too quickly.  So he got out his video game and played it.  Mom had to stop for gas one time right before we made it to the Mississippi state line.  We always honk the horn when we cross over into Mississippi, but she said she was not going to do that since it was now getting dark and it might upset other drivers.  I have a very smart mom.

Part 2

Soon enough we were at my grandmother's.  Mom had made us pack one light bag with just enough for each of us our night clothes, and a clean outfit for the next day.  That way we didn't have to take so much out at my grandmother's house.  We were ready for a light soup supper and off to bed.

Before we knew it, it was daylight again. Mom was hustling us out of bed and into the kitchen for breakfast. She said to eat hearty as we had many more miles to go before we reached our final destination. So thankful that my grandmother cooked her best oatmeal for us topped with cinnamon, brown sugar, strawberries, and whipped cream! Who could ask for anything more? Yummy!!

Then it was load back into the car and get on the road. This time Mom found an oldies radio station and she was singing along with Patsy Cline, Tennessee Ernie Ford, and Frank Sinatra. Talk about strange music that none of us knew except her! Valerie and I played a game of travel trivia which was sort of fun and of course, Daniel, was back on his video games!

For lunch we stopped at a roadside park and had the sandwiches our grandmother had packed for us along with an apple and sweet iced tea. When we got back on the road, not a sound could be heard. I figured out later that all of us kids had fallen asleep.

A loud bang woke us as Mom clapped her hands and proclaimed our arrival to the Holiday Inn at Disneyworld! I could not tell you who was the most excited as we were all yelling sounds of glee and running around the car to get our luggage out. Mom registered us for our room and we were giggling uncontrollably.

Part 3

When we were settled in to our room, Mom explained the sleeping arrangements. Valerie and I would get one of the queen size beds to share, Daniel would get the fold out couch in the living area, and Mom would get the other bed. She said that is night number one, then we will switch on the second night. I love it when my mom thinks of everyone and being fair to all. We were so happy we could have slept on the floor and not minded!! Mom called Dad to let him know we made it safe and sound. Then she called our grandmother, too. She also called Valerie's mom in the hospital so Valerie could talk to her and let her know all was well. Valerie's mom's health was improving daily, too.

Mom ordered pizza for us the first night. We went to bed without any complaining, so excited to be going to Disneyworld the next day!

Mom had picked up a map of the park when she had registered us, so she was busy planning our day while we were falling asleep.

The morning came with a clap and thunder outside of our room. What was going on, we had wondered? Mom explained that it was raining and that we would have breakfast in the hotel lobby and then see what happened. She did tell us that the hotel manager had explained to her that quite often the rains would start and stop during the summers at Kissimmee, Florida. We were not too disappointed after she said that. The hotel offers a free breakfast for everyone. That was definitely a plus in Mom's opinion.

Sure enough after we had eaten the sun came out. The hotel offered a trolley bus to the theme parks, so we opted to take that rather than worrying about parking and walking. Disneyworld stays open all day and late into the evening. Mom said she had mapped out our route to take so we could get to see most everything in our two days along with purchasing us the fast passes to avoid long line delays.

What a cool Mom, right?

Part 4

The awesome view, the rides, the larger than life Disney characters, people laughing and having fun everywhere. Yes, Welcome to Disneyworld! First we started following the crowds that were going down the main street with shops galore. Then Mom got out her map and starting us on our route. By lunchtime, we had already seen more than imaginable. We had ridden the Liberty Square Riverboat, gone to the Swiss Family Treehouse, enjoyed the birds at the Enchanted Tiki Room, and countless of stops to listen to theatrical groups perform. Mom had thought of packing a lunch, but had decided against that. We had hot dogs, chips and a soda. Mom said the prices might be a bit high, but it was well worth it!

In the afternoon, the rain began to return, so we went inside a western style dance hall and listened to a group of singers dance and perform. It was really quite entertaining. Then it was time for more rides. Space Mountain was indeed worth it! Scary, and adventurous and well, mostly scary! My little brother couldn't go it and he pouted about that. So we switched directions and went to a kind of petty zoo afterwards, and to ride the Mad Tea Party (Dad's Teacups) to keep him happy. Valerie and I did not mind a bit. Mom steadily had her phone out taking pictures to post and to make copies for us.

Needless to say, by the end of the day, we were all exhausted and a little sun burned, too. Mom said we would stay the second night for the parade and fireworks. She said it was time to call it a day. We all moaned, but happily boarded the trolley back to our hotel. Once at the hotel, we settled for the buffet dinner. They let kids eat free at this hotel if you choose the buffet.

That night we all chatted about the rides and all of the attractions we saw. Mom didn't even have to tell us to go to bed. We bathed and took to the sheets! The morning was just around the corner.

Part 5

Again on the second day, we had the free breakfast and rode the trolley. It wasn't raining this time at all. Mom got out her map and we began our day. Daniel wanted to go back and ride the Mad Tea Party again, but thankfully Mom said no to that.

We were able to go to Splash Mountain, the Jungle Cruise, the 7 Dwarf's Mine Train and much more. Mom did make a request of her own. She wanted to meet Mickey and Minnie Mouse who were scheduled to appear outside of the Cinderella Castle. She also said she wanted to listen to the Enchanted Tales with Belle and ride the Prince Charming Regal Carrousel. What a crazy silly Mom!

What we didn't know was that she had a plan. It was right after we left the carrousel that we heard fantastic sounds coming down the main street. Yes, parade time right before our eyes. Mom told us to come and sit. There we were on the side of the castle sitting on the ledge in perfect view of the parade. We asked her how she knew to stop there. She said one of the hotel clerks had told her how to find the spot and when to be there. The parade was magnificent to say the least. The characters actually stopped in front of us and performed. Wow! We couldn't have planned it any better.

After the parade we went to A Pirate's Adventure and Tomorrowland Speedway, andBig Thunder Mountain. Mom said we needed to head toward the front entrance as it was time for fireworks and we needed to be ready. We got there just in time. The lights lit up the sky behind the Cinderella Castle and throughout Disneyworld. Just picture it!

What a perfect ending to our vacation.

**13. If you were the author, how would you change your story?**

> **Write at least two sentences to show what you would do differently. Write your answer in the box below.**

## Celia Cruz

She was born in Havana, Cuba in 1925. She was told by her grandmother that she could sing before she could talk. Her grandmother used to laugh and tell the family that she practiced her singing at night. (She was thought to have cried most of the night.) Cruz' work in radio during the 1940's in Cuba led to her fame and she traveled throughout Latin America with a female band. She won her first award singing on an amateur hour TV show. Cruz sang a version of a tango song that was very popular in Cuba.

In the 1950's Celia Cruz joined the Sonora Mantancera as a lead female singer. Then she was able to go to the Tropicana, the best establishment for Cuban music. If you performed at the Tropicana, you had made it in the singing world of Cubans.

She then went to Mexico for a one year contract right before Fidel Castro took over Cuba. She and her band never returned. Cruz moved to New York in 1961. By this time she was a well- known Cuban singer and independent from her band. She became known as the "Salsa Queen" due to her style of music. During the 1990's she gained great popularity among the younger generations, as her music reappeared. Cruz has been honored by five Presidents of the United States. She died of brain cancer in 2003, but her music and legend continue to thrive throughout the world.

**14. If you were to be a musician such as Celia Cruz, what type of music would you perform, where and why? Write your answer in the box below.**

**Question 15 is based on the story below**

### The Endangered Species Act.

The Act was originated in 1973, and is one of many US environmental laws passed in the 1970's. The law protects species from extinction. The United States Fish and Wildlife Service and the National Oceanic and Atmospheric Administration help to administer the act.

It was amended in 1978 to add economic considerations and again in 1982 which prevented economic considerations.

To be considered for listing, the species must meet one of five criteria (section 4(a)(1)):
1. There is the present or threatened destruction, modification, or curtailment of its habitat or range.
2. An over utilization for commercial, recreational, scientific, or educational purposes.
3. The species is declining due to disease or predation.
4. There is an inadequacy of existing regulatory mechanisms.
5. There are other natural or manmade factors affecting its continued existence.

15. **In thinking about and considering types of endangered species, animals in particular, which one would you most be concerned with?**

    **Which of the 5 listed criteria supports your concern? Write your answer in the box below.**

# CHAPTER 1 → Lesson 11: Visual Connections

## Question 1 is based on the story below

### Mary loves writing stories

"The Elephant Who Saw the World," Mary started speaking. It was Friday, and the students had to share their creative writing stories of the week.

Mary loved writing, and this part of the week, when they were able to make up stories for creative writing, was her favorite part. She enjoyed it so much that she became really good at it. When she was home on the weekends and she didn't have much homework, she would sit in her room for hours and create stories to share with her friends and family. Her parents always supported her and were her biggest fans.

However, there was one part about every Friday at school that Mary did not enjoy, and that was when she had to share her story in front of the class. The teacher made all of the children share on Friday afternoons, and this made Mary very nervous. She was shy, and although she knew her teacher was right, she didn't like it.

After sitting and listening to the other children's share, Mary finally heard her name called. She knew it was her turn to share. She got out of her seat slowly, walked to the front of the room and began.

## 1. Which picture below best represents what's happening in the story?

Ⓓ None of the above

**2. Which text below best represents what is happening in the picture?**

Ⓐ  Thelma watched her two baby lions, Louis and Lisa as they played. They were playing well until they started fighting over something the zoo keeper had thrown into the enclosure.

Ⓑ  Thelma watched her two baby meerkats, Louis and Lisa, as they played. They were playing well until they started fighting over something the zoo keeper had thrown into the enclosure.

Ⓒ  Thelma watched her two baby monkeys, Louis and Lisa, as they played. They were playing well until they started fighting over something the zoo keeper had thrown into the enclosure.

Ⓓ  Thelma watched her two baby koala bears, Louis and Lisa, as they played. They were playing well until they started fighting over something the zoo keeper had thrown into the enclosure.

**3. Which paragraph would be an appropriate description for the picture above?**

Ⓐ One day last spring I was out walking as it was a beautiful spring day. I came across an emp-ty  forest and heard a noise. It sounded like a baby but it couldn't have been a baby since there was no one else there. I walked over to where I thought the noise was coming from and stopped in front of a large hollow tree. It looked as if it had been there for a very long time. I stopped and listened. I heard the noise again and it was definitely coming from inside the tree. I looked inside and I saw a little kitten.

Ⓑ One day last spring I was out walking as it was a beautiful spring day. I came across an empty parking lot and heard a noise. It sounded like a baby but it couldn't have been a baby since there was no one else there. I walked over to where I thought the noise was coming from and stopped in front of a large box. It looked like some thing someone may have used for moving. I stopped and listened. I heard the noise again and it was definitely coming from inside the box. I looked inside and I saw a little kitten.

Ⓒ One day last spring I was out walking as it was a beautiful spring day. I came across a construction site and heard a noise. It sounded like a baby but it couldn't have been a baby since there was no one else there. I walked over to where I thought the noise was coming from and stopped in front of a large cement pipe. It looked like some thing they might use to transport water underground. I stopped and listened. I heard the noise again and it was defi-nitely coming from inside the pipe. I looked inside and I saw a little kitten.

Ⓓ At first the kitten was scared but eventually, with lots of coaxing, the kitten came to one of the open ends of the tree. I was able to see that it was a little black and white kitten who was probably very hungry and scared. I took the kitten home and it became my companion from that day on.

## 4. Which of the statements below most accurately reflects the picture?

Ⓐ  Many people like to act, even if they don't act very well. Acting helps them express how they are feeling. Sometimes acting makes them feel happy. Not everyone wants to be a professional, though. Professional actors like to entertain other people. Their skill is usually a combination of talent and training.

Ⓑ  Many people like to dance, even if they don't dance very well. Dancing helps them express how they are feeling. Sometimes dancing makes them feel happy. Not every one wants to be a professional, though. Professional dancers like to entertain other people. Their skill is usually a combination of talent and training.

Ⓒ  Many people like to sing, even if they don't sing very well. Singing helps them express how they are feeling. Sometimes singing makes them feel happy. Not everyone wants to be a professional, though. Professional singers use their voices to entertain other people. Their skill is usually a combination of talent and training.

Ⓓ  Their skill is usually a combination of talent and training. Most professional dancers work with a coach. They usually start training at a young age. Many of them get their first experience by being in school musicals. Talent and training are not enough to make a successful career, though. Young people who want to be dancers should also have poise, good stage presence, creativity, and the ability to deal with change. They must be healthy and strong, too.

## 5. Which paragraph would be an appropriate description for the picture above?

Ⓐ   Summer is probably my favorite season. One of my most favorite things to do is to go watch a sandcastle building contest they have every year in San Diego, California. We can see amazing sandcastles that people spend hours and days building. This year one of the winners of the contest made this really large superhero to honor their love of comic books.

Ⓑ   Summer is probably my favorite season. One of my most favorite things to do is to go watch a sandcastle building contest they have every year in San Diego, California. We can see amazing sandcastles that people spend hours and days building. This year one of the winners of the contest made this really long snake to honor their Mexican heritage.

Ⓒ   Summer is probably my favorite season. One of my most favorite things to do is to go watch a sandcastle building contest they have every year in San Diego, California. We can see amazing sandcastles that people spend hours and days building. This year one of the winners of the contest made this really big pyramid to honor their Egyptian heritage.

Ⓓ   Summer is probably my favorite season. One of my most favorite things to do is to go watch a sandcastle building contest they have every year in San Diego, California. We can see amazing sandcastles that people spend hours and days building. This year one of the winners of the contest made this really long dragon to honor their Chinese heritage.

**Sandy's Soccer**

Sandy Thomas enrolled in soccer when she was in first grade. She had loved to watch the soccer games on TV with her dad. Sandy's dad was a high school soccer coach. It was his passion, as well as hers. Sandy was elated when she convinced her parents to let her play soccer rather than take ballet. Her friends were astonished as they had all signed up for ballet and expected her to, as well.

The team she was on this year was called, The Blue Jets. She was playing her favorite position, goalie. She practices at home with a goal her dad made for her. He tries to make the goal and she blocks it almost every time.

**6. If the pattern stays exactly the same, what will game 3 score results be? Fill in the chart.**

| Game # | Team Blue Jets | Opposing Team | Difference + or - |
|--------|---------------|---------------|-------------------|
| 1 | 10 | 8 | +2 |
| 2 | 8 | 6 | +2 |
| 3 | | | |

**7. Choose a team sport and write a sentence telling what position you would play and how you would practice with a family member or a friend.**

Write your answer in the box below.

**Question 8 and 9 are based on the passage below**

### Going Mudding with Dad

Jeff and his dad love to go mudding on their four wheelers. Mudding is great fun, but can be dangerous! Jeff has his own four wheeler, too. It is not as massive as his dad's but can go fast and sling mud everywhere. Mudding has become a sort of sports in the swamp country in Louisiana where they live. So picture this in your mind. A four wheeler with a kid on it going through muddy paths covered in moss and vines. The mud is thick and water is everywhere. Get the picture, if you like mud like they do, it is a blast. The object of mudding is to see who can go the fastest, beat the other "mudders" while getting the most mud and filth on them as well.

There are several things to remember and keep in mind when preparing to drive and while driving four wheelers through mud. First, never go out alone. Buddy up is the best policy. Always wear plenty of clothing. Jeff and his dad wear long sleeve shirts, jeans, and high top hunting boots. Never go on a four wheeler without wearing a helmet for protection. Most of them have seat belts, so buckle up. Take water or a vitamin sports drink and a healthy snack with you. Keep a first aid kit in your four wheeler, too. If you are going out on a path that has several trails, take strips of cloth and tie on branches along the way to find your way back. Be sure to inspect your vehicle before going out. Check the basic like oil, gas, clean off any mud left before hand and make sure that your vehicle starts and stops when needed. While driving do not turn your four wheeler too sharp at any time as this could cause it to flip over. If the curve ahead of you looks sharp, slow down before you approach, or you might have an accident, as well. Safety is more important than winning or being the muddiest one out there!

Then hit the trails, have fun and enjoy the mud!

**8. If you were to go bike riding, which of the tips for mudding that were listed in the passage could apply? List three. Write your answer in the box below.**

**9. Find and write the two sentences in the first paragraph that help you to visualize mudding.**

**Question 10 is based on the poem below**

## YOUNG NIGHT THOUGHT

All night long and every night,
When my mama puts out the light
I see the people marching by,
As plain as day, before my eye.
Armies and emperors and kings,
All carrying different kinds of things,
And marching in so grand a way,
You never saw the like by day.
So fine a show was never seen
At the great circus on the green;
For every kind of beast and man
Is marching in that caravan.
At first they move a little slow,
But still the faster on they go,
And still beside them close I keep
Until we reach the Town of Sleep.

By Robert Louis Stevenson

10. **The poet uses many descriptions in his poem to help the reader picture what he is referring to.**

   **Draw a picture or write what you are seeing in your mind as you read this poem.**

**Question 11 and 12 based on the passage below**

## Roses are Red

Everyone knows the poem that goes- Roses are Red, Violets are blue, Sugar is sweet and so are you!

But I am not talking poetry right now. I am talking about the roses that Aunt Molly has in her yard.

Yeah, you see the pictures of them. Aren't they so beautiful? How does she get them that way?

Notice the two pictures on the page. The white roses come from a huge rose bush. I call it a tree it is so big! My aunt started that one with a branch cut off of our Great Grandma Witt's rose bush down in Centerville. She brought it home when Great Grandma was still alive. Grandma Witt told her to cut it off, wrap it in wet paper towels, put it in a bucket of red clay dirt from her front yard and take it home. So my aunt did.

When she got home with it, she dug a deep hole in her backyard. She put the clay dirt in first, then made another hole in the middle of that. Next, she put in rose fertilizer to help it grow. Then she put in the branch from the rose bush. After that, she pushed the dirt in real tight. When she got ready to water it, she didn't water it straight at the branch. Instead, she watered it slightly to the side of the hole at an angle. She also took a banana peel the next day and wrapped it around where the bottom of the branch was at. An old man had told her to do that whenever she planted rose bushes. I had no idea that you could grow a rose bush just from a branch. You can. The rose bush will start to make new roots under the soil. Bingo, a rose bush!

Now, look at the second red rose picture. This is a rose bush from Tyler, Texas. That town is world famous for growing the best roses. Aunt Molly bought that one about a year ago. It was on sale, she said, or she would never have paid full price for it. She put it on the side of her house near the carport. She had wanted to grow roses there for a long time. At first, she told me that it was not looking very healthy, and she knew why it had been on sale. However, she kept pampering it, adding fresh clay soil around it. Of course, she had to do the banana peel thing to it, too! During the winter, Aunt Molly was afraid it was dead. But to her surprise, it came back bigger than ever. She said it produces cluster roses almost every week.

Well, apparently she knows how to grow roses. It all seems to work just fine for Aunt Molly.

**11. What did you notice about the two pictures that are the same? Write your answer in the box below.**

**12. What might be different? Write your answer in the box below.**

## CHAPTER 1 → Lesson 12: Comparing and Contrasting

**Question 1 is based on the passage below**

### Fred Goes to the Dentist

Fred had never been to the dentist. All of his life he had heard horror stories about the buzzing drills, the huge needles, and the scary tools that the dentist used to torture his patients. Since none of his teeth were hurting, Fred just couldn't understand why his mom was insisting on taking him to the dentist. She told him that it was important to visit the dentist each year to have his teeth checked and cleaned. This seemed silly to Fred because he cleaned his teeth everyday by brushing and flossing them, but nothing would change his mother's mind. He found it hard to believe that she would think it was a good idea to take him somewhere to be tortured. However, he had no choice but to go.

On the way to the dentist, Fred's imagination went wild. He pictured walking into a room with a huge chair that the dentist would strap him to. He could just see the dentist pulling out a huge drill and drilling his tooth while his mother and several others held him in the chair. By the time he got to the dentist's office, he was shaking all over.

Surprisingly, the office was nothing like he expected. The dentist was friendly, and the chair was comfortable. It didn't have any straps. He looked around the room and didn't see any huge drills or torture devices. He was relieved when all the dentist did was look in his mouth, show him how to properly brush and floss his teeth, and give him a balloon. His mom made another appointment to have his teeth cleaned in six months. Maybe this wouldn't be as bad as he had thought it would be.

1. **Compare the way Fred felt about going to the dentist before his visit to the way he felt after his first visit.**

   Ⓐ  Fred was excited about going but became afraid once he arrived.
   Ⓑ  Fred was afraid of going and was even more afraid after he met the dentist.
   Ⓒ  Fred was afraid of going but felt relieved after he met the dentist.
   Ⓓ  Fred was excited about going and loved it once he arrived.

# Timothy

**Passage 1:**

Timothy got a job walking dogs each morning. When school started this year, everyone encouraged him to quit his job, but he decided to keep it. He knew it would be hard to get up every morning at 5 a.m. in order to get all of the dogs walked and then go to school all day. Additionally, he planned to sing in the chorus, play basketball, and be a mentor in the tutoring program this year. He knows it will not be easy, but he thinks his hard work will be worth it. He is trying to save enough money to go to a youth camp next summer.

**Passage 2:**

Adam likes to spend time with his friends. If he is not with them, he is texting them or playing games with them online. Adam is always busy. He cannot stand to sit around and do nothing. In fact, the only time he is still is when he is sleeping. Adam plays football, basketball, soccer, and baseball. He loves to be involved in whatever is going on at school or at the town's youth center. He spends a lot of his time encouraging people to recycle and even volunteers at the youth center. Although he loves spending time with his friends, he is willing to give up time with them to help others.

**Passage 3:**

Stanley loves to stay at home. He enjoys activities that can be done alone such as reading, drawing, and spending time with his dogs. Most days after school you can find him at home enjoying one of his favorite activities. He also thinks recycling is important and makes sure his family does it. Although he likes being alone, he enjoys volunteering at the youth center with his brother. He thinks it is important to make a difference in the lives of others, which is why he thinks he would like to be a doctor. Adam and Stanley may be different in many ways, but they join together and make a difference in their community.

## 2. If you compare Timothy and Adam, which statement is correct?

Ⓐ Timothy participates in extracurricular activities, but Adam does not.
Ⓑ Timothy does not participate in extracurricular activities, but Adam does.
Ⓒ Timothy and Adam both participate in extracurricular activities.
Ⓓ Neither Timothy nor Adam participates in extracurricular activities.

**3. If you contrast Timothy and Stanley, which statement is correct?**

Ⓐ Stanley participates in many extracurricular activities such as sports and chorus, but Timothy does not.

Ⓑ Stanley and Timothy both participate in extracurricular activities such as sports and chorus.

Ⓒ Neither Stanley nor Timothy participates in extracurricular activities.

Ⓓ Stanley enjoys solitary activities such as drawing, but Timothy enjoys group activities such as chorus and sports.

**4. Compare and contrast Adam and Stanley. Which statement is true?**

Ⓐ Both Adam and Stanley believe in recycling.

Ⓑ Neither Adam nor Stanley believes in recycling.

Ⓒ Adam believes in recycling, but Stanley does not.

Ⓓ Adam does not believe in recycling, but Stanley does.

### Question 5 is based on the passage below

This year Jim and I had the most wonderful vacation. Especially, compared to the one we took last year. We went to Hawaii, which was a better place to visit than last year's hunting lodge in Alaska. The hotel we stayed in was a luxury suite; it included a big screen TV with all of the movie channels, a hot tub on the balcony, a small kitchen stocked with local fruits and vegetables, and a huge bed shaped like a pineapple. The weather in Hawaii was superb. We enjoyed many hours on the beach sunbathing and playing volleyball. When we were not on the beach, we were in the ocean swimming or riding the waves on a surf board. Each night we enjoyed eating and dancing with all of our friends at a luau. Our week in Hawaii rushed by, making us wish we had planned a two-week vacation. Without a doubt, we will be going back to Hawaii next year for our vacation.

The hunting lodge in Alaska had a shower with hardly any warm water, a small cooler for our food, and cots to sleep on each night. But, the room wasn't even the worst part of the vacation. The weather was terrible; it rained the entire time we were there. Even with the rain, our guide expected us to go on an all-day fishing trip that was part of our vacation package. All we caught on that fishing trip was a cold from the rain. After the third day in Alaska, we decided to end our nightmare, cut our trip short, and head for home.

**5. Compare and contrast the Alaskan and Hawaiian vacations. Which statement is correct?**

Ⓐ Both had beautiful hotel rooms with nice accommodations.

Ⓑ The weather in Alaska was beautiful, but it rained the entire time they were in Hawaii.

Ⓒ The Hawaiian vacation was much more enjoyable than the Alaskan vacation.

Ⓓ The Alaskan vacation was much more enjoyable than the Hawaiian vacation.

"Dad and I need to go out of town this weekend," said Mom. "We'll be back on Monday, so the three of you are going to spend the weekend with your two aunts. "

Lindsay, Scarlet, and Austin loved their aunts and were really excited. They ran upstairs and started getting their things together to take with them. They put everything in one bag that they would need for school. They were going to stay with Aunt Margaret for two nights and the last night with their Auntie Josephine.

At the end of the school day, the children came running out of classroom doors from all different directions. Aunt Margaret was waiting for her nieces and nephew at the entrance of the school. She was wearing a bright red suit with a sparkly cat pin on it. She also had on a proper wool hat to match. She noticed a scuff on her shoes when her nieces and nephew ran up to her.

She cried, "Oh, my goodness! I am so happy you are here. The children at your school are just a bunch of toughies. I was nearly trampled while I was standing here! Let's get into the car." Aunt Margaret pointed to a large, green, four-door station wagon that was parked in the lot.

The next day, a funny-sounding honk came from the front of the house. The children ran outside and saw Auntie Jo sitting in her convertible. She was wearing a big cowboy hat. She wore a pair of polka dot shorts with a too large shirt.

**6. Compare and contrast the way the two different aunts dressed.**

Ⓐ  Auntie Jo and Aunt Margaret dressed the same.
Ⓑ  Auntie Jo dressed very casually while Aunt Margaret dressed very formally.
Ⓒ  Auntie Jo was wearing a skirt and Aunt Margaret was wearing a dress.
Ⓓ  None of the above

**7. Compare and contrast the cars that the aunts drove.**

Ⓐ  Auntie Jo had a  convertible, and Aunt Margaret had a station wagon.
Ⓑ  The two aunts had the same car.
Ⓒ  Auntie Jo had a sedan, and Aunt Margaret had a convertible.
Ⓓ  Neither Aunt liked to wear skirts or dresses.

The red tail hawk noticed something was happening to all of the other animals living in Running Brook during the spring. The birds seemed to be losing their feathers. The bears were losing their fur. Mountain goats were complaining that their feet hurt. The beavers had cavities, and the deer all seemed to be catching cold. The red squirrels had gotten so fat that they almost could not make it across the road.

Hawk made an observation. He was pretty sure that everything started happening when the town's first fast food restaurant opened. Forest Fawn thought he brought a great idea to the town and that he could make some extra money. He opened an eatery where food was easy to prepare, order, and eat quickly. Forest Fawn knew how difficult it was to find food during the winter months. He thought that he was doing his friends a favor.

The restaurant sold birdseed in five different flavors. Forest Fawn sold artificially flavored honey, salmon cakes, and deep-fried berries for the bears. Salted tree moss with lichen-flavored chips was on the shelf for the mountain goats and deer.

**8. What was Hawk's theory of what was causing the animals' complaints?**

   Ⓐ   Birds were losing their feathers, and bears were losing patches of fur.
   Ⓑ   Beavers got cavities, and deer had colds.
   Ⓒ   Bad things were happening to the animals because of the food that they were eating.
   Ⓓ   The squirrels were getting fat and the mountain goats complained about their feet.

**9. Compare what happened to the beavers and the birds.**

   Ⓐ   The birds lost their feathers, and the beavers had cavities.
   Ⓑ   The birds had cold, and the beavers lost their fur.
   Ⓒ   The birds liked the candy, and the beavers liked the syrup
   Ⓓ   The birds had sore feet and the beavers gained weight.

Beatrice was so excited. This was truly a special day for her. She looked down and saw that her cup was sparkling with clean and cold water. She couldn't believe that it was real! She had never seen water like this before. Slowly, she took a sip and it tasted so fresh. Her mother had always told her about the importance of water.

Beatrice used to get water from a ditch near her home. Also, they could walk for miles to reach other areas with water. The water wasn't very clean in the stream. In fact, most of the time, the water had a putrid smell and was brown in color. Beatrice and her family knew it wasn't acceptable but they didn't have any choice. The water that they drank was unclean, making Beatrice feel sick often.

The water they mostly use is from streams, rivers, and lakes and is used for cooking, taking baths, and washing clothes. This water is contaminated with chemicals in the products they use and can cause diseases, such as typhus, cholera, dysentery, and malaria.

**10. How did Beatrice get her water in the past compared to how she gets her water now?**

Ⓐ  They have always gotten their water from a faucet in their kitchen.
Ⓑ  They used to get it from the well and now they'll get it from the faucet.
Ⓒ  They used to get it from the dirty stream, and now they will have a well in the village.
Ⓓ  None of the above

## GRAINS, GRAINS, GRAINS

Everyone knows that grains are an important healthy part of a good diet.  It is important to make sure that you are eating the right amount of grains daily.

To make sure this happens include grains in half of your diet each day. Whole grain and wheat help to keep your digestive system in order and run smoothly as well.

Did you know that whole grains and whole grain foods are made up of all three layers of the grain seed or kernel?

Here are the layers and explanations that will help you to understand.

1. The bran (outer layer): give you all of the fiber as well as B vitamins; minerals such as magnesium, iron and zinc, and some protein.
2. The endosperm (middle layer): makes up for most of the weight of the grain and is made up mainly of carbohydrate and protein.

3. The germ (inner layer): has B vitamins, unsaturated fats, vitamin E, and minerals.

Most whole grains are quite tasty such as brown rice, barley, whole oats or oatmeal, wheat and rye breads.

When you go shopping with your parents, do the healthy choice thing and read labels.

Whole grain foods will have the words 'whole' or 'whole grain' followed by the name of the grain as one of the first ingredients.

**11. How can you help when you are out shopping with your parents to be sure healthy choices are made? Write your answer in the box below.**

> [blank answer box]

**Question 12 and 13 are based on the passage below**

### John F. Kennedy and Martin Luther King, Jr.

**John F. Kennedy (John Fitzgerald "Jack" Kennedy)** (May 29, 1917 – November 22, 1963)

President John F. Kennedy, our 35th President of the United States, has often been referred to as simply JFK. He was President from January 1961 until he was assassinated in November 1963. He is known for his famous quote, "Ask not what your country can do for you. Ask what you can do for your country." He was the youngest US President elected and the only Roman Catholic to serve office. He is also the only US President to win the famed Pulitzer's Prize.

He is well known for his advancements in aiding the Civil Rights Movement. During his term, the Peace Corps was established, the "New Frontier" domestic program, and the Cuban Missile Crisis also occurred.

He was killed by Lee Harvey Oswald in Dallas, Texas. It is thought that there was a conspiracy to commit the murder. Jack Ruby then killed Oswald in a jail corridor. The majority of Americans alive during the time believed that it was not done simply by just one man.

**Martin Luther King, Jr.** (1929-1968)

Martin Luther King, Jr. was born in 1929 in Atlanta, Georgia. He was the son of a Baptist preacher and became a Baptist minister himself, too. He followed the beliefs of Gandhi to be non-violent in his actions. He was the greatest supporter of the Civil Rights Movement during his time. He believed in boycotting, refusing to buy merchandise from those people who were considered racists. He was known for the March on Washington for Jobs and Freedom in 1963. King became a sort of national hero for the movement of African-Americans.

He is best known today for this and for his historic speech, "I Have a Dream". Martin Luther King, Jr. won the Nobel Peace Prize in 1964. The Civil Rights Act was passed that year, and he was the greatest influence in its passing. He was against discrimination of all kinds, but especially that against the African-American population. He was killed in 1968.

**12. In what ways do you find both President Kennedy and Martin Luther King, Jr. alike? List three and Write your answer in the box below.**

13. **Had you been alive during this time, what do you think your thoughts might be in ways to promote civil rights to all? Could these thoughts still help today?**

**Write two sentences in the box below to show how you would feel then and how you could help then and now.**

---

**Question 14 and 15 based on the passage below**

**Lionel Sosa and Sam Walton**

Lionel Sosa grew up in San Antonio, Texas. He was expected to follow his family tradition and learn a trade and become a Democrat. However, he chose to follow the ideal of the American Dream and also to become a Republican.

In doing so, he ran a small ad- agency. It was then that US Senator John Tower employed Sosa's company to run his election ad campaign. This gained Tower his re-election by focusing on the Hispanic vote. Sosa was then approached by clients such as Dr Pepper to help gain the Latino market sales. Sosa and Associates became the largest and most profitable US Hispanic ad agency in the country.

Since then, he was able to work on many presidential campaigns including that of Ronald Reagan.

He now spends his retirement time painting and writing.

**Sam Walton (1918-1992)** founded Walmart and Sam's Club. He opened the first Wal-Mart Discount City in 1962 after having several franchise Ben Franklin stores. His main effort was to market American made products. Although after his death, this practice was not continued. He placed his stores close to distribution centers, thereby having stores in multiple areas, not just in major cities.

He was listed as the richest man in the US from 1982 to 1988. Walmart and Sam's Club stores operate in the US and in 15 other countries including, Canada, Japan, Mexico, and the UK.

**14. How do you think the two men were alike in the business deals? Write your answer in the box below.**

**15. How did they differ? Write your answer in the box below.**

<br>

---

**Question 16 is based on the poem below**

### The Fish

wade
through black jade.
    Of the crow-blue mussel-shells, one keeps
    adjusting the ash-heaps;
        opening and shutting itself like

an
injured fan.
    The barnacles which encrust the side
    of the wave, cannot hide
        there for the submerged shafts of the

sun,
split like spun
    glass, move themselves with spotlight swiftness
    into the crevices—
        in and out, illuminating

the
turquoise sea
     of bodies. The water drives a wedge
     of iron through the iron edge
        of the cliff; whereupon the stars,

pink
rice-grains, ink-
     bespattered jelly fish, crabs like green
     lilies, and submarine
        toadstools, slide each on the other.

All
external
     marks of abuse are present on this
     defiant edifice—
        all the physical features of

ac-
cident—lack
     of cornice, dynamite grooves, burns, and
     hatchet strokes, these things stand
        out on it; the chasm-side is

dead.
Repeated
     evidence has proved that it can live
     on what can not revive
        its youth. The sea grows old in it.

## 15. Part A

**If you were to write such a poem, not using rhyming patterns, what might you write about? Write your answer in the box below.**

┌─────────────────────────────────────────┐
│                                         │
│                                         │
│                                         │
│                                         │
│                                         │
│                                         │
└─────────────────────────────────────────┘

**Part B**

Give at least two lines of your poem. Write your answer in the box below.

# End of Reading Literature

# Chapter 2 - Reading Informational Text

## Lesson 1: It's All in the Details

### Question 1 and 2 are based on the passage below

The ostrich is the largest bird in the world, but it cannot fly. Its legs are so strong and long that it can travel faster by running. Ostriches use their wings to help them gather speed when they start to run. They also use them as brakes when turning and stopping.

Ostriches have been known to run at speeds of 60 miles per hour. This is faster than horses and matches the average speed of vehicles on a highway.

These huge birds stand as tall as horses and sometimes weigh as much as 298 pounds. In North Africa, they are often seen with other larger animals.

The zebra, which is also a fast runner, seems to be one of their favorite companions.

An ostrich egg weighs one pound, which is as much as two dozen chicken eggs. Ostrich eggs are delicious and are often used for food by people in Africa. The shells are also made into cups and beautiful ornaments.

**1. Why is it a good thing that the Ostrich can run, rather than fly?**

- Ⓐ  The Ostrich does not enjoy flying.
- Ⓑ  The Ostrich is able to fly.
- Ⓒ  The Ostrich does not want to fly.
- Ⓓ  The Ostrich can travel faster by running.

**2. Devon says that Ostriches are shy and solitary birds. Which detail in the text proves him wrong?**

Ⓐ "Ostrich eggs are delicious and are often used for food by people in Africa."
Ⓑ "An ostrich egg weighs one pound."
Ⓒ "These huge birds stand as tall as a horse."
Ⓓ "The zebra, which is also a fast runner, seems to be one of their favorite companions."

**Question 3 is based on the passage below**

The blue whale is quite an amazing creature. It is a mammal that lives its entire life in the ocean. The size of its body is also amazing. This whale can grow up to 98 feet long and weigh as much as 200 tons. It is the largest known animal to have ever existed. Its body is long and elegantly tapered, unlike other whales which have a rounder, stockier build. The way that they are built, along with their extreme size, gives them a unique look. It also gives them the ability to move gracefully at greater speeds. Normally they travel around 12 mph, but they slow to 3.1 mph when feeding. They can even reach speeds up to 31 mph for short periods of time! Although they are extremely large animals, they eat small shrimp-like creatures called krill. Since the krill are so small, the blue whale eats about four tons daily as they swim deep in the ocean.

Blue whales do not live in tight-knit groups called pods like other whales. They live and travel alone or with one other whale. While traveling through the ocean, they come to the top to breathe air into their lungs through blowholes. They come from under the ocean, spitting water out of their blowholes. Then they roll and re-enter the water with a grand splash of their large tails. They make loud, deep, and rumbling low-frequency sounds that travel great distances. This allows them to communicate with other whales as far as 100 miles away. Their cries can be felt as much as heard. This resonating call makes them the loudest animal on Earth. If you ever have the opportunity to see or hear a blue whale, it will be an experience you will not soon forget.

**3. Angel argues that the blue whale is a solitary creature. What evidence from the text best supports his point?**

Ⓐ "Blue whales do not live in tight-knit groups called pods like other whales. They live and travel alone or with one other whale."
Ⓑ "This whale can grow up to 98 feet long and weigh as much as 200 tons. It is the largest known animal to have ever existed."
Ⓒ "They make loud, deep, and rumbling low-frequency sounds that travel great distances. This allows them to communicate with other whales as far as 100 miles away."
Ⓓ "Although they are extremely large animals, they eat small shrimp-like creatures called krill."

If you join our music club, you will receive 4 free CDs. These CDs are yours to keep even if you decide to cancel your membership. If you choose to stay a member and buy just 2 CDs at the regular price, you will get to choose 3 more CDs to keep for free. After your first purchase you will receive 10 points for every CD you buy after that. When you collect 30 points, you get to choose another free CD! If you want to earn even more free CDs, then have your friends join, too. When a friend joins and gives your name, you will get 3 more free CDs. The best part is that you get 3 free CDs each time you have another friend join our club, so join today and start collecting your favorite CDs.

4. **What detail from the text encourages music club members to get their friends to join the club?**

   Ⓐ  "If you join our music club, you will receive 4 free CDs."
   Ⓑ  "After your first purchase you will receive 10 points for every CD you buy after that."
   Ⓒ  "If you want to earn even more free CDs, then have your friends join, too."
   Ⓓ  "The best part is that you get 3 free CDs each time you have another friend join our club, so join today and start collecting your favorite CDs."

Have you ever wondered what happened to the dinosaurs that once roamed the Earth? Well, scientists have developed several theories throughout the years. One such theory is that a gigantic meteorite crashed into our planet, causing a massive dust cloud to cover the Earth. The dust cloud was so enormous that it blocked the rays of the Sun from reaching Earth. This caused all of the plants to die. With nothing to eat, the herbivores died. The large carnivores also died, leaving the planet without dinosaurs.

5. **Amelia asserts that dinosaurs definitely died because a giant meteorite crashed into Earth. What key words from the text would help Terrance to make a counterpoint?**

   Ⓐ  "One idea..."
   Ⓑ  "...a giant meteorite crashed into our planet"
   Ⓒ  "...leaving the planet with no dinosaurs."
   Ⓓ  This caused all of the plants to die.

**Question 6 is based on the passage below**

Do you like frogs? Do you know what a spring peeper is?

Spring peepers are tiny little tree frogs that live in wooded areas near ponds. Although these frogs are tiny, only about an inch big, they make a very loud sound. They are found mostly in the central and eastern parts of the United States. So, when the weather begins to get warmer after winter, these little frogs start to sing. Their "peep," which is why they are called spring peepers, can be heard for miles around. They live near ponds so they can lay their eggs in the water.

When the weather starts getting colder again, the spring peepers start to go into hiding. They hibernate under logs or any other place they can find in the forest to protect them from the cold. For example, sometimes they hide under fallen leaves or even in a small hole in the ground.

**6. Which paragraph contains details that support Monique's idea that people are most likely to see spring peepers during warm weather months?**

Ⓐ Paragraphs 1 and 2
Ⓑ Paragraphs 1 and 3
Ⓒ Paragraph 3
Ⓓ Paragraphs 2 and 3

**Question 7 is based on the passage below**

Most people think of koalas as koala bears, but they are not bears. They are marsupials and are in the same family as the wombat. Koalas live in a special place called a eucalyptus forest. They can be found in eastern and southeastern Australia. Adult koalas are one of only three animals that can live on a diet of eucalyptus leaves. These leaves contain 50% water. The eucalyptus leaves are mostly the main source of water for koalas.

The koala is a marsupial which means the baby crawls into a pocket, called a pouch, on the mother's tummy as soon as it is born. Baby koalas are called "joeys." When they are born, they cannot see, have no hair, and are less than one inch long. They stay in their mother's pouch for the next six months. First the mother feeds them milk. Then she feeds them a food called "pap" in addition to milk. Joeys continue to drink the mother's milk until they are a year old. The young koala will remain with its mother until another joey is born and comes into the pouch.

**7. What detail in the text explains why someone is not likely to see a koala in northwestern Australia?**

Ⓐ Koalas live in a special place called a eucalyptus forest.
Ⓑ They are marsupials and are in the same family as the wombat.
Ⓒ Koalas live...in eastern and south-eastern Australia.
Ⓓ When they are born, they are blind, hairless, and less than one inch long.

**Question 8 and 9 are based on the passage below**

There are four types of tissues that are created as cells join together and work as a group. Each type of tissue has a unique structure and does a specific job. Muscle tissue is made up of long, narrow muscle cells. Muscle tissue makes the body parts move by tightening and relaxing. Connective tissue is what holds up the body and connects its parts together. The bone is made up of connective tissue. Nerve tissue is made up of long nerve cells that go through the body and carry messages. Epithelial tissue is made of wide, flat epithelial cells. This tissue lines the surfaces inside the body and forms the outer layer of the skin. Groups of tissue join together to form the organs in the body such as the heart, liver, lungs, brain, and kidneys just to name a few. Then these organs work to-gether to form the body systems. Each system works together, and with the other systems of the body.

**8. What job does muscle tissue perform in the body?**

&#9398; It holds up the body.
&#9399; It allows the body to move
&#9400; It allows messages to travel through the body.
&#9401; It forms the outer layer of skin.

**9. What job does the epithelial tissue perform?**

&#9398; It holds up the body.
&#9399; It allows the body to move.
&#9400; It allows messages to travel through the body.
&#9401; It forms the outer layer of skin.

**Question 10 is based on the passage below**

2362 West Main Street
Jojo, TX 98456

June 16, 2017

Dear Mr. Seymour:

I ordered a Magic Racing Top from your company. The toy was delivered to me today in a package that was badly damaged. I took a picture of the box before I opened it, which I am sending to you as proof of the damage. The toy inside was broken due to the damage of the package during shipping.

This toy was to be a gift for my friend's birthday. There is not enough time before his party to wait for a replacement toy; therefore, I no longer need the toy. I would like you to refund my money. Please send me a prepaid shipping label if you would like me to return the broken toy. Thank you for handling this matter for me. I look forward to hearing from you and hope we can satisfactorily resolve this problem.

Sincerely,
Tim West

**10. Dominique argues that the writer of this letter was pleased with the toy company because he says, "please," and "if you would like." Does this evidence do a good job of supporting her argument?**

Ⓐ  Yes. These are very polite words, so he is clearly pleased with the toy company.
Ⓑ  Yes.  He also says, "Thank you for handling this matter for me."
Ⓒ  No. He is being polite, but he also says the package he ordered was, "badly damaged," and, "I would like you to refund my money."
Ⓓ  No. He wants to satisfactorily resolve the problem.

# CHAPTER 2 → Lesson 2: The Main Idea

## Question 1 and 2 are based on the passage below

The ostrich is the largest bird in the world, but it cannot fly. Its legs are so strong and long that it can travel faster by running. Ostriches use their wings to help them gather speed when they start to run. They also use them as brakes when turning and stopping.

Ostriches have been known to run at speeds of 60 miles per hour. This is faster than horses and matches the average speed of vehicles on a highway.

These huge birds stand as tall as horses and sometimes weigh as much as 298 pounds. In North Africa, they are often seen with other larger animals.

The zebra, which is also a fast runner, seems to be one of their favorite companions.

An ostrich egg weighs one pound, which is as much as two dozen chicken eggs. Ostrich eggs are delicious and are often used for food by people in Africa. The shells are also made into cups and beautiful ornaments.

## 1. What is the most appropriate title for this passage?

Ⓐ The Ostrich
Ⓑ The Bird that Cannot Fly
Ⓒ The Ostrich Egg
Ⓓ The Largest Bird in the World

## 2. What is the main idea of the passage?

Ⓐ Ostriches are great because their eggs are delicious.
Ⓑ The ostrich is the largest bird and can run very fast.
Ⓒ The ostrich is the largest bird but it cannot fly.
Ⓓ The ostrich lives in Africa.

**Question 3 is based on the passage below**

Did you know that the coconut tree is very useful to people? Each part of the tree can be used for many different purposes. The coconut fruit, which we get from the tree, is very nutritious and is used to cook varieties of food. Coconut milk, which is taken from the coconut, tastes very delicious. It is used to prepare a variety of sweet dishes.

Oil can be extracted from a dried coconut. Coconut oil is a very good moisturizer. It is used in many beauty products like body wash, face wash, shampoos, and conditioners. The oil is also used for cooking of tropical foods. Some coconut trees grow straight and tall, and some trees are very short. Coconut trees do not have branches. They have long leaves which grow right at the top of the tree. The leaves have many different uses. Leaf ribs are made into brooms. The fiber obtained from the outer cover of the nut is used for mattresses and rugs. The trunk is used to make logs for small boats. It is also used for firewood. The sweet water of the tender coconut quenches thirst during the hot summer months and it is also very healthy.

## 3. What is the most appropriate title for this passage?

Ⓐ The Coconut Tree and Its Uses
Ⓑ Trees of the Rainforest
Ⓒ Foods that We Get from the Coconut
Ⓓ Tall Coconut Trees

## 4. What would be the main idea of the below story?

Beatrice was so excited. This was truly a special day for her. She looked down and saw that her cup was sparkling with clean and cold water. She couldn't believe it was real as she had never seen water like that before. She slowly took a sip and it tasted so fresh. Her mother always told her how important water is.

The only way that Beatrice was able to get her water in the past was from the dirty water in a ditch not far from her home. Otherwise, they would have to walk for miles to reach other areas that had water. The water there wasn't very clean, either. In fact, most of the time, this water had a horrible smell and was brownish in color. Beatrice and her family knew it wasn't great but they didn't have any choice. The water that they drank from was contaminated making Beatrice feel sick often.

The water they mostly use is from streams, rivers, and lakes and is used for cooking, taking baths, and washing clothes. This water is contaminated from chemicals in the products they use and can cause diseases, such as typhus, cholera, dysentery, and malaria.

 Ⓐ Beatrice never had water that tasted so good before.
 Ⓑ Beatrice is happy that she and her family will finally have clean drinking water.
 Ⓒ Beatrice and her family get their water from the murky stream near the home.
 Ⓓ Contaminated water often carries diseases and people can become very ill.

## 5. Which detail in the below passage tells us that the soil is being polluted?

Pollution hurts the world around us. It upsets the balance of nature, which is very important for our survival. The problems in the environment affect in four areas. The areas affected are the soil, water, air and sound. Large amounts of trash from factories and houses can cause land pollution. Chemicals used in farming pollute the soil. Plastics are wasteful products. Too many animals needing to eat and the cutting down of trees creates deserts and wastelands. Deserts already cover 40 percent of the Earth's surface. Waste in water makes it unhealthy and harmful. Plants and animals in the water are harmed because of the tons of oil that is spilled into the seas and oceans. The air that we breathe is polluted by smoke and dust in the atmosphere. Lung illnesses can occur when the air is polluted. Noise pollution in cities has grown intensely. Pollution has become a serious and invasive problem around the globe.

 Ⓐ the oil spills in the seas and oceans.
 Ⓑ smoke and dust in the air
 Ⓒ large amounts of trash from factories and houses
 Ⓓ global warming

Beautiful seashells that are washed ashore on beaches by ocean waves have always amazed people. Shells come in a collection of shapes, sizes, and colors. Shells are actually made by marine creatures to serve as their homes. Seashells are quite simply skeletons of mollusks. Mollusks are a class of water animals that have soft bodies and hard outer coverings, called shells. People have bony skeletons on the inside and soft bodies on the outside. But mollusks do just the opposite. Shells protect these soft-bodied animals from rough surfaces that can harm their bodies. Shells also protect mollusks from predators.

Shells are durable and last longer than the soft-bodied animals that make and wear them. Shells may be univalve or bivalve. Univalve shells are made up of just one unit. Bivalve shells have two units or two halves. Snails have univalve shells and oysters have bivalve shells.

**6. The main role of a seashell is:**

    Ⓐ  to look beautiful
    Ⓑ  to serve as a home for mollusks
    Ⓒ  to float to the shores
    Ⓓ  to be collected by divers

Sacagawea is a famous Native American from the Shoshone tribe. She became famous when she helped two male explorers named Lewis and Clark, find their way through the unknown west. When she was 12 years old, she was kidnapped by an enemy Native American tribe called the Hidatsa. Then, legend has it, the chief of the Hidatsa tribe sold Sacagawea into slavery.

In 1804, she became a translator and guide for a group of explorers led by Lewis and Clark. She helped them find their way from near the Dakotas to the Pacific Ocean. She became a famous Native American in our history for being brave and helping these men discover unknown territory.

**7. What would be a good title for the above story?**

    Ⓐ  Sacagawea: A Shoshone Woman
    Ⓑ  Sacagawea: An Amazing Woman
    Ⓒ  Sacagawea: Kidnapped by the Hidatsa
    Ⓓ  Sacagawea: Sold to a Fur Trader

**8. What is the main idea of the story above?**

    Ⓐ  Sacagawea's life was amazing.
    Ⓑ  Sacagawea was a woman who did so many things that women didn't do at the time.
    Ⓒ  Sacagawea helped two men explore the west.
    Ⓓ  What Sacagawea did will be remembered forever.

## 9. What is the main idea of the below passage?

A Bichon frise is an unusual breed of dog. It has white fluffy hair and tiny, black eyes. Years ago, this funny little breed was used as a circus dog. Many people keep this breed as pets, because it is hypo-allergenic. This means that people with allergies aren't allergic to this breed. They don't shed, so they won't leave hair all over your house.

   Ⓐ  A Bichon frise is a unique breed of dogs.
   Ⓑ  A Bichon frise was used as a circus dog.
   Ⓒ  A Bichon frise is hypoallergenic.
   Ⓓ  A Bichon frise has white hair and black eyes.

## 10. Which detail supports the idea that scientists believe a meteorite crashed into the planet and killed off the dinosaurs?

Have you ever thought about what happened to the dinosaurs that once roamed the Earth? Well, scientists have developed several ideas throughout the years. One idea is that a giant meteorite crashed into our planet and caused a huge dust cloud to cover the Earth. The dust cloud was so enormous that it kept the Sun's rays from reaching Earth. This caused all of the plants to die. With nothing to eat, the herbivores died. The large carnivores also died, leaving the planet without dinosaurs.

   Ⓐ  Scientists have developed several ideas through the years.
   Ⓑ  Have you ever thought about what happened to the dinosaurs that once roamed the Earth?
   Ⓒ  The dust cloud was so enormous that it kept the Sun's rays from reaching Earth.
   Ⓓ  The planet was left without dinosaurs.

## CHAPTER 2 → Lesson 3: Using Details to Explain the Text

**Question 1 and 2 are based on the passage below**

### Digestive System

The digestive system is made up of the esophagus, stomach, liver, gall bladder, pancreas, large and small intestines, appendix, and rectum. Digestion actually begins in the mouth when food is chewed and mixed with saliva. Muscles in the esophagus push food into the stomach. Once there, it mixes with digestive juices. While in the stomach, food is broken down into nutrients, good for you, and turned into a thick liquid. The food then moves into the small intestine where more digestive juices complete breaking it down. It is in the small intestine that nutrients are taken into the blood and carried throughout the body. Anything left over that your body cannot use goes to the large intestine. The body takes water from the leftovers. The rest is passed out of your body.

**1. What event begins the digestive process?**

Ⓐ  The small intestine absorbing nutrients.
Ⓑ  Muscles in the esophagus pushing food into the stomach.
Ⓒ  Chewing food and allowing it to mix with saliva.
Ⓓ  Nutrients are taken into the blood.

**2. How do nutrients that are absorbed from food move through the body?**

Ⓐ  They develop the ability to swim through the body's fluids in a tiny school bus.
Ⓑ  The digestive juices in the small intestine break them down.
Ⓒ  They move through the esophagus and into the stomach.
Ⓓ  They are absorbed into the blood, which carries them to other parts of the body.

**Question 3 and 4 are based on the passage below**

The blue whale is quite an amazing creature. It is a mammal that lives its entire life in the ocean. The size of its body is also amazing. This whale can grow up to 98 feet long and weigh as much as 200 tons. It is the largest known animal to have ever existed. Its body is long and elegantly tapered, unlike other whales which have a rounder, stockier build. The way that they are built, along with their extreme size, gives them a unique look. It also gives them the ability to move gracefully at greater speeds. Normally they travel around 12 mph, but they slow to 3.1 mph when feeding. They can even reach speeds up to 31 mph for short periods of time! Although they are extremely large animals, they eat small shrimp-like creatures called krill. Since the krill are so small, the blue whale eats about four tons daily as they swim deep in the ocean.

Blue whales do not live in tight-knit groups called pods like other whales. They live and travel alone or with one other whale. While traveling through the ocean, they come to the top to breathe air into their lungs through blowholes. They come from under the ocean, spitting water out of their blowholes. Then they roll and re-enter the water with a grand splash of their large tails. They make loud, deep, and rumbling low-frequency sounds that travel great distances. This allows them to communicate with other whales as far as 100 miles away. Their cries can be felt as much as heard. This resonating call makes them the loudest animal on Earth. If you ever have the opportunity to see or hear a blue whale, it will be an experience you will not soon forget.

## 3. How do blue whales breathe?

Ⓐ  They use their blowholes to process oxygen found at deep ocean depths.
Ⓑ  They spit water out of their blowholes and then rise to the surface to breathe air.
Ⓒ  They rise to the surface, spit water out of their blowholes, and then breathe air in through their blowholes.
Ⓓ  They roll and re-enter the water with a grand splash of their large tail.

## 4. How are blue whales able to communicate with other whales from great distances?

Ⓐ  They make a loud, deep, low frequency sound that is able to travel as much as 100 miles under water.
Ⓑ  They use tiny whale telephones.
Ⓒ  They send a high frequency sound that only other whales are able to hear.
Ⓓ  Their cries can be heard but never felt.

> ### Question 5-7 are based on the passage below

All matter, which makes up all things, can be changed in two ways: chemically and physically. Both chemical and physical changes affect the state of matter. Physical changes are those that do not change the actual substance. For example, clay will flatten if squeezed, but it will still be clay. Changing the shape of clay is a physical change and does not change the matter's identity. Chemical changes turn the matter into something new. For example, when paper is burned, it becomes ash and will never be paper again. The difference between them is that physical changes are temporary or only last for a little while. Chemical changes are permanent, which means they last forever. Physical and chemical changes both affect the state of matter.

**5. Which sentence below explains the concept of physical change?**

Ⓐ Physical change occurs when matter goes through a change that makes something new.
Ⓑ Physical change occurs when a person gains or loses weight.
Ⓒ Physical change is change that occurs naturally and affects the state of matter.
Ⓓ Physical change is change that does not make something new.

**6. Which sentence below explains the concept of chemical change?**

Ⓐ Chemical change is change that does not make something new.
Ⓑ Chemical changes occur when something new is made
Ⓒ Chemical change occurs when someone mixes unknown chemicals in a beaker.
Ⓓ Chemical change occurs when clay is flattened or squeezed.

**7. What is the primary difference between physical and chemical change?**

Ⓐ Physical changes affect the state of matter, while chemical changes do not.
Ⓑ Chemical changes are temporary, while physical changes are permanent.
Ⓒ Physical changes are temporary, while chemical changes are permanent.
Ⓓ Chemical and physical changes make something entirely new.

**Question 8 is based on the passage below**

### Lewis and Clark

Sacagawea, also spelled *Sacajawea*, is best known for her role in helping Meriwether Lewis and William Clark during their journey to explore the American West. They set out on their journey on May 14, 1804. They left from near Wood River, Illinois; it was during winter in South Dakota when they met Sacagawea. They reached the Pacific Ocean on the coast of Oregon in November 1805.

The journey was unique. The new frontier was full of unknown native people and the land was dangerous. Without the help of someone who knew the land, Lewis and Clark may not have made it to the Pacific.

Sacagawea was the young Shoshone wife of a French-Canadian fur trapper named Toussaint Charbonneau. Together, she and her husband served as interpreters, guides, and negotiators for Lewis and Clark. Their friendship with Clark was so strong that when they returned, they moved to his hometown of St. Louis. Clark became the guardian of her children after her death.

8. **Which of the following sentences best explains how important Sacagawea was to Lewis and Clark's expedition?**

Ⓐ Sacagawea was a member of the Shoshone tribe of Native Americans.

Ⓑ Because they were travelling unknown territory, they needed the help of a person who knew about the people that they would encounter and the land that they would navigate.

Ⓒ Sacagawea could not have aided the Lewis and Clark expedition without the help of her husband, who was an experienced fur trapper.

Ⓓ Sacagawea was Shoshone by birth and married to a French-Canadian man, and she spoke two languages.

> **Question 9 and 10 are based on the passage below**

There are many theories about how dinosaurs came to be extinct. Scientists do not all agree about what may have happened. The most recent idea says that a giant meteorite crashed into the earth. It kicked up enough dust and dirt that the Sun's rays did not reach Earth for a very long time. This prevented plants from making their own food via photosynthesis. Plant-eaters and then, meat-eaters died due to a lack of food.

The other leading idea says that dinosaurs died out when the Earth went through a time of volcanoes erupting. Like the meteorite idea, it is thought that the volcanoes spewed enough ash into the air that the Sun's rays were blocked. This also caused plant and animal life to die.

9. **According to the passage, how can lack of sunlight cause animals to become extinct?**

Ⓐ It disrupts the food chain starting with producers. If plants die out, then plant-eaters have nothing to eat. If plant-eaters starve and die out, then meat-eaters have nothing to eat and also die.

Ⓑ Dinosaurs became extinct because of widespread volcanic eruptions that blocked sunlight from reaching Earth. When this happened, plants died, beginning a disruption of the food chain that dinosaurs didn't survive.

Ⓒ One theory suggests a meteorite caused dinosaur extinction, while another claims widespread volcanic eruptions caused the animals to die. Both theories, however, center around the idea that plants did not get needed sunlight and plant-eating and meat-eating animals died as a result.

Ⓓ It creates a shadow over the entire planet which makes everything very cold. This extreme cold keeps the animals from being able to hunt or eat.

## 10. Do all scientists agree about how dinosaurs became extinct?

Ⓐ No. The text explains that there are many theories on dinosaur extinction and describes two of them.

Ⓑ No. Some scientists believe dinosaurs died when a giant meteorite crashed into earth, while others blame extraterrestrials.

Ⓒ Yes. The scientific community has debated several possibilities, and they agree that dinosaurs died out as the result of widespread volcanic eruptions.

Ⓓ Yes. The scientists have argued but finally agree that the dinosaurs became extinct when a meteor crashed into Earth.

## CHAPTER 2 → Lesson 4: What Does it Mean?

### Question 1 is based on the passage below

The blue whale is quite an amazing creature. It is a mammal that lives its entire life in the ocean. The size of its body is also amazing. This whale can grow up to 98 feet long and weigh as much as 200 tons. It is the largest known animal to have ever existed. Its body is long and elegantly tapered, unlike other whales which have a rounder, stockier build. The way that they are built, along with their extreme size, gives them a unique look. It also gives them the ability to move gracefully at greater speeds. Normally they travel around 12 mph, but they slow to 3.1 mph when feeding. They can even reach speeds up to 31 mph for short periods of time! Although they are extremely large animals, they eat small shrimp-like creatures called krill. Since the krill are so small, the blue whale eats about four tons daily as they swim deep in the ocean.

Blue whales do not live in tight-knit groups called pods like other whales. They live and travel alone or with one other whale. While traveling through the ocean, they come to the top to breathe air into their lungs through blowholes. They come from under the ocean, spitting water out of their blowholes. Then they roll and re-enter the water with a grand splash of their large tails. They make loud, deep, and rumbling low-frequency sounds that travel great distances. This allows them to communicate with other whales as far as 100 miles away. Their cries can be felt as much as heard. This <u>resonating</u> call makes them the loudest animal on Earth. If you ever have the opportunity to see or hear a blue whale, it will be an experience you will not soon forget.

**1. What is the meaning of the word resonating?**

Ⓐ low
Ⓑ loud
Ⓒ silent
Ⓓ quiet

### Question 2 and 3 are based on the passage below

Have you ever thought about what happened to the dinosaurs that once roamed the Earth? Well, scientists have developed several ideas throughout the years. One idea is that a giant meteorite crashed into our planet and caused a huge dust cloud to cover the Earth. The dust cloud was so enormous that it kept the Sun's rays from reaching Earth. This caused all of the plants to die. With nothing to eat, the <u>herbivores</u> died. The large <u>carnivores</u> also died, leaving the planet without dinosaurs.

2. **What is the meaning of the word herbivore?**

Ⓐ  a type of plant
Ⓑ  an animal that eats only plants
Ⓒ  a type of storm
Ⓓ  an animal that eats only meat

3. **What is the meaning of the word carnivores?**

Ⓐ  a type of plant
Ⓑ  an animal that eats only plants
Ⓒ  a type of storm
Ⓓ  an animal that eats only meat

4. **The rain danced on the roof, tapping a happy tune.**
   **The sentence above gives human qualities to the rain. This is called:**

Ⓐ  Onomatopoeia
Ⓑ  Personification
Ⓒ  Assonance
Ⓓ  Alliteration

## Question 5 is based on the passage below

In the United States today, we are starting to see more and more of a problem with children who are overweight. Doctors and other health care professionals are trying to do something about it. They are recommending healthier foods and encouraging children get daily <u>vigorous</u> exercise. They also recommend that children go outside and play instead of sitting in front of the tv. They have suggested that children get at least an hour of exercise a day by participating in activities like jumping rope, cycling, or basketball, movement that makes the heart beat faster. This kind of exercise is known as aerobic exercise. Something else they recommend is for children to do exercises that strengthen the bones and muscles. There are a lot of ways that children can do this. One way is running.

5. **What is the meaning of "vigorous" in the above text?**

Ⓐ  slow
Ⓑ  growing well
Ⓒ  energetic, forceful
Ⓓ  weak

**6. What word in the sentence below helps you understand what reimburse means?**

People who travel on business are usually <u>reimbursed</u> for their travel expenses; that is, they are repaid for money that they have spent for the company.

- Ⓐ expenses
- Ⓑ representatives
- Ⓒ repaid
- Ⓓ business

**Question 7 is based on the passage below**

Many years ago there weren't any self-serve grocery stores. Shoppers were served by clerks who chose products for them. When the first self-serve market was opened, no one thought that it would be successful. Owners of the full-service grocery stores laughed at the idea and said that the public would probably <u>boycott</u> the stores.

Clarence Saunders, the man who came up with this innovative system, thought that he could save money by having shoppers help themselves from the open shelves. He was warned by many of his competitors that customers would <u>boycott</u> this type of grocery store and put him out of business.

**7. What is the meaning of the word boycott in the above text?**

- Ⓐ to only go to this store and shop there
- Ⓑ to get a lot of money
- Ⓒ to lose a lot of money
- Ⓓ to refuse to buy something

**8. Which words in the below text help to understand the meaning of copra?**

We get a lot of <u>copra</u> from the Malay Peninsula. <u>Copra</u> is dried coconut meat which is used for making coconut oil. We use coconut oil for cooking and as an ingredient in many beauty products.

- Ⓐ coconut oil
- Ⓑ coconut meat
- Ⓒ Malay Peninsula
- Ⓓ beauty products

## 9. What is the meaning of the underlined word?

The first review of *Despicable Me* was <u>favorable</u>. Many people attended and enjoyed the movie.

Ⓐ clear
Ⓑ negative
Ⓒ positive
Ⓓ unsure

## 10. The bomb exploded with a loud BOOM! Did you hear the snake hiss as it crawled along the ground?
Boom and hiss are words that imitate the noise made. This is called:

Ⓐ Onomatopoeia
Ⓑ Personification
Ⓒ Assonance
Ⓓ Alliteration

## CHAPTER 2 → Lesson 5: How is it Written?

**Question 1 and 2 are based on the passage below**

The blue whale is quite an amazing creature. It is a mammal that lives its entire life in the ocean. The size of its body is also amazing. This whale can grow up to 98 feet long and weigh as much as 200 tons. It is the largest known animal to have ever existed. Its body is long and elegantly tapered, unlike other whales which have a rounder, stockier build. The way that they are built, along with their extreme size, gives them a unique look. It also gives them the ability to move gracefully at greater speeds. Normally they travel around 12 mph, but they slow to 3.1 mph when feeding. They can even reach speeds up to 31 mph for short periods of time! Although they are extremely large animals, they eat small shrimp-like creatures called krill. Since the krill are so small, the blue whale eats about four tons daily as they swim deep in the ocean.

Blue whales do not live in tight-knit groups called pods like other whales. They live and travel alone or with one other whale. While traveling through the ocean, they come to the top to breathe air into their lungs through blowholes. They come from under the ocean, spitting water out of their blowholes. Then they roll and re-enter the water with a grand splash of their large tails. They make loud, deep, and rumbling low-frequency sounds that travel great distances. This allows them to communicate with other whales as far as 100 miles away. Their cries can be felt as much as heard. This resonating call makes them the loudest animal on Earth. If you ever have the opportunity to see or hear a blue whale, it will be an experience you will not soon forget.

**1. The author used which text structure when writing this passage?**

Ⓐ Problem and solution
Ⓑ Cause and effect
Ⓒ Sequence
Ⓓ Descriptive

**2. A report that explains how animal cells and plant cells are alike and how they are different would be written using which of the text structures?**

Ⓐ Cause and effect
Ⓑ Compare and contrast
Ⓒ Problem and solution
Ⓓ Sequence or chronological

**Question 3 is based on the passage below**

**Grandma's Chocolate Cake**
1 ¾ cups all-purpose flour
2 cups white sugar
2 sticks of room temperature butter
2 eggs
¾ cup cocoa powder
1 cup milk
1 tsp. vanilla extract
1 tsp. salt

Preheat oven to 350 degrees F.
Butter and flour two 8 inch cake pans.
Combine eggs, sugar, milk, vanilla extract, and butter. Beat until smooth.
Sift together the flour, salt, and cocoa powder.
Slowly add the sifted dry ingredients to the wet ingredients.
Mix until batter is smooth.
Pour the batter into the floured and greased cake pans.
Bake for 35 to 40 minutes.
Cool in pans on cooling rack for 30 minutes.
Ice cake with your favorite frosting.

**3. Which text structure is used in the second half of the above recipe?**

Ⓐ Cause and effect
Ⓑ Compare and contrast
Ⓒ Problem and solution
Ⓓ Sequence

**Question 4 is based on the paragraph below**

All matter, which makes up all things, can be changed in two ways: chemically and physically. Both chemical and physical changes affect the state of matter. Physical changes are those that do not change the actual substance. For example, clay will flatten if squeezed, but it will still be clay. Changing the shape of clay is a physical change and does not change the matter's identity. Chemical changes turn the matter into something new. For example, when the paper is burned, it becomes ash and will never be paper again. The difference between them is that physical changes are temporary or only last for a little while. Chemical changes are permanent, which means they last forever. Physical and chemical changes both affect the state of matter.

### 4. What type of structure did they use to write this paragraph?

Ⓐ  Compare and contrast
Ⓑ  Cause and effect
Ⓒ  Sequence
Ⓓ  Problem and solution

### Question 5 and 6 are based on the passage below

#### Sacagawea

Sacagawea is a famous Native American woman from the Shoshone tribe. She became famous when she helped two male explorers named Lewis and Clark, find their way through the unknown west. When she was 12 years old, she was kidnapped by an enemy of the Shoshone tribe called the Hidatsa. Legend has it, that the chief of the Hidatsa tribe sold Sacagawea into slavery.

In 1804, she became a translator and guide for a group of explorers led by Lewis and Clark. She helped them find their way from near the Dakotas to the Pacific Ocean. She became a famous Native American woman in US history for being brave and helping these explorers discover unknown territory.

### 5. How is the text written?

Ⓐ  Compare and contrast
Ⓑ  Cause and effect
Ⓒ  Sequence
Ⓓ  Problem and solution

### 6. What type of writing is the text above?

Ⓐ  Descriptive
Ⓑ  Informative
Ⓒ  Persuasive
Ⓓ  Narrative

Every day after school when I get home, I get certain ingredients to make myself a snack. I get the peanut butter, jelly, and bread and put everything on the counter. Peanut butter and jelly sandwiches are my favorite! Then, I take the lid off all the jars. Next, I take a big spoonful of peanut butter and spread it on one side of the bread and another big spoonful of jelly on the other. After that, I put the two pieces of bread together to make my super yummy peanut butter and jelly sandwich. I can enjoy my snack while starting my homework. It always tastes so good! Each time it seems as if it is the best peanut butter and jelly sandwich I have ever eaten.

**7. What is the text structure of the above passage?**

Ⓐ  Cause and effect
Ⓑ  Compare and contrast
Ⓒ  Problem and solution
Ⓓ  Chronological

**8. If the title of an essay was, "Should Students be Allowed to Have Cell Phones in Elementary School?" What type of writing would it be?**

Ⓐ  Comparative
Ⓑ  Informative
Ⓒ  Narrative
Ⓓ  Persuasive

**9. If the title of an essay was "Two Places I've Visited Recently," what type of writing will it be?**

Ⓐ  Persuasive
Ⓑ  Informative
Ⓒ  Comparative
Ⓓ  Narrative

**10. If a title of an essay was "How I Spent My Summer Vacation," what type of writing would it be?**

Ⓐ  Persuasive
Ⓑ  Informative
Ⓒ  Narrative
Ⓓ  Poetry

## CHAPTER 2 → Lesson 6: Comparing Different Versions of the Same Event

> **Question 1-3 are based on the passage below**

### The Parade: A Firsthand Account

When I got there I was dressed from head to toe in sparkly sequins and itchy tights, and I held my baton like a pro. I lined up with others in my squad and we began marching through the streets while the marching band played in front of us. I saw the crowds of people waving and smiling. At first, their happy faces made it seem less cold, but by the second mile the happy faces did not soothe the blisters on my feet. I threw my twirling baton into the air, and this time I did not catch it. In fact, when I turned to retrieve it, I tripped on the girl behind me and caused quite a situation. I was so embarrassed that I contemplated never showing my face again.

### The Parade: A Secondhand Account

I read about the Thanksgiving parade in our school newspaper today. It was held downtown last Saturday morning to honor the American holiday that occurs every year on the third Thursday in November. There was a marching band, floats from all of the local businesses, a step team, a ballet studio, and baton twirlers. The temperature outside was forty five degrees, but the sun was shining brightly and helped warm over 600 people who came out to see the parade. All in all, the parade was a huge success, and the city plans to hold it again next year.

**1. How is the focus of the firsthand account different from the secondhand account?**

Ⓐ   The firsthand account focuses on the parade itself, while the secondhand account focuses on the weather on the day of the parade.
Ⓑ   The firsthand account has a wide focus that represents the parade as a whole, while the secondhand account is narrow and only talks about the crowd who attended the parade.
Ⓒ   The firsthand account is more accurate, while the secondhand account is based on rumor.
Ⓓ   The firsthand account focuses only on the personal experience of the speaker, while the secondhand account gives general information from the newspaper report about the parade.

**2. How are the firsthand account and the secondhand account alike?**

Ⓐ   They both consider the parade a huge success.
Ⓑ   They both give specific information about the number of people in attendance.
Ⓒ   They both discuss the baton twirlers' sequin costumes.
Ⓓ   They both discuss the weather, the marching band, the baton twirlers, and the crowd.

**3. How are the firsthand account and the secondhand account different?**

Ⓐ The firsthand account is more personal and includes the speaker's feelings about the parade, while the secondhand account is more objective and includes mostly facts about the parade.

Ⓑ The firsthand account includes more details about the parade, while the secondhand account is more of a broad summary.

Ⓒ The firsthand account is true, while the secondhand account gives false information.

Ⓓ The firsthand account discusses the origins of the parade, while the secondhand account is from a newspaper.

## Question 4-6 are based on the passage below

### The Inauguration of Barack Obama: A Firsthand Account

When Barack Obama was inaugurated as America's first African-American president, I was watching from my TV only a couple of miles away. It was a cold, cold, cloudy day, but thousands and thousands of people climbed on jam-packed metro train cars, and busses. Some even walked across the Key Bridge from Arlington, Virginia to get into Washington, D.C. I saw groups of people moving down the street outside of my apartment. They had homemade signs in puffy jackets and happy faces. I wondered what they would eat. I also wondered where they would sleep. I watched from of my warm living room with what I imagined to be, a much better view of a new President taking the oath of office.

### The Inauguration of Barak Obama: A Secondhand Account

Barak Obama was inaugurated as our nation's 44th president on Tuesday, January 20, 2009. It was the most attended event in Washington, D.C.'s history. The inauguration was held during the celebration of the 200th year of Abraham Lincoln's birthday. There were many mentions of Lincoln throughout the event. Obama was even sworn into office using the same Bible Lincoln used when he became President.

The event offered welcoming remarks, the oath of office, and an inaugural address. There was music by Aretha Franklin, Yo Yo Ma, and other talented artists. The night was celebrated with a series of inaugural balls, which the new First Family attended.

**4. How are the two accounts similar?**

Ⓐ They both detail the events of election night.

Ⓑ They both give important details about the inauguration itself.

Ⓒ They both tell true events on the day of Barack Obama's first inauguration.

Ⓓ They both talk about the importance of Abraham Lincoln.

**5. How are the two accounts different?**

Ⓐ The details in the secondhand account may not be accurate, while the details in the firsthand account have been verified to be true.

Ⓑ The secondhand account is more personal than the firsthand account.

Ⓒ The firsthand account is longer than the secondhand account.

Ⓓ The details in the firsthand account are limited only to what the speaker witnessed, while the secondhand account gives more specific details concerning the inauguration.

**6. What is the difference in focus between the two accounts?**

Ⓐ The firsthand account focuses on the practical details concerning the people in attendance, while the secondhand account focuses on the details of the inauguration event.

Ⓑ The firsthand account focuses on important details, while the secondhand account is focused on less significant details.

Ⓒ The secondhand account focuses on biographical details about Obama's life, while the first-hand account focuses on details like the music that played at the inauguration.

Ⓓ Both accounts have the same focus.

> **Question 7-9 are based on the passage below**

### John Glenn's Return to Space: a Firsthand Account

President Bill Clinton, The White House, Washington, D.C.

Dear Mr. President,

    This is certainly a first for me, writing to a President from, space, and it may be a first for you in receiving an E mail direct from an orbiting spacecraft.

    In any event, I want to personally thank you and Mrs. Clinton for coming to the Cape to see the launch. I hope you enjoyed it just half as much as we did on board.. It is truly an awesome experience from a personal standpoint, and of even greater importance for all of the great research projects we have on Discovery. The whole crew was impressed that you would be the first President to personally see a shuttle launch and asked me to include their best regards to you and Hillary. She has discussed her interest in the space program with Annie on several occasions, and I know she would like to be on a flight just like this.

    We have gone almost a third of the way around the world in the time it has taken me to write this letter, and the rest of the crew is waiting. Again, our thanks and best regards. Will try to give you a personal briefing after we return next Saturday.

Sincerely,

John Glenn

Margie S. Keller
Admin Officer
Astronaut Office
281-244-8991

### John Glenn's Return to Space: a Secondhand Account

In October of 1998, John Glenn returned to space aboard the space shuttle Discovery. It was on that mission that the first American to orbit the Earth made history again by becoming the oldest man to fly in space. He was a U.S. Senator from Ohio at the time. President Bill Clinton attended the launch as the first U.S. President to do so.

**7. What is the difference in focus between the firsthand and secondhand account above?**

   Ⓐ  The firsthand account and the secondhand account have the same focus.
   Ⓑ  The firsthand account is more accurate than the secondhand account.
   Ⓒ  The firsthand account focuses on providing information to President Bill Clinton, while the secondhand account focuses on details about John Glenn.
   Ⓓ  The firsthand account is an actual letter and the second is as well.

**8. How are the two accounts similar?**

   Ⓐ  They both give information about President Clinton being the first U.S. President to personally see a launch.
   Ⓑ  They both include information about the date of the historic mission.
   Ⓒ  They both detail the important research being conducted on the mission.
   Ⓓ  The firsthand account is an article and the second is an actual letter.

**9. How are the two accounts different?**

   Ⓐ  The firsthand account is a letter and tells a little bit about Glenn's personal experience, while the secondhand account is an informational paragraph and was most likely written by some one who did not know John Glenn.
   Ⓑ  The firsthand account discusses John Glenn's return to space in 1998, while the secondhand account discusses his first orbit around Earth in 1962.
   Ⓒ  The firsthand account is written in complete sentences, while the secondhand account is written in short, note-like form.
   Ⓓ  The firsthand account is an article and the second is an actual letter.

**10. What is the difference between a firsthand account and secondhand account of an event or occurrence?**

   Ⓐ  Firsthand accounts are written by people who witness an event first, while secondhand accounts are written by people who witness the event second.
   Ⓑ  Firsthand accounts are written by people who witnessed the event, while secondhand accounts are written by people who learned details of the event from other sources.
   Ⓒ  Firsthand accounts are true, while secondhand accounts are usually made up.
   Ⓓ  Firsthand accounts are primary documents and secondhand accounts are not.

**Question 11 is based on the paragraph below**

In the United States today, we are starting to see more and more of a problem with children who are overweight. Doctors and even the President's wife are trying to do something about it. They are recommending healthier foods and that children get daily exercise. They recommend that children go outside and do things instead of sitting in front of the tv. They have suggested that children get at least an hour of exercise a day by doing things like jumping rope or cycling, or anything else that makes their heart beat faster. This kind of exercise is known as aerobic exercise. They also recommend that children do exercises that strengthen the bones and muscles. There are lots of ways children can do this. Running is one example.

**11. Which style of narration is used in the above text? Explain.**

## CHAPTER 2 → Lesson 7: Using Text Features to Gather Information

**Question 1-3 are based on the passage below**

There are four types of tissues that are created as cells join together and work as a group. Each type of tissue has a unique structure and does a specific job. Muscle tissue is made up of long, narrow muscle cells. Muscle tissue makes the body parts move by tightening and relaxing. Connective tissue is what holds up the body and connects its parts together. The bone is made up of connective tissue. Nerve tissue is made up of long nerve cells that go through the body and carry messages. Epithelial tissue is made of wide, flat epithelial cells. This tissue lines the surfaces inside the body and forms the outer layer of the skin. Groups of tissue join together to form the organs in the body such as the heart, liver, lungs, brain, and kidneys just to name a few. Then these organs work together to form the body systems. Each system works together, and with the other systems of the body.

| Muscle Tissue | Connective Tissue | Nerve Tissue | Epithelial Tissue |
|---|---|---|---|
| - long, narrow cells | - holds up the body | - long cells | - wide, flat cells |
| - contracts and relaxes causing movement | - connects body parts together | - carries messages throughout the body | - lines inside surfaces |
| | | | - forms outer skin layer |

1. **How does the chart help the reader understand the functions of each of the four types of tissues?**

    Ⓐ  It adds details not mentioned in the text so the reader can gather more information.
    Ⓑ  It elaborates on details mentioned in the text.
    Ⓒ  It changes some of the details mentioned in the text.
    Ⓓ  It clarifies the details mentioned in the text by categorizing them by tissue type.

2. **Which types of tissue have similarly shaped cells?**

    Ⓐ  epithelial tissue and connective tissue
    Ⓑ  muscle tissue and connective tissue
    Ⓒ  connective tissue and nerve tissue
    Ⓓ  muscle tissue and nerve tissue

3. **To help the reader visualize what each tissue looks like, what would be the BEST visual aid to include with this text?**

Ⓐ  A drawing of the heart, liver, lungs, brain, and kidneys
Ⓑ  A microscopic views of each type of tissue
Ⓒ  A diagram of a nerve cell
Ⓓ  A chart providing information about each type of tissue

### Question 4 is based on the passage below

Most people think of koalas as koala bears, but they are not bears. They are marsupials and are in the same family as the wombat. Koalas live in a special place called a eucalyptus forest. They can be found in eastern and southeastern Australia. Adult koalas are one of only three animals that can live on a diet of eucalyptus leaves. These leaves contain 50% water. The eucalyptus leaves are mostly the main source of water for koalas.

The koala is a marsupial which means the baby crawls into a pocket, called a pouch, on the mother's tummy as soon as it is born. Baby koalas are called "joeys." When they are born, they cannot see, have no hair, and are less than one inch long. They stay in their mother's pouch for the next six months. First the mother feeds them milk. Then she feeds them a food called "pap" in addition to milk. Joeys continue to drink the mother's milk until they are a year old. The young koala will remain with its mother until another joey is born and comes into the pouch.

4. **Which picture or illustration would not help the reader understand the above text and should not be included?**

Ⓐ  a picture of an adult koala
Ⓑ  a picture of a newborn 'joey'
Ⓒ  a picture of a polar bear
Ⓓ  a map showing areas where koalas are found naturally

### Question 5 is based on the paragraph below

The digestive system is made up of the esophagus, stomach, liver, gall bladder, pancreas, large and small intestines, appendix, and rectum. Digestion actually begins in the mouth when food is chewed and mixed with saliva. Muscles in the esophagus push food into the stomach. Once there, it mixes with digestive juices. While in the stomach, food is broken down into nutrients, good for you, and turned into a thick liquid. The food then moves into the small intestine where more digestive juices complete breaking it down. It is in the small intestine that nutrients are taken into the blood and carried throughout the body. Anything left over that your body cannot use goes to the large intestine. The body takes water from the leftovers. The rest is passed out of your body.

**5. What visual aid should be included with the above text to enhance student understanding?**

Ⓐ a diagram of the digestive system
Ⓑ a diagram of the mouth
Ⓒ a diagram of food
Ⓓ a diagram of stomach tissue

**Question 6 is based on the passage below**

### Sacagawea

Sacagawea is a famous Native American woman from the Shoshone tribe. She became famous when she helped two male explorers named Lewis and Clark, find their way through the unknown west. When she was 12 years old, she was kidnapped by an enemy of the Shoshone tribe called the Hidatsa. Legend has it, that the chief of the Hidatsa tribe sold Sacagawea into slavery.

In 1804, she became a translator and guide for a group of explorers led by Lewis and Clark. She helped them find their way from near the Dakotas to the Pacific Ocean. She became a famous Native American woman in US history for being brave and helping these explorers discover unknown territory.

**6. Which of the pictures below best represents what is being explained in the text?**

Ⓐ

Ⓑ

Ⓒ

Ⓓ None of the above

## Question 7 is based on the passage below

The blue whale is quite an amazing creature. It is a mammal that lives its entire life in the ocean. The size of its body is also amazing. This whale can grow up to 98 feet long and weigh as much as 200 tons. It is the largest known animal to have ever existed. Its body is long and elegantly tapered, unlike other whales which have a rounder, stockier build. The way that they are built, along with their extreme size, gives them a unique look. It also gives them the ability to move gracefully at greater speeds. Normally they travel around 12 mph, but they slow to 3.1 mph when feeding. They can even reach speeds up to 31 mph for short periods of time! Although they are extremely large animals, they eat small shrimp-like creatures called krill. Since the krill are so small, the blue whale eats about four tons daily as they swim deep in the ocean.

Blue whales do not live in tight-knit groups called pods like other whales. They live and travel alone or with one other whale. While traveling through the ocean, they come to the top to breathe air into their lungs through blowholes. They come from under the ocean, spitting water out of their blowholes. Then they roll and re-enter the water with a grand splash of their large tails. They make loud, deep, and rumbling low-frequency sounds that travel great distances. This allows them to communicate with other whales as far as 100 miles away. Their cries can be felt as much as heard. This resonating call makes them the loudest animal on Earth. If you ever have the opportunity to see or hear a blue whale, it will be an experience you will not soon forget.

**7. What would be an important illustration or picture to include with this article?**

Ⓐ a picture of the ocean
Ⓑ a picture of a pod of whales
Ⓒ a picture of an adult blue whale
Ⓓ a picture of a whaling ship

## Question 8 is based on the passage below

The following excerpt is from the November 12, 1892, edition of "Golden Days" magazine. It explains how condensed milk was made: The process very simple, the fresh milk is put into a great copper tank with a steam jacket. It is heated and sugar is added. The mixture is then moved into a vacuum tank, where evaporation is produced by heat.

The vacuum tank will hold approximately nine thousand quarts. It has a glass window at the top, through which the operator in charge monitors it. He can tell by the appearance of the milk when to shut off the steam. This must be done at just the right moment or else the batch will be spoiled.

Next, the condensed milk is drawn into forty-quart cans, set in very cold spring water to revolve rapidly by a mechanism so that the contents may cool evenly.

Ice is put into the milk to bring it down to the proper temperature if it is not cold enough. Finally the market sized tin cans are filled with the milk by a machine, which automatically pours exactly sixteen ounces of milk. There is a worker placing the cans beneath the spout while another worker removes them once they are filled.

**8. Which text feature would be most helpful for the reader to understand the process of making condensed milk?**

Ⓐ a numbered list of steps with illustrations for each step
Ⓑ a timeline of the events in the process
Ⓒ a map of where evaporated milk was made in 1892
Ⓓ a picture of an evaporated milk can

**Question 9 is based on the details below**

**BETWEEN WOOD AND FIELD. Arrange the wall tents with flys and set up with stakes.**

**THE TENT "GREEN."** These are conical wall tents that accommodate eight cots. They are not easy to put up and give little head room.

**Well-built floors keep out the damp ground, and make the supports level and steady.**

**9. These photographs and captions are most likely included in which of the following texts?**

Ⓐ a recipe book for outdoorsmen
Ⓑ a guide to city life
Ⓒ a guide to Girl Scout camps
Ⓓ a fishing guide

Caterpillar feeds on a milkweed leaf as it prepares to begin its transition

Caterpillar attached to leaf as it changes to the chrysalis phase

The transition stage

The chrysalis

**10. What would these photographs and captions be most helpful in explaining?**

Ⓐ  all about plants
Ⓑ  a very hungry caterpillar
Ⓒ  how a caterpillar begins its transformation into a butterfly
Ⓓ  how a caterpillar goes to sleep each night

**Question 11 is based on the passage below**

Do you like frogs? Do you know what a spring peeper is?

Spring peepers are tiny little tree frogs that live in wooded areas near ponds. Although these frogs are tiny, only about an inch big, they make a very loud sound. They are found mostly in the center or Eastern part of the United States. So, when the weather begins to get warmer after winter, these little frogs start to sing. Their "peep", which is why they are called spring peepers, can be heard for miles around. They live near ponds so they can lay their eggs in the water.

When the weather starts getting colder again, the spring peepers start to go into hiding. They hibernate under logs or any other place they can find in the forest to protect them from the cold. For example, sometimes they hide under fallen leaves or even in a small hole in the ground.

**11. Which picture below best illustrates what the text is about.**

Ⓓ None of the above

**Question 12 is based on the passage below**

### Geologic Maps

As we all know, there are maps of many kinds. Most of us are familiar with maps that show us location of places, such as the map of the United States. However, other maps show other thing. A geological map show where rocks and faults are at, as well as their location in an area. Then the map has various colors to show different information. It also includes many symbols. The geological map helps us to understand the earth beneath us, so we can understand the world around us better.

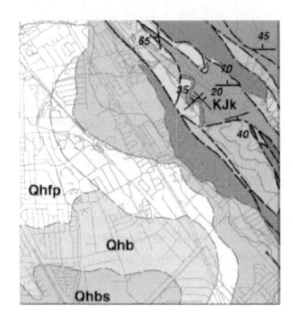

Notice the shaded areas on this map taken from the US Geological Survey website. Each area is colored to match the type of geological unit (volume of a certain kind of rock of a given age range). For example, one area might be colored bright orange to show a sandstone of one age while another might be pale brown to show another sandstone of a different age.

The geologists name and define the geological units they find. They determine everything they do based on their findings of rocks and the ages of the rocks. These continue to change as more investigations are completed. The science of geology can be quite interesting.

**12. While reading about geological maps compare the information to the information on the map of United States**

**Write a sentence in the box below explaining the differences in the types of maps.**

## CHAPTER 2 → Lesson 8: Finding the Evidence

### Question 1 and 2 are based on the passage below

The blue whale is quite an amazing creature. It is a mammal that lives its entire life in the ocean. The size of its body is also amazing. This whale can grow up to 98 feet long and weigh as much as 200 tons. It is the largest known animal to have ever existed. Its body is long and elegantly tapered, unlike other whales which have a rounder, stockier build. The way that they are built, along with their extreme size, gives them a unique look. It also gives them the ability to move gracefully at greater speeds. Normally they travel around 12 mph, but they slow to 3.1 mph when feeding. They can even reach speeds up to 31 mph for short periods of time! Although they are extremely large animals, they eat small shrimp-like creatures called krill. Since the krill are so small, the blue whale eats about four tons daily as they swim deep in the ocean.

Blue whales do not live in tight-knit groups called pods like other whales. They live and travel alone or with one other whale. While traveling through the ocean, they come to the top to breathe air into their lungs through blowholes. They come from under the ocean, spitting water out of their blowholes. Then they roll and re-enter the water with a grand splash of their large tails. They make loud, deep, and rumbling low-frequency sounds that travel great distances. This allows them to communicate with other whales as far as 100 miles away. Their cries can be felt as much as heard. This resonating call makes them the loudest animal on Earth. If you ever have the opportunity to see or hear a blue whale, it will be an experience you will not soon forget.

1. **Which statement did the writer of this passage use to support his opinion that the size of a blue whale's body is amazing?**

   Ⓐ The blue whale is quite an extraordinary creature.
   Ⓑ Its body is long and elegantly tapered, unlike other whales which have a rounder, stockier body.
   Ⓒ This whale can grow up to 98 feet long and weigh as much as 200 tons, making it the largest known animal to have ever existed.
   Ⓓ Their build, along with their extreme size, gives them a unique appearance and the ability to move gracefully and at greater speeds than one might imagine.

2. **What evidence does the author provide in the second paragraph that supports the fact that whales communicate with one another?**

Ⓐ Blue whales live and travel alone or with one other whale.

Ⓑ They emerge from the ocean, spewing water out of their blowhole, roll over, and re-enter the water with a grand splash of their tail.

Ⓒ They make loud, deep, and rumbling low-frequency sounds that travel great distances, which allow them to communicate with other whales as much as 100 miles away.

Ⓓ Their cries can be felt as much as heard.

**Question 3 and 4 are based on the letter below**

2362 West Main Street
Jojo, TX 98456

June 16, 2017

Dear Mr. Seymour:

I ordered a Magic Racing Top from your company. The toy was delivered to me today in a package that was badly damaged. I took a picture of the box before I opened it, which I am sending to you as proof of the damage. The toy inside was broken due to the damage of the package during shipping.

This toy was to be a gift for my friend's birthday. There is not enough time before his party to wait for a replacement toy; therefore, I no longer need the toy. I would like you to refund my money. Please send me a prepaid shipping label if you would like me to return the broken toy. Thank you for handling this matter for me. I look forward to hearing from you and hope we can satisfactorily resolve this problem.

Sincerely,
Tim West

3. **What evidence does the writer of this letter offer to support his claim that the package arrived damaged?**

Ⓐ The toy was broken.

Ⓑ He wanted a replacement or a refund.

Ⓒ He is sending a picture of the damaged package.

Ⓓ He wants to satisfactorily resolve the problem.

**4. The author does not want a replacement toy. What reason does he give for not wanting a replacement?**

Ⓐ  The package was damaged during shipping.
Ⓑ  The toy was a gift, and there is not enough time to ship a replacement.
Ⓒ  The toy is broken.
Ⓓ  He requests a prepaid shipping label to return the toy.

**Question 5 is based on the passage below**

### Digestive System

The digestive system is made up of the esophagus, stomach, liver, gall bladder, pancreas, large and small intestines, appendix, and rectum. Digestion actually begins in the mouth when food is chewed and mixed with saliva. Muscles in the esophagus push food into the stomach. Once there, it mixes with digestive juices. While in the stomach, food is broken down into nutrients, good for you, and turned into a thick liquid. The food then moves into the small intestine where more digestive juices complete breaking it down. It is in the small intestine that nutrients are taken into the blood and carried throughout the body. Anything left over that your body cannot use goes to the large intestine. The body takes water from the leftovers. The rest is passed out of your body.

**5. What evidence does the writer provide to support the fact that everything eaten is not used by the body for nutrients?**

Ⓐ  Digestion actually begins in the mouth when food is chewed and mixed with saliva.
Ⓑ  The food then moves into the small intestine where more digestive juices complete breaking it down.
Ⓒ  It is in the small intestine that nutrients are taken into the blood and carried throughout the body.
Ⓓ  Anything left over that the body cannot use goes to the large intestine. The body takes water from those leftovers. The rest is passed out of the body.

Smoking is a cheesy (icky) habit. It not only damages your health, but it also affects the way an individual looks and smells. People who smoke have dreadful breath that's comparable to a dirty ashtray, but it is not only their breath that smells awful. Their clothes and hair smell smoky, and if this isn't bad enough, smoking can cause their teeth to turn yellow.

6. Above is a section from a persuasive essay written to encourage people not to smoke. What evidence does the writer provide that supports the claim that smoking affects the way you look?

   (A) Smoking is a cheesy (icky) habit.
   (B) People who smoke have dreadful breath.
   (C) Their clothes and hair smell smoky.
   (D) Smoking can cause their teeth to turn yellow.

7. Above is a section from a persuasive essay written to encourage people not to smoke. Which statement does not provide evidence that supports the claim that smoking causes you smell bad?

   (A) People who smoke have dreadful breath thats comparable to a dirty ashtray.
   (B) Eating onions also may cause you to have bad breath.
   (C) It is not only people's breath that smells bad.
   (D) Their clothes and hair also smell like smoke.

Drinking alcohol and driving is a dangerous combination. This is because alcohol affects the nervous system. Alcohol can make an individual act silly and laugh at situations that are not funny. Alcohol slows down the brain. This can cause the driver to have a slowed reaction time and to have difficulty thinking accurately. It causes a motorist to not be able to make quick, clear decisions about traffic and road conditions. Alcohol's effect on the brain can cause a lack of coordination. This can lead to a driver to weaving in many directions on the road. It can cause a driver to have trouble applying the brakes when needed. Any one of these reactions can easily cause an accident that can be harmful to themselves and others.

8. **Above is a section from a persuasive essay written to encourage people not to drink. What statement does not provide evidence supporting the writer's claim that drinking alcohol and driving is dangerous?**

Ⓐ Alcohol can make an individual act silly and laugh at situations that are not funny.
Ⓑ Alcohol slows down the brain.
Ⓒ Alcohol's effect on the brain causes lack of coordination.
Ⓓ This can lead a driver weaving in many directions on the road or have trouble applying the brakes when needed.

### Question 9 is based on the paragraph below

Dr. Johnson thinks that everyone should take responsibility for preserving the toad species. By not mowing certain areas of our lawns, special areas of wild grass can be kept for toads. This practice may help to preserve the species. According to Dr. Johnson, dangerous chemicals found in pesticides and fertilizers are the reason that the toads are disappearing. The chemicals affect the food chain and kill the insects that toads eat. Dr. Johnson believes that the toads can be saved if we keep a space in our yards and stop using chemical fertilizers.

9. **What would be an appropriate title for the above text?**

Ⓐ Please Stop Mowing Your Lawn
Ⓑ Don't Let Toads Disappear
Ⓒ Please Stop Using Fertilizers
Ⓓ Dr. Johnson and the Toad

In the United States today, we are starting to see more and more of a problem with children who are overweight. Doctors and other health care professionals are trying to do something about it. They are recommending healthier foods and encouraging children get daily vigorous exercise. They also recommend that children go outside and play instead of sitting in front of the tv. They have suggested that children get at least an hour of exercise a day by participating in activities like jumping rope, cycling, or basketball, movement that makes the heart beat faster. This kind of exercise is known as aerobic exercise. Something else they recommend is for children to do exercises that strengthen the bones and muscles. There are a lot of ways that children can do this. One way is running.

**10. What is the main idea of the above text?**

Ⓐ  Doctors want you to move.
Ⓑ  It is very important for kids to exercise daily.
Ⓒ  Jumping and other activities help make bones strong.
Ⓓ  Any physical exercise can help make the heart beat stronger.

Rosa Parks is famous for her actions during the Civil Rights movement. Although she initially dropped out of high school, she went back later to earn her high school diploma when she was around 20 years old. At that time, not many people in Montgomery, Alabama finished school. Thanks to her diploma, she was able to get a job at Maxwell Field, an air force base not far from her home. During the time Rosa worked on the military base, President Roosevelt decided that military bases could not be segregated. This meant that workers of different race could be together which wasn't the way it was outside the base. Segregation laws separated people of different races in all public places. So, on the bus that Rosa had to take home, she had to ride in the back.

**11. Which details above help to explain segregation?**

Ⓐ Rosa Parks was one of the few people in Montgomery who had her high school diploma.
Ⓑ She worked at Maxwell Field.
Ⓒ Segregation laws said that Rosa had to ride in the back of the city buses.
Ⓓ Rosa boarded the city bus, paid her fare, and moved to the back of the bus.

## CHAPTER 2 → Lesson 9: Integrating Information

**Question 1-3 are based on the passage below**

### *On the Trail: an Outdoor Book for Girls* by Adelia Beard and Lina Beard

For any journey, by rail or by boat, one has a general idea of the direction to be taken, the character of the land or water to be crossed, and of what one will find at the end. So it should be in striking the trail. Learn all you can about the path you are to follow. Whether it is plain or obscure, wet or dry; where it leads; and its length, measured more by time than by actual miles. A smooth, even trail of five miles will not consume the time and strength that must be expended upon a trail of half that length which leads over uneven ground, varied by bogs and obstructed by rocks and fallen trees, or a trail that is all up-hill climbing.

### *How to Camp Out* by John M. Gould

Think over and decide whether you will walk, go horseback, sail, camp out in one place, or what you will do; then learn what you can of the route you propose to go over, or the ground where you intend to camp for the season. If you think of moving through or camping in places unknown to you, it is important to learn whether you can buy provisions and get lodgings along your route. See some one, if you can, who has been where you think of going, [Pg 10]and put down in a note-book all he tells you that is important.

**1. Which sentence below integrates information from the above texts?**

Ⓐ Hiking over logs or fallen trees is harder than hiking an even, clear trail.
Ⓑ You should talk to someone who has been where you plan to go so you can get information and tips that will be helpful in planning your camping trip.
Ⓒ Hiking over uneven land will take longer than going the same distance over flat land.
Ⓓ When planning a camping trip, it is important to plan by considering both the type of the trail you will travel and whether you will walk or ride on horseback.

**2. Which paragraph below combines information from the above texts?**

Ⓐ Camping is terribly difficult, and only true experts should try to camp overnight.
Ⓑ If you plan to camp somewhere you've never been, you should learn everything you can about the trail. Find out what the land is like and where you can buy supplies along the way.
Ⓒ Only boys can go on long camping trips across bogs or uneven land.
Ⓓ You should always take a notebook on your camping trips to write about your trip and draw pictures of plants and animals you see.

## 3. Which pair of sentences shows similar information found in both texts?

Ⓐ "Learn all you can about the path you are to follow."
"Learn what you can of the route that you propose to go over."

Ⓑ "So it should be in striking the trail."
"Think over and decide whether you will walk, go horseback, sail, camp out in one place, or what you will do…"

Ⓒ "A smooth, even trail of five miles will not consume the time and strength that must be expended upon a trail of half that length which leads over uneven ground…"
"… It is important to learn whether you can buy provisions and get lodgings along your route."

Ⓓ All of the above

### Question 4 and 5 are based on the passage below

## The Amazing Peacock

Did you know that the term, "peacock" only refers to the male of its species? A female peafowl is actually called a "peahen." Peacocks are native to India and other parts of Southeast Asia and are known for their brilliantly colored feathers. Their bodies can be thirty-five to fifty inches, while their beautiful tails can be as long as five feet! People admire peacocks for their beautiful feathers, but the tails also serve a purpose. The peacocks' tails help peahens choose their mates!

## The Peafowl and It's Magnificent Tail

Peafowls are glorious animals and have long been admired by humans for their beautiful and brightly colored tail feathers. Their tails do not reach their full length until the peacock is four or five years old. When this happens, the peacock will strut day after day in hopes of attracting a mate. Peafowl are actually a kind of pheasant. Some are natives of India, while others come from Sri Lanka, Myanmar (Burma), or Java. Peafowl are some of the largest flying birds around!

## 4. Which paragraph below integrates information from both texts above?

Ⓐ The peafowl, more commonly known as the peacock, has beautiful tail feathers.
Those feathers can grow to be around five feet long, but their growth usually does not peak until the peacock is four or five years old.
Ⓑ Peacocks are wonderful creatures. They come from India, and their bodies can grow to be thirty-five to fifty inches long.
Ⓒ Peacocks like to strut around all day with their beautiful feathers spread wide for all to see. This is what helps them to find a mate.
Ⓓ None of the above

## 5. Which sentence below combines information from both texts above?

Ⓐ Peacocks have been admired by humans for over a thousand years because their tail feathers are so beautiful.

Ⓑ "Peafowl" actually refers to both the male and female of its species, while "peacock" is the correct term for the male only.

Ⓒ Peacocks are enormous.

Ⓓ With bodies as big as thirty-five to fifty inches and tails as long as five feet, peacocks are some of the largest flying birds you will ever see.

### Question 6-8 are based on the passage below

## Sacagawea

Sacagawea is a famous Native American woman from the Shoshone tribe. She became famous when she helped two male explorers named Lewis and Clark, find their way through the unknown west. When she was 12 years old, she was kidnapped by an enemy of the Shoshone tribe called the Hidatsa. Legend has it, that the chief of the Hidatsa tribe sold Sacagawea into slavery.

In 1804, she became a translator and guide for a group of explorers led by Lewis and Clark. She helped them find their way from near the Dakotas to the Pacific Ocean. She became a famous Native American woman in US history for being brave and helping these explorers discover unknown territory.

## Lewis and Clark

Sacagawea, also spelled *Sacajawea*, is best known for her role in helping Meriwether Lewis and William Clark during their journey to explore the American West. They set out on their journey on May 14, 1804. They left from near Wood River, Illinois; it was during winter in South Dakota when they met Sacagawea. They reached the Pacific Ocean on the coast of Oregon in November 1805.

The journey was unique. The new frontier was full of unknown native people and the land was dangerous. Without the help of someone who knew the land, Lewis and Clark may not have made it to the Pacific.

Sacagawea was the young Shoshone wife of a French-Canadian fur trapper named Toussaint Charbonneau. Together, she and her husband served as interpreters, guides, and negotiators for Lewis and Clark. Their friendship with Clark was so strong that when they returned, they moved to his hometown of St. Louis. Clark became the guardian of her children after her death.

**6. Which of the following sentences integrates information from both texts above?**

(A) Despite being kidnapped and sold into slavery at the age of 12, Sacagawea went on to guide and befriend Meriwether Lewis and William Clark on their journey of exploration from South Dakota to the Pacific Ocean in Oregon.

(B) Sacagawea is a famous and brave Shoshone Indian who helped guide Lewis and Clark on their journey to find new territory.

(C) Sacagawea developed such a strong bond with William Clark that after the expedition she moved to his city and even left her children in his care when she died.

(D) Sacagawea was kidnapped by the Hidatsa in 1804.

**7. Which of the following sentences combines information from both texts above?**

(A) Sacagawea was a Shoshone princess who very slyly took charge of one of the most famous explorations in American History.

(B) Sacagawea did serve as interpreter and guide, but it was merely her presence that showed William's and Clark's peaceful intentions when the expedition encountered new tribes.

(C) At twelve, Sacagawea was kidnapped and sold to a French-Canadian man; but she eventually married the fur trapper, Toussaint Charbonneau, and together they became part of an expedition that will live on in history.

(D) Sacagawea was kidnapped by the Hidatsa in 1804.

**8. Which of the following sentences combines information from both texts above?**

(A) Sacagawea was a member of the Shoshone tribe of Native Americans.

(B) Sacagawea was brave because she was kidnapped as a child, went on a treacherous and historic journey across the American West, and also ventured to live in a new city.

(C) Sacagawea could not have aided the Lewis and Clark expedition without the help of her husband, who was an experienced fur trapper.

(D) Sacagawea was kidnapped by the Hidatsa in 1804.

## One Theory on Dinosaur Extinction

Have you ever thought about what happened to the dinosaurs that once roamed the Earth? Well, scientists have developed several ideas throughout the years. One idea is that a giant meteorite crashed into our planet and caused a huge dust cloud to cover the Earth. The dust cloud was so enormous that it kept the Sun's rays from reaching Earth. This caused all of the plants to die. With nothing to eat, the herbivores died. The large carnivores also died, leaving the planet without dinosaurs.

## Dinosaur Die-out: Competing Theories

There are many theories about how dinosaurs came to be extinct. Scientists do not all agree about what may have happened. The most recent idea says that a giant meteorite crashed into the earth. It kicked up enough dust and dirt that the Sun's rays did not reach Earth for a very long time. This prevented plants from making their own food via photosynthesis. Plant-eaters and then, meat-eaters died due to a lack of food.

The other leading idea says that dinosaurs died out when the Earth went through a time of volcanoes erupting. Like the meteorite idea, it is thought that the volcanoes spewed enough ash into the air that the Sun's rays were blocked. This also caused plant and animal life to die.

## 9. Which of the following paragraphs integrates information from both of the above texts?

Ⓐ Dinosaurs are thought to have become extinct 65 million years ago, but some scientists theorize that they are still roaming remote parts of the Amazon Rainforest.

Ⓑ Dinosaurs became extinct because of widespread volcanic eruptions that blocked sunlight from reaching Earth. When this happened, plants died, beginning a disruption of the food chain that dinosaurs didn't survive.

Ⓒ One theory suggests a meteorite caused dinosaur extinction, while another claims widespread volcanic eruptions caused the animals to die. Both theories, however, center around the idea that plants did not get needed sunlight, and plant-eating and meat-eating animals died as a result.

Ⓓ None of the above

**10. Which of the following sentences integrates information from both of the above texts?**

&#9400; Several theories exist about how dinosaurs became extinct; but the two main theories are that either a meteorite crashing into Earth or a series of massive volcanic eruptions caused the animals to die out.

&#9401; Dinosaurs may have become extinct because a giant meteorite crashed into the Earth somewhere near the Gulf of Mexico, but scientists are not sure.

&#9402; If producers are unable to get sunlight, photosynthesis can't take place. This means plant-eating animals do not have food, thus meaning that meat-eating animals will not have food either.

&#9403; All of the above

# End of Reading Informational Text

# Chapter 3 - Language

## Lesson 1: Pronouns

**1. Choose the correct pronoun to complete the sentence.**

Bobby and I have practice every day. The 7th graders practice first and their practice always runs long. I live closer but Bobby is on my team, so ___ walk to the games together.

Ⓐ  I
Ⓑ  we
Ⓒ  us
Ⓓ  they

**2. Choose the correct pronoun to complete the sentence.**

My father asked me to bring _____ book inside.

Ⓐ  he
Ⓑ  him
Ⓒ  his
Ⓓ  us

**3. Choose the correct pronoun to complete the sentence.**

I would like you to meet Jamie. _____ is my best friend.

Ⓐ  He
Ⓑ  Him
Ⓒ  Its
Ⓓ  Their

**4. Choose the correct pronoun to complete the sentence.**

My dogs love to play with _____ squeaky toys.

Ⓐ  his
Ⓑ  its
Ⓒ  their
Ⓓ  them

**5. Choose the correct pronoun to complete the sentence.**

The little girl put _____ doll in the toy box before going to bed.

Ⓐ she
Ⓑ its
Ⓒ their
Ⓓ her

**6. Choose the correct pronoun to complete the sentence.**

The dancers practice every night in order to learn _____ dance steps.

Ⓐ its
Ⓑ them
Ⓒ their
Ⓓ our

**7. Choose the appropriate pronoun.**

Kelly and I have been going to dances for two years now, but her little sister wants to come with us this time. This is _____ first time at a school dance.

Ⓐ her
Ⓑ my
Ⓒ she
Ⓓ it

**8. Complete the sentence with the appropriate pronoun.**

_____ went hiking in the mountains together.

Ⓐ His
Ⓑ Her
Ⓒ They
Ⓓ Them

## 9. Choose the correct pronoun.

I baked fancy Christmas cupcakes for my teacher. She is my favorite teacher and I couldn't wait until Monday to give them to _____.

Ⓐ she
Ⓑ him
Ⓒ he
Ⓓ her

## 10. Choose the correct pronoun.

Alice and Jennifer like going ice skating. _____ are going to the ice skating rink this afternoon.

Ⓐ Their
Ⓑ They
Ⓒ Them
Ⓓ Her

## 11. Choose the appropriate pronoun. Fill in the blank by choosing the correct answer from the options given below

_____ have been going to school together since first grade.

Ⓐ Them
Ⓑ He
Ⓒ Him
Ⓓ They

## 12. Choose the pronoun that fits in the blank above. Fill in the blank by choosing the correct answer from the options given below

Please bring the remote control to _____.

Ⓐ me
Ⓑ I
Ⓒ they
Ⓓ we

# CHAPTER 3 → Lesson 2: Progressive Verb Tense

**1. Choose the correct progressive verb tense.**

Efrain, accompanied by his parents, _____ to Europe this summer.

Ⓐ are traveling
Ⓑ will be traveling
Ⓒ was traveling
Ⓓ is traveling

**2. Choose the correct verb to complete the sentence.**

Darrel and I _____ the football game with friends this Friday night.

Ⓐ is attending
Ⓑ am attending
Ⓒ was attending
Ⓓ will attend

**3. Choose the sentence that has the proper progressive verb tense.**

Ⓐ Minnie, Jill, and Sandra are singing the birthday song to Ann right now.
Ⓑ Bob, Jim, and Harry have played baseball next summer.
Ⓒ One of my five hamsters might get out of the cage tomorrow night.
Ⓓ Twenty-five dollars are too much to charge for that bracelet.

**4. Choose the sentence that has proper verb tense.**

Ⓐ Everyone in my neighborhood, including the woman with nine dogs, were walking each night after dinner.
Ⓑ Contestants from Europe, America, and Germany are competing in last year's contest.
Ⓒ Neither of the girls is planning to audition for the school play today.
Ⓓ No one in my history class wishes that we had more homework each night.

## 5. Choose the correct one.

Jenny, one of my many friends, _____ to buy a new car this summer with money she earns during this school year at her baby-sitting job.

Ⓐ will be saving
Ⓑ is saving
Ⓒ am saving
Ⓓ be hoping

## 6. What could be the correct form of the sentence?

The cheerleader, who was cheering for her team, wore one of the team's new uniforms.

Ⓐ The cheerleader, who was cheering for her team, were dressed in one of the team's new uniforms.
Ⓑ The cheerleader, who was cheering for her team, was wearing one of the team's new uniforms.
Ⓒ The cheerleader, who were cheering for her team, were wearing one of the team's new uniforms.
Ⓓ The cheerleaders, who was cheering for her teams, will be wearing one of the teams new uniforms.

## 7. What could be the correct form of the sentence?

The trees that keeps waved in the wind on the side of the street show how forceful the wind is.

Ⓐ The trees that waved in the wind on the side of the street show how forceful the wind is.
Ⓑ The trees that will be waving in the wind on the side of the street show how forceful the wind is.
Ⓒ The trees that keep waving in the wind on the side of the street show how forceful the wind is.
Ⓓ The trees that waving in the wind on the side of the street shows how forceful the wind is.

## 8. Choose the correct sentence.

The world change so rapidly that we can hardly keep up.

Ⓐ The world will be changing so rapidly that we can hardly keep up.
Ⓑ The world change so rapidly that we can hardly keep up.
Ⓒ The world is changing so rapidly that we can hardly keep up.
Ⓓ The worlds change so rapidly that we can hardly keep up.

**9. Choose the correct sentence.**

She sitted at the table by the window when the waiter approached.

Ⓐ  She sitting at the table by the window when the waiter approached.
Ⓑ  She was sitting at the table by the window when the waiter approached.
Ⓒ  She is sitting at the table by the window when the waiter approached.
Ⓓ  Shes will be sitting at the table by the window when the waiter approached.

**10. Which verb best completes the sentence?**

Kenji and Briana _____ at recess when their parents pick them up for their doctor appointments.

Ⓐ  play
Ⓑ  will play
Ⓒ  will be playing
Ⓓ  were playing

## CHAPTER 3 → Lesson 3: What's the Verb?

**1. In the below sentence, find the simple predicate.**

"I picked it up on the beach last weekend."

Ⓐ picked it up
Ⓑ I
Ⓒ I picked it
Ⓓ picked

**2. Choose the correct word to fill in the blank.**

I heard a sound. Did you _____ a sound?

Ⓐ hearing
Ⓑ heard
Ⓒ hear
Ⓓ will hear

**3. Choose the correct verb for the below sentence.**

Mary sang in the school choir last year, but this year she _____ in the church choir.

Ⓐ sung
Ⓑ had sang
Ⓒ is singing
Ⓓ has sung

**4. Choose the verbs from the sentence below.**

At the game last week, Lauren hit the ball over the fence and scored the winning run.

Ⓐ ball, fence
Ⓑ hit, scored
Ⓒ winning, run
Ⓓ over, run

**5. Choose the correct verb for the sentence below.**

I _____ so nervous about standing in front of the class and reciting my poem today that my hands are shaking.

Ⓐ  are
Ⓑ  is
Ⓒ  were
Ⓓ  am

**6. Choose the simple predicate from the sentence below.**

My mother finished the work on my sister's tomato costume for the play.

Ⓐ  play
Ⓑ  finished
Ⓒ  costume
Ⓓ  work

**7. Choose the sentence that uses a present tense verb.**

Ⓐ  I stood outside and watched the lunar eclipse with my family.
Ⓑ  The farmer will be planting corn this year instead cotton and soybeans.
Ⓒ  Randy and Paul are sitting in the bus at the end of the line.
Ⓓ  You had to go to detention today because you forgot to do your homework.

**8. Choose the verb in the sentence below.**

My grandmother's love for flowers shows in her beautiful painting.

Ⓐ  shows
Ⓑ  love
Ⓒ  beautiful
Ⓓ  painting

**9. Choose the correct verb to complete the below sentence.**

I saw a bear and her cubs as they walked through the forest. Did you _____ them?

Ⓐ  seeing
Ⓑ  seen
Ⓒ  saw
Ⓓ  see

**10. Choose the sentence that is written in past tense.**

Ⓐ The sea gulls swooped down suddenly and captured the unsuspecting fish.
Ⓑ My mother says that everyone will be in a hurry to finish their shopping today.
Ⓒ Although he wants to buy a computer, Bill plans to buy a new cell phone instead.
Ⓓ I do not know the answer to that question, but I will find the answer before our next class.

**11. What is the entire verb phrase in this sentence?**

The kids at my school have all mysteriously disappeared!

Ⓐ have disappeared
Ⓑ have all
Ⓒ have all disappeared
Ⓓ have mysteriously

**12. Identify the simple predicate in the sentence below.**

This morning I cleaned my room.

Ⓐ This
Ⓑ morning
Ⓒ cleaned
Ⓓ room

## CHAPTER 3 → Lesson 4: Modal Auxiliary Verbs

**1. Which sentences contain an auxiliary verb?**

(1) Rae and her mother need to find a birthday gift for Rae's father, Joseph. (2) They discussed shopping online, walking to the store in their neighborhood, or going to the mall to find the gift. (3) Because Rae's mother suffers from arthritis, I don't think they will walk to the store to buy the gift. (4) They may decide it's most efficient to buy the gift online.

   Ⓐ sentence 1
   Ⓑ sentences 2 and 3
   Ⓒ sentence 4
   Ⓓ sentences 3 and 4

**2. What is the purpose of the modal auxiliary verb, "may," in the sentence?**

Oliver may go to school tomorrow if his fever has dissipated.

   Ⓐ It is being used to express doubt.
   Ⓑ It is being used to talk about a future event with uncertainty.
   Ⓒ It is being used to talk about something that will definitely happen.
   Ⓓ It is being used to talk about something that definitely will not happen.

**3. Replace "can" with the correct verb in the sentence.**

Liam can have taken the test before he went on vacation, but he did not inform his teacher about the trip in advance.

   Ⓐ will
   Ⓑ must
   Ⓒ can't
   Ⓓ could

**4. What is the auxiliary modal verb in the sentence?**

Dana had to leave the party when her mother called to inform her of an emergency at home.

   Ⓐ called to
   Ⓑ at
   Ⓒ had to
   Ⓓ will

**5. Choose the sentence that contains a modal auxiliary verb.**

Ⓐ You shouldn't have handled your disagreement with physical violence.
Ⓑ I want to have a birthday party.
Ⓒ Everyone needs to look up.
Ⓓ That is the most beautiful painting I have ever seen.

**6. Choose the sentence that contains a modal auxiliary verb.**

Ⓐ You are a very good reader.
Ⓑ Sara is having a great time on her Hawaiian vacation.
Ⓒ I am not a big fan of Justin Beiber.
Ⓓ You could be a really good student if you applied yourself to your studies.

**7. Choose the sentence that contains a modal auxiliary verb.**

Ⓐ Jerome has potential to be an excellent science fiction writer.
Ⓑ Margaret is the most beautiful dancer on the stage.
Ⓒ I shall never think another bad thought again.
Ⓓ Jenny is eating a sandwich for dinner.

**8.** (1)If I could dine with any person, living or dead, I would choose Maya Angelou. (2)She endured hardships in her life but went on to become one of the most influential literary figures of the 20th century. (3)I will ask her what inspired her most.

**"Will" is not the best verb choice in the 3rd sentence.**

**What word should the speaker have used instead to express possibility rather than certainty?**

Ⓐ can
Ⓑ may
Ⓒ shall
Ⓓ would

**9. Why did Marvin's mother respond this way?**

"Can you hand me that apple?" Marvin asked his mother.
"Yes," she answered. But she didn't move a muscle.

Ⓐ She had an extremely long and tiring day at work. Marvin's mother did not want to hand him the apple.

Ⓑ Marvin's mother recognizes she can hand him the apple and knows there is a better way for him to ask using the word "will".

Ⓒ Marvin's mother does not approve of apples.

Ⓓ She thinks Marvin should have to get his own apple.

**10. Choose the sentence that correctly uses a modal auxiliary verb.**

Ⓐ I might have to see a doctor if this headache does not go away.

Ⓑ I shall all the items on the menu.

Ⓒ She musted remembered to lock the front door before leaving for work each day.

Ⓓ Her might need to go to the school for a conference tomorrow.

# CHAPTER 3 → Lesson 5: Adjectives and Adverbs

**1. Identify the _adverb_ used in <u>sentence 2</u>.**

(1) Mary went to visit her grandmother last weekend. (2) She likes to visit her grandmother frequently. (3) While visiting, they enjoy walking. (4) They strolled in the beautiful park and talked. (5) Mary and her grandmother enjoyed their visit.

Ⓐ likes
Ⓑ visit
Ⓒ frequently
Ⓓ her

**2. Identify the _adjective_ used in <u>sentence 4</u>.**

(1) Mary went to visit her grandmother last weekend. (2) She likes to visit her grandmother frequently. (3) While visiting, they enjoy walking. (4) They strolled in the beautiful park and talked. (5) Mary and her grandmother enjoyed their visit.

Ⓐ strolled
Ⓑ beautiful
Ⓒ park
Ⓓ talked

**3. Identify an _adjective_ in the below sentence.**

Zelda and her family visited the Jackson Zoo last weekend although it was alarmingly cold and rainy.

Ⓐ last
Ⓑ although
Ⓒ and
Ⓓ cold

**4. Identify the _adjective_ in the below sentence.**

The fastest runner in our school practices frequently in order to increase his speed.

Ⓐ fastest
Ⓑ practices
Ⓒ frequently
Ⓓ increase

**5. Choose the appropriate word for the sentence below.**

I think that my daughter is the _____ girl in the world.

- Ⓐ beautifulest
- Ⓑ beautifuler
- Ⓒ most beautiful
- Ⓓ more beautiful

**6. Choose the correct _comparative adjective_ to complete the below sentence.**

The wind was much _____ than it was last weekend.

- Ⓐ cold
- Ⓑ coldest
- Ⓒ more cold
- Ⓓ colder

**7. Choose the proper comparative adjective to complete the below sentence.**

While standing at the intersection, I heard a loud noise and turned my head to see the _____ wreck imaginable.

- Ⓐ horrificest
- Ⓑ most horrificest
- Ⓒ more horrificest
- Ⓓ most horrific

**8. What's the correct order of adverbs in the sentence below?**

The huge tiger hungrily and stealthily walked in the black, spiky bush getting ready to pounce.

- Ⓐ huge, spiky
- Ⓑ hungrily and stealthily
- Ⓒ stealthily and hungrily
- Ⓓ black spiky

## 9. What is the adjective in sentence 1?

(1) Lindsay, Laine, and John were excited. (2) Each put their things in an overnight bag. (3) They were going to spend two nights with Aunt Margaret, and the next night with their Auntie Jo.

Ⓐ John
Ⓑ Lindsay
Ⓒ Laine
Ⓓ excited

## 10. What is one of the adjectives in sentence 3?

(1) Lindsay, Laine, and John were excited. (2) They put their things in his or her overnight bag. (3) They were going to spend two nights with Aunt Margaret, and the next night with their Auntie Jo, who was their mom's sister.

Ⓐ aunt
Ⓑ they
Ⓒ two
Ⓓ mom's

## 11. Fill in the blank using the correct adjective from the options given below.

It was determined that James was the _____ runner on our track team.

Ⓐ most fast
Ⓑ fastest
Ⓒ most fastest
Ⓓ faster

## CHAPTER 3 → Lesson 6: Prepositional Phrases

**1. Choose the sentence that contains a prepositional phrase.**

Ⓐ  The monkey was washing its paws.
Ⓑ  The lion jumped into the pool of cool water.
Ⓒ  That is the most beautiful dog I have ever seen.
Ⓓ  When you decide, let me know.

**2. Identify the prepositional phrase in the below sentence.**

You will find the new notebooks underneath the journals.

Ⓐ  will find
Ⓑ  notebooks underneath
Ⓒ  new notebooks
Ⓓ  underneath the journals

**3. Choose the sentence that contains a prepositional phrase.**

Ⓐ  Please put your paper down so that others won't see your answers.
Ⓑ  Because he doesn't have enough money to buy ice cream, he must do without.
Ⓒ  Do not leave for school without your lunch box.
Ⓓ  Please don't forget to let the dog in.

**4. Choose the sentence that contains a prepositional phrase.**

Ⓐ  When entering the room, Ana tripped on the rug and fell.
Ⓑ  I want to see the Rocky Mountains.
Ⓒ  Everyone needs to look up.
Ⓓ  That is the most beautiful painting I have ever seen.

**5. Identify the prepositional phrase in the below sentence.**

Finding his money, Lee and Jose rushed to join their friends at the fair.

Ⓐ  finding his money
Ⓑ  rushed to join
Ⓒ  their friends
Ⓓ  at the fair

**6. Identify the sentence that contains two prepositional phrases.**

Ⓐ Terrance went into the room to get his book.
Ⓑ Terrance went into the room.
Ⓒ Terrance went into the room and sat in his favorite chair.
Ⓓ Terrance sat in his favorite chair to read.

**7. Identify the prepositional phrase in the below sentence.**

The puppy barked loudly and chased the kitten across the yard.

Ⓐ barked loudly
Ⓑ chased across
Ⓒ barked loudly and chased
Ⓓ across the yard

**8. Identify the sentence that contains a prepositional phrase.**

Ⓐ The intoxicating aroma filled the air.
Ⓑ The aroma coming from the kitchen was inviting.
Ⓒ I forgot to purchase a loaf of bread.
Ⓓ A lovely young woman watched as the band marched.

**9. Identify the sentence that does not contain a prepositional phrase.**

Ⓐ Are you going to let him answer the question?
Ⓑ The answer to the question was wrong.
Ⓒ The teacher put a huge red checkmark on my paper.
Ⓓ The questions on this test were very difficult.

**10. Identify the prepositional phrase in the sentence below.**

The fox chased the deer down the trail.

Ⓐ chased the deer
Ⓑ the fox
Ⓒ down the trail
Ⓓ the deer down

## 11. Which sentence does not contain a prepositional phrase?

Ⓐ No, Mr. Johnson doesn't go to the library.
Ⓑ Jenny and Andy hiked through the valley.
Ⓒ They will not go to the beach because of the rain.
Ⓓ I sent all the packages.

## 12. Which sentence does not contain a prepositional phrase?

Ⓐ I wish that my children wouldn't fight with each other.
Ⓑ My little dog likes to sit on the couch.
Ⓒ I will eat cereal for breakfast this morning.
Ⓓ It is very hot outside today.

## CHAPTER 3 → Lesson 7: Complete Sentences

**1. Which answer choice corrects this run-on sentence?**

Jordan wants to go outside and play with her neighbor her mother said she had to clean up her room first.

Ⓐ Jordan wants to go outside and play with her neighbor, but her mother said she had to clean up her room first.

Ⓑ Jordan wants to go outside and play but her mother won't let her.

Ⓒ Jordan wants, to go outside and play with her neighbor but her mother said she had to clean up her room first.

Ⓓ Jordan wants to go outside. And play with her neighbor. But her mother said she had to clean up her room first.

**2. Which answer choice corrects the run-on sentence below?**

George Washington Carver is best known for his work with peanuts but he also taught his students about crop rotation that's when farmers plant different crops each year to avoid draining the soil of its nutrients.

Ⓐ George Washington Carver is best known for his work with peanuts, but he also taught his students about crop rotation, that's when farmers plant different crops each year to avoid draining the soil of its nutrients

Ⓑ George Washington Carver is best known for his work with peanuts, but he also taught his students about crop rotation. That's when farmers plant different crops each year to avoid draining the soil of its nutrients.

Ⓒ George Washington Carver is best known for his work with peanuts. But he also taught his students about crop rotation. That's when farmers plant different crops each year to avoid draining the soil of its nutrients

Ⓓ George Washington Carver is best known for his work with peanuts but he also taught his students about crop rotation that's when farmers plant different crops each year to avoid draining the soil of its nutrients

**3. Which answer choice is a fragment, rather than a complete sentence?**

Ⓐ Be careful what you wish for.
Ⓑ He should not run with scissors.
Ⓒ If you can't say something nice.
Ⓓ Don't say anything at all.

**4. What would transform this fragment into a complete sentence?**

Three ways to transfer heat.

Ⓐ Replacing the period with a question mark at the end of the sentence
Ⓑ Adding "convection, conduction, and radiation" to the end of the sentence.
Ⓒ Adding "There are" to the beginning of the sentence.
Ⓓ Nothing. The sentence is complete already.

**5. Which sentence is a fragment, rather than a complete sentence?**

(1)Producers make their own food from the sun during a process called photosynthesis. (2)The Greek root, "photo," means "light." (3)Means "to put together." (4)So "photosynthesis" means "to put together with light," which is exactly what plants do when they make their own food.

Ⓐ Sentence 1
Ⓑ Sentence 2
Ⓒ Sentence 3
Ⓓ Sentence 4

6. **Choose the best edited version of the paragraph below. Pay attention to run-on sentences and fragments.**

(1)Jawaad held his head high. (2)As he strode to the front of the classroom to present his research report. (3)The report compared the Norse god, Thor, to the Marvel Comic version of Thor. (4)He was proud of his work and thought the class would really enjoy it.

Ⓐ Jawaad held his head high. As he strode to the front of the classroom to present his research report. The report compared the Norse god, Thor, to the Marvel Comic version of Thor. He was proud of the work and thought the class would really enjoy it.

Ⓑ Jawaad held his head high. As he strode to the front of the classroom to present his research report, the report compared the Norse god, Thor, to the Marvel Comic version of Thor. He was proud of the work and thought the class would really enjoy it.

Ⓒ Jawaad held his head high. As he strode to the front of the classroom to present his research report. The report compared the Norse god, Thor, to the Marvel Comic version of Thor he was proud of the work and thought the class would really enjoy it.

Ⓓ Jawaad held his head high as he strode to the front of the classroom to present his research report. The report compared the Norse god, Thor, to the Marvel Comic version of Thor. He was proud of the work and thought the class would really enjoy it.

7. **Choose the run-on sentence.**

Ⓐ Felix has a mischievous spirit he is somehow quite well-behaved.
Ⓑ Margaret is the most beautiful dancer on the stage.
Ⓒ The sky was the limit for a bright, energetic, young prodigy like Ben.
Ⓓ None of the above

8. **Identify the run-on sentence.**

(1)If I could dine with any person, living or dead, I would choose Maya Angelou. (2)She endured hardships in her life but went on to become one of the most influential literary figures of the 20th century. (3)I would ask her what inspired her most.

Ⓐ Sentence 1
Ⓑ Sentence 2
Ⓒ Sentence 3
Ⓓ None of the above

**9. What would transform the fragment into a complete sentence?**

A really great pair of shoes.

Ⓐ A really great pair of shoes, two ironed shirts, and two pairs of dress pants.
Ⓑ A really great pair of shoes should be both stylish and comfortable.
Ⓒ Doesn't need a really great pair of shoes.
Ⓓ My friend's really great pair of shoes.

**10. Choose the complete sentence.**

Ⓐ While she is a very sweet puppy, I can't justify adopting her.
Ⓑ While she is a very sweet puppy.
Ⓒ Because my apartment is too small.
Ⓓ I can't justify adopting this puppy my apartment is too small.

## CHAPTER 3 → Lesson 8: Frequently Confused Words

**1. Choose the correct word to complete the sentence.**

Divya and her family celebrate Diwali, a traditional festival in _____ culture.

Ⓐ their
Ⓑ they're
Ⓒ there
Ⓓ the're

**2. Choose the correct word to complete the sentence.**

Place your projects over _____ until it's time to present.

Ⓐ their
Ⓑ they're
Ⓒ there
Ⓓ the're

**3. Choose the correct word to complete the sentence.**

Gretchen and Laura are thankful _____ able to peer edit each other's writing.

Ⓐ their
Ⓑ they're.
Ⓒ there
Ⓓ the're

**4. Choose the best edited version of the sentence.**

We're going too my grandmother's house for Thanksgiving, but we'll be driving back home on Friday.

Ⓐ We're going two my grandmother's house for Thanksgiving, but we'll be driving back home on Friday.
Ⓑ Were going too my grandmother's house for Thanksgiving, but we'll be driving back home on Friday.
Ⓒ We're going to my grandmother's house for Thanksgiving, but we'll be driving back home on Friday.
Ⓓ The sentence is correct already.

## 5. What error did the writer make?

I assumed the mall would be crowded today. Were are all the people?

Ⓐ She wrote a run-on sentence.
Ⓑ She spelled "assumed" incorrectly.
Ⓒ She used "were" instead of "where."
Ⓓ She wrote a fragment.

## 6. Which word best completes the sentence?

We don't have any milk or bread, so _____ going to the grocery store right this instant.

Ⓐ were
Ⓑ we're
Ⓒ where
Ⓓ there

## 7. What error did the writer make?

I can't take another breathe until I know how this book will end.

Ⓐ She should have used the word, "breath," rather than "breathe."
Ⓑ She should never hold her breath because she could faint.
Ⓒ She should have used "took," rather than "take."
Ⓓ She should have used "an other" instead of "another."

## 8. Choose the correct word to complete the sentence.

Amal _____ his exam with flying colors. He knew it was because he studied so hard.

Ⓐ pessed
Ⓑ pest
Ⓒ past
Ⓓ passed

**9. Choose the correct word to complete the sentence.**

I have to _____ that science does not come easily for me. If I want to do well I will have to work at it.

Ⓐ except
Ⓑ accept
Ⓒ expect
Ⓓ exccept

**10. Choose the correct sentence.**

Ⓐ We base our school rules around the common principal that everyone should be treated with respect.
Ⓑ The principal called Evelyn to her office to reward her for perfect attendance.
Ⓒ Jamar was extatic when he was chosen as a principle dancer in the ballet.
Ⓓ Kelsey became the most principaled person at the school.

## CHAPTER 3 → Lesson 9: How is it Capitalized?

**1. Identify the words that need to be capitalized in the below sentence.**

Although spring and summer are my favorite seasons, our family gathering on thanksgiving makes november my favorite month.

Ⓐ Spring, November
Ⓑ Thanksgiving, November
Ⓒ Summer, Thanksgiving
Ⓓ Seasons, November

**2. Correctly capitalize the underlined portion of the below address.**

<u>dr. j. howard smith</u>
1141 east palm street
washington, la 98654

Ⓐ Dr. J. Howard Smith
Ⓑ DR. J. Howard Smith
Ⓒ Dr. J. howard smith
Ⓓ Dr. j. Howard Smith

**3. Correctly capitalize the underlined portion of the below address.**

dr. j. howard smith
<u>1141 east palm street</u>
washington, la 98654

Ⓐ 1141 east Palm Street
Ⓑ 1141 East palm Street
Ⓒ 1141 east palm Street
Ⓓ 1141 East Palm Street

**4. Correctly capitalize the underlined portion of the below address.**

dr. j. howard smith
1141 east palm street
<u>washington, la 98654</u>

Ⓐ  Washington, LA 98654
Ⓑ  Washington, La 98654
Ⓒ  washington, LA 98654
Ⓓ  washington, La 98654

**5. Edit the below sentence for capitalization. Choose the sentence that is written correctly.**

Next Semester, I plan to take English, History, Math, Spanish, and Music.

Ⓐ  Next Semester, I plan to take English, History, Spanish, math and music.
Ⓑ  Next semester, I plan to take English, History, Spanish, Math and Music.
Ⓒ  Next semester, I plan to take english, history, spanish, Math and music.
Ⓓ  Next semester, I plan to take English, history, Spanish, math and music.

**6. Choose the title of the book that has correct capitalization.**

In Mrs. Hart's English class, we are reading <u>the indian in the cupboard</u>.

Ⓐ  <u>The Indian In The Cupboard</u>
Ⓑ  <u>The Indian in the Cupboard</u>
Ⓒ  <u>The indian in the Cupboard</u>
Ⓓ  <u>the Indian in the Cupboard</u>

**7. Choose the correctly capitalized version of the below sentence.**

The entire family is excited and looking forward to our visit with aunt jenny, my uncle, my grandfather, and grandma.

Ⓐ  The entire Family is excited and looking forward to our visit with Aunt jenny, my uncle, my grandfather, and Grandma.
Ⓑ  The entire family is excited and looking forward to our visit with Aunt jenny, my uncle, my Grandfather, and Grandma.
Ⓒ  The entire family is excited and looking forward to our visit with Aunt Jenny, my uncle, my grandfather, and Grandma.
Ⓓ  The entire family is excited and looking forward to our visit with aunt Jenny, my Uncle, my Grandfather, and Grandma.

**8. Choose correctly capitalized version of the below letter closing.**

yours truly,
timmy newlin

Ⓐ Yours Truly,
   Timmy Newlin

Ⓑ yours truly,
   Timmy Newlin

Ⓒ Yours truly,
   Timmy Newlin

Ⓓ Yours truly,
   Timmy newlin

**9. Which words should be capitalized?**

the chicago river runs into the mississippi valley waterways.

Ⓐ The, Chicago
Ⓑ The, Chicago River
Ⓒ The, Chicago River, Mississippi
Ⓓ The, Chicago River, Mississippi Valley

**10. Which word in the below sentence should be capitalized?**

I love these lime green nike shoes that my grandma got me for my birthday.

Ⓐ Grandma
Ⓑ Birthday
Ⓒ Nike
Ⓓ Shoes

**11. Which word in the sentence below should be capitalized?**

One of my favorite authors, Ernest hemingway, wrote some amazing books and short stories.

Ⓐ  authors
Ⓑ  hemingway
Ⓒ  favorite
Ⓓ  The sentence is correct.

**12. Which word in the sentence below should be capitalized?**

Beau is having his birthday party at the Stone County City pool.

Ⓐ  Birthday
Ⓑ  Party
Ⓒ  Pool
Ⓓ  The sentence is correct.

## CHAPTER 3 → Lesson 10: What's the Punctuation?

**1. Choose the sentence that is punctuated correctly.**

Ⓐ   Before I go to bed each night I brush my teeth.
Ⓑ   The rabbit scampered across the yard, and ran into the woods.
Ⓒ   I don't like to watch scary movies but I like to read scary books.
Ⓓ   Our teacher gave us time to study before she gave us the test.

**2. Choose the sentence that correctly punctuates a quotation.**

Ⓐ   "Did you remember to lock the door," asked Jenny?
Ⓑ   "Did you remember to lock the door? asked Jenny."
Ⓒ   Jenny asked "Did you remember to lock the door?"
Ⓓ   Jenny asked, "Did you remember to lock the door?"

**3. Choose the sentence that contains a punctuation error.**

Ⓐ   Cindy wants to go to the mall this afternoon, but her mother will not let her.
Ⓑ   Wendy stayed up all night completing her science project, but forgot to take it with her.
Ⓒ   Henry forgot to close the gate securely, so his dog escaped from the backyard.
Ⓓ   Jimmy and John joined the Army; Billy and George joined the Navy.

**4. What is the correct way to write the sentence below?**

Do you know Shel Silverstein's poem The Boa Constrictor our teacher asked.

Ⓐ   "Do you know Shel Silverstein's poem 'The Boa Constrictor'?" our teacher asked.
Ⓑ   "Do you know Shel Silverstein's poem "The Boa Constrictor"? our teacher asked.
Ⓒ   "Do you know Shel Silverstein's poem The Boa Constrictor"? our teacher asked.
Ⓓ   "Do you know Shel Silverstein's poem The Boa Constrictor" she asked?

**5. What is the correct way to write the sentence below?**

Of all the poems in his latest book she said this is my favorite. It's really very funny she added.

Ⓐ  "Of all the poems in his latest book" she said "this is my favorite." "It's really very funny she added."

Ⓑ  "Of all the poems in his latest book," she said, "this is my favorite. It's really very funny," she added.

Ⓒ  "Of all the poems in his latest book she said this is my favorite. It's really very funny she added."

Ⓓ  "Of all the poems in his latest book," she said "this is my favorite. "It's really very funny" she added.

**6. What is the correct way to write the sentence below?**

Tom's English professor asked him what was wrong.

Ⓐ  The sentence is correct.

Ⓑ  Tom's English professor asked him "what was wrong?"

Ⓒ  "Tom's English professor asked him what was wrong."

Ⓓ  Tom's English professor, asked him, what was wrong.

**7. Choose the sentence that correctly punctuates the above sentence.**

Coco Chanel my best friends dog loves to play chase with me when I visit.

Ⓐ  Coco Chanel, my best friends dog, loves to play chase with me when I visit

Ⓑ  Coco Chanel, my best friend's dog, loves to play chase with me, when I visit.

Ⓒ  Coco Chanel, my best friend's dog, loves to play chase with me when I visit.

Ⓓ  Coco Chanel, my best friend's dog loves to play chase, with me when I visit.

**8. Which sentence below is written correctly?**

We are having broccoli and beets roast chicken and ice cream for dinner.

Ⓐ  We are having broccoli, and beets, roast chicken, and ice cream for dinner.

Ⓑ  We are having broccoli and beets, roast chicken, and ice cream for dinner.

Ⓒ  We are having broccoli, and beets, roast, chicken, and ice cream for dinner.

Ⓓ  We are having broccoli and beets, roast chicken and ice cream for dinner.

**9. Which sentence below is written correctly?**

A famous basketball player Kobe Bryant won many MVP awards.

Ⓐ   A famous basketball player Kobe Bryant won many MVP awards.
Ⓑ   A famous basketball player, Kobe Bryant won many MVP awards.
Ⓒ   A famous basketball player, Kobe Bryant, won many MVP awards.
Ⓓ   A, famous basketball player, Kobe Bryant, won many MVP awards.

**10. Which sentence below has the correct end punctuation?**

Ⓐ   Their cat is black!
Ⓑ   Help, a clown is chasing me!
Ⓒ   Are you sure that goes there!
Ⓓ   I wish I knew what time it was!

# CHAPTER 3 → Lesson 11: Conjunctions and Interjections

(1) Mary went to visit her grandmother last weekend. (2) She likes to visit her grandmother frequently. (3) While visiting, they enjoy walking. (4) They strolled in the beautiful park and talked. (5) Mary and her grandmother enjoyed their visit.

## 1. Which sentences contain a conjunction?

(A) sentences 1 and 2
(B) sentences 2 and 3
(C) sentences 3 and 4
(D) sentences 4 and 5

## 2. Identify the conjunction in the below sentence.

Billy does not like to play basketball, nor does he enjoy watching it on TV.

(A) not
(B) nor
(C) does
(D) to

## 3. Identify the subordinating conjunction in the below sentence.

As soon as I finish my homework, I am going to watch my favorite TV show.

(A) soon
(B) as soon as
(C) to
(D) to watch

## 4. Identify the coordinating conjunction in the below sentence.

Zelda and her family visited the Jackson Zoo last weekend although it was cold and rainy.

(A) last
(B) although
(C) and
(D) cold

**5. Identify the <u>subordinating conjunction</u> in the above sentence.**

Zelda and her family visited the Jackson Zoo last weekend although it was cold and rainy.

(A) last
(B) although
(C) and
(D) cold

**6. Choose the compound sentence that uses the proper coordinating conjunction.**

(A) My favorite food is pizza, or Jenny's favorite food is tacos.
(B) The junior high baseball game was exciting, nor the varsity game was even better.
(C) I forgot to do my math homework, but I am being sent to detention.
(D) I love horseback riding, so I am looking forward to the trail ride this weekend.

**7. Identify the <u>interjection</u> in the below sentence.**

No, you cannot go to the mall with your friends this weekend because we are going to visit Grandma and Grandpa.

(A) no
(B) to
(C) because
(D) and

**8. Identify the <u>coordinating conjunction</u> in the below sentence.**

No, you cannot go to the mall with your friends this weekend because we are going to visit Grandma and Grandpa.

(A) no
(B) to
(C) because
(D) and

**9. Identify the subordinating conjunction in the below sentence.**

No, you cannot go to the mall with your friends this weekend because we are going to visit Grandma and Grandpa.

Ⓐ no
Ⓑ to
Ⓒ because
Ⓓ and

**10. Identify the interjection in the below sentence.**

Wow! That was the most amazing trick I have ever seen.

Ⓐ most
Ⓑ amazing
Ⓒ that
Ⓓ wow

**11. Go put on either your shoes and your boots.**

**Fix the sentence by replacing and with an appropriate conjunction.**

## CHAPTER 3 → Lesson 12: How is it Spelled?

**1. Choose the correctly spelled word that best completes the sentence.**

Vargas asked his partner, "Could you please _____ your question to make it easier to understand?"

- Ⓐ clearify
- Ⓑ Clerify
- Ⓒ carefully
- Ⓓ clarify

**2. Find the misspelled word.**

- Ⓐ ostrich
- Ⓑ vehicel
- Ⓒ wings
- Ⓓ horse

**3. Which of the following words are spelled correctly?**

- Ⓐ pollution
- Ⓑ polution
- Ⓒ plloution
- Ⓓ polltion

**4. Choose the word that is incorrectly spelled in the below sentence.**

Mom asked the mayor, "Do you beleive in ghosts?"

- Ⓐ asked
- Ⓑ mayor
- Ⓒ beleive
- Ⓓ ghosts

**5. Choose the word that is correctly spelled.**

- Ⓐ monkies
- Ⓑ strawberrys
- Ⓒ cherrys
- Ⓓ donkeys

**6. Choose that word that is incorrectly spelled in the below sentence.**

Nicky set the table for dinner, but she forgot to place knifes at each place setting.

Ⓐ dinner
Ⓑ knifes
Ⓒ setting
Ⓓ table

**7. Choose the word that is not spelled correctly.**

Ⓐ collaterol
Ⓑ enthusiasm
Ⓒ infrequently
Ⓓ vigorous

**8. Choose the sentence with the misspelled word.**

Ⓐ Rosemary skipped across the room to give her grandfather a hug.
Ⓑ I bought a beautiful new aquarium for my goldfish while at the flea market.
Ⓒ After tripping in the cafeteria and spilling her tray, Mary ran from the room crying.
Ⓓ When I opened the box, I realized that the attachment I wanted was sold seperately and not included in the package.

**9. Choose the sentence that contains a misspelled word.**

Ⓐ Our class just completed a study on the lifecycle of butterflies.
Ⓑ The delivery man stacked the packages and boxxes in his truck.
Ⓒ The turtle jumped from its log, creating quite a splash.
Ⓓ When firefighters were able to contain the flames, the crowd cheered.

**10. Which word below is spelled correctly?**

Ⓐ nerrate
Ⓑ nihrayt
Ⓒ narrete
Ⓓ narrate

**11. Unscramble the word IWLD**

**12. Unscramble the word FWEOLR**

**13. Fill in the missing vowels to make a proper word.**

r ___ m _____ _____ n

- Ⓐ romoin
- Ⓑ rimain
- Ⓒ remain
- Ⓓ ramian

**14. Fill in the missing vowels to make a proper word.**

____ v _____ n _____ _____

- Ⓐ ivinae
- Ⓑ avinie
- Ⓒ avenue
- Ⓓ evenie

## CHAPTER 3 → Lesson 13: Word Choice: Attending to Precision

**1. Choose the word that best completes the sentence.**

Alexander _____ into the living room to show off his new suit. He had a very high opinion of himself!

Ⓐ walked
Ⓑ strutted
Ⓒ trudged
Ⓓ waddled

**2. Choose the word that best completes the sentence.**

Collecting the garbage was _____ work, but Tom was happy to do it. The job wore on his body, especially during the hottest days of summer, but he knew he was providing an important public service to his community.

Ⓐ uncomfortable
Ⓑ grueling
Ⓒ bad
Ⓓ stupid

**3. Choose the word that best completes sentence.**

Dante was _____ about his award for most improved swimmer. He had never wanted any-thing more!

Ⓐ peaceful
Ⓑ happy
Ⓒ elated
Ⓓ disappointed

**4. Choose the word that best completes the sentence.**

The baby babbled sweetly, making it difficult for her mother to be upset about the _____mess she had made when she threw spaghetti all over the kitchen.

Ⓐ gigantic
Ⓑ big
Ⓒ wide
Ⓓ deep

**5. Choose the word that best completes the sentence.**

The defendant's fingerprint at the scene of the crime was the most _____ evidence in the trial. The jury had no choice but to convict her.

Ⓐ worst
Ⓑ damaging
Ⓒ bad
Ⓓ wonderful

**6. Choose the word that best completes the sentence.**

Shelby was a _____. She was fiesty, and she did not let anyone push her around.

Ⓐ ham
Ⓑ scrooge
Ⓒ shrinking violet
Ⓓ fireball

**7. Choose the word that best completes the sentence.**

The girls _____ to the front of the crowd to get a glimpse of their favorite boy band.

Ⓐ walked
Ⓑ skipped
Ⓒ dove
Ⓓ clambered

**8. Anne is paying attention to choosing precise words in her writing. Which sentence should she use in her personal narrative to describe the overflowing bathtub?**

Ⓐ The water <u>dripping</u> over the edge reminded her of a waterfall.
Ⓑ The water <u>spraying</u> over the edge reminded her of a waterfall.
Ⓒ The water <u>bubbling</u> over the edge reminded her of a waterfall.
Ⓓ The water <u>cascading</u> over the edge reminded her of a waterfall.

9. Riley is paying attention to choosing precise words in his writing. Which sentence should he use to help persuade the reader to recycle?

Ⓐ Recycling <u>cuts down on</u> the amount of waste that goes into landfills each year.
Ⓑ Recycling <u>helps us put a little bit less</u> waste into landfills each year.
Ⓒ Recycling <u>reduces</u> the amount of waste that goes into landfills each year.
Ⓓ Recycling <u>makes us put not as much</u> waste into landfills each year.

10. **Choose the word that best completes the sentence.**

Janet _____ with delight when she called her mother to say she had been accepted to her top choice college.

Ⓐ squealed
Ⓑ spoke
Ⓒ sneezed
Ⓓ growled

# CHAPTER 3 → Lesson 14: Punctuating for Effect!

1. **Choose the punctuation that means Jermain's mother is speaking to him.**

   Jermaine mother said you have to clean your room.

   Ⓐ Jermaine mother said you have to clean your room.
   Ⓑ "Jermaine, Mother said you have to clean your room."
   Ⓒ Jermaine Mother said, "You have to clean your room."
   Ⓓ "Jermaine," Mother said, "you have to clean your room."

2. **Choose the punctuation that means a third character is shouting at Jermaine to tell him his mother said to clean his room.**

   Jermaine mother said you have to clean your room.

   Ⓐ "Jermaine," Mother said, "you have to clean your room!"
   Ⓑ "Jermaine, Mother said you have to clean your room!"
   Ⓒ "Jermaine," Mother said, "you have to clean your room?"
   Ⓓ "Jermaine, Mother said you have to clean your room."

3. **Choose the most appropriate end punctuation.**

   Dante was elated about his award for most improved swimmer. He had never wanted anything more

   Ⓐ .
   Ⓑ ?
   Ⓒ !
   Ⓓ $

4. **Choose the sentence that is punctuated correctly.**

   Ⓐ The tiger crept carefully through the jungle?
   Ⓑ The tiger crept carefully through the jungle!
   Ⓒ The tiger crept carefully through the jungle
   Ⓓ The tiger crept carefully through the jungle.

## 5. Choose the appropriate end punctuation for sentence 1.

James was furious when Gemma squirted ketchup all over his new white shirt(1) Sheesh (2) What did Gemma expect to happen (3)

Ⓐ   .
Ⓑ   !
Ⓒ   ?
Ⓓ   *

## 6. Choose the appropriate end punctuation for sentence 2.

James was furious when Gemma squirted ketchup all over his new white shirt(1) Sheesh (2) What did Gemma expect to happen (3)

Ⓐ   .
Ⓑ   !
Ⓒ   ?
Ⓓ   *

## 7. Choose the appropriate end punctuation for sentence 3.

James was furious when Gemma squirted ketchup all over his new white shirt(1) Sheesh (2) What did Gemma expect to happen (3)

Ⓐ   .
Ⓑ   !
Ⓒ   ?
Ⓓ   *

## 8. Which punctuation best follows "Wow"?

Wow( ) I can't believe I am going to compete in the national chess competition for my age group!

Ⓐ   .
Ⓑ   !
Ⓒ   ?
Ⓓ   &

**9. Which of the following sentences is not punctuated correctly?**

Ⓐ Gee whiz!
Ⓑ I can't believe my good fortune!
Ⓒ Why does water evaporate faster when the sun is out!
Ⓓ Clean your room this instant!

**10. Which of the following sentences is punctuated correctly?**

Ⓐ She startled me when she jumped out of the bushes!
Ⓑ I'm so hungry I'm afraid I won't make it to lunch?
Ⓒ Our teacher is an amazing #storyteller
Ⓓ This is my favorite time of year, "Jenny said."

# CHAPTER 3 → Lesson 15: Finding the Meaning

**1. What does the word _extracted_ mean in the below sentence?**

The milk is extracted from the coconut, which is used to prepare a variety of dishes and sweets.

Ⓐ  To put in
Ⓑ  To take out of something
Ⓒ  To make
Ⓓ  To throw out

**2. Using context clues from the below sentence, the word _despondent_ means:**

The poor woman was despondent after losing everything she owned in the fire.

Ⓐ  excited
Ⓑ  questioning
Ⓒ  disheartened
Ⓓ  radiant

**3. Based on the below sentence, console means:**

My father tried to <u>console</u> me after my dog died, but nothing he did made me feel better.

Ⓐ  entertain
Ⓑ  comfort
Ⓒ  talk to
Ⓓ  explain

**4.** The sleepy kittens crawled into bed with their mother. They quickly nestled cozily beside her and went to sleep.

**The word _nestled_ means:**

Ⓐ  purred softly
Ⓑ  lay down
Ⓒ  leaned against
Ⓓ  snuggled up to

**5. Based on the below sentence, the best meaning for the word _gawked_ is:**

Larry gawked in wide-eyed astonishment at the woman wearing the glass hat with fish swimming in it.

Ⓐ  glanced at
Ⓑ  stared intensely
Ⓒ  laughed at
Ⓓ  yelled at

**6. The word _cease_ means:**

If the talking does not cease immediately, you will have 50 additional math problems for homework.

Ⓐ  become less noisy
Ⓑ  continue
Ⓒ  decrease
Ⓓ  stop

**7. The word _weary_ means:**

The young men rode their bikes 60 miles to the fair. They did not stop for a break the entire trip. Once they arrived, they were too weary to walk around and enjoy the rides, so they simply lounged on the bleachers and watched the quilt judging contest.

Ⓐ  excited
Ⓑ  tired
Ⓒ  energized
Ⓓ  enthusiastic

**8. The word _lounged_ means:**

The young men rode their bikes 60 miles to the fair. They did not stop for a break the entire trip. Once they arrived, they were too weary to walk around and enjoy the ride, so they simply lounged on the bleachers and watched the quilt judging contest.

Ⓐ  watched
Ⓑ  sat rigidly
Ⓒ  stood
Ⓓ  relaxed

9. **Based on the context clues in the below sentence, the best meaning of the word** _plummeted_ **is:**

At the football game Friday night, Bill broke his leg when he plummeted to the ground from the top of the bleachers.

Ⓐ floated
Ⓑ drifted
Ⓒ slipped
Ⓓ plunged

10. **According to the sentence below, the word** _frigid_ **means:**

The weather man is predicting several days of frigid temperatures in the mountains. After watching the weather report, I decided to pack thermal shirts and pants, wool sweaters, gloves, and my warmest coat for the camping trip this weekend.

Ⓐ rising
Ⓑ freezing
Ⓒ warm
Ⓓ chilly

## CHAPTER 3 → Lesson 16: Same Word Different Meanings

**1. Choose the correct meaning for the word 'ornaments' in the following sentence.**

The shells are also made into cups and ornaments.

Ⓐ  a statue
Ⓑ  cap
Ⓒ  books
Ⓓ  jewelry worn by women

**Question 2 is based on the poem below**

I found a shell, a curly one;
Lying on the sand.
I picked it up and took it home,
Held tightly in my hand.

Mommy looked at it and then,
She held it to my ear,
And from the shell there came a song
Soft and sweet and clear.

I was surprised, I listened hard,
And it was really true:
If you can find a nice big shell,
You'll hear the singing too.

--- Unknown

**2. In the poem find the word that means 'hard outer covering'.**

Ⓐ  song
Ⓑ  sweet
Ⓒ  shell
Ⓓ  soft

(1) Jim was given the Most Valuable Player award at the banquet last night. (2) Everyone agreed that he was the best batter on the team this year. (3) Because he won the award, Mindy wanted to give him a surprise party. (4) She invited all of his friends and even baked him a cake. (5) In the end, the surprise was on Mindy because she had put salt in the batter instead of sugar.

**3. The meaning of the word 'batter' in sentence 2 is:**

Ⓐ   a mixture for baking
Ⓑ   to damage
Ⓒ   user of a baseball bat
Ⓓ   to hit repeatedly

**4. The meaning of the word 'batter' in sentence 5 is:**

Ⓐ   a mixture for baking
Ⓑ   to damage
Ⓒ   user of a baseball bat
Ⓓ   to hit repeatedly

### Question 5-7 are based on the details below

(1) Kelly and her sister picked strawberries today. (2) When they arrived home, they decided to make strawberry jam. (3) They had picked so many strawberries that they wouldn't all fit in the pot they had chosen. (4) Kelly got a large spoon and began to jam the strawberries into the pot. (5) Once they were cooked, she then put them into the blender. (6) Her mother warned her not to put too much into the blender because it would cause it to jam. (7) To prevent this from happening, Kelly blended the berries in small batches. (8) Once the berries were blended, they realized how late it was. (9) They asked their mother if she would finish for them so that they could go to the jam session their favorite band was having. (10) She agreed, and they happily left to join their friends.

**5. Choose the meaning of the word 'jam' in sentence 2.**

Ⓐ   to pack tightly
Ⓑ   a fruit spread like jelly
Ⓒ   become stuck
Ⓓ   an informal gathering of musicians

**6. Choose the meaning of the word 'jam' in sentence 4.**

Ⓐ to pack tightly
Ⓑ a fruit spread like jelly
Ⓒ become stuck
Ⓓ an informal gathering of musicians

**7. Choose the meaning of the word 'jam' in sentence 6.**

Ⓐ to pack tightly
Ⓑ a fruit spread like jelly
Ⓒ become stuck
Ⓓ an informal gathering of musicians

**8. (1) I cannot stand to waste my time waiting in line. (2) It hurts my back to stand for so long.**
**In sentence 1, the word stand means:**

Ⓐ tolerate or endure
Ⓑ to undergo
Ⓒ a small rack or table
Ⓓ to maintain an upright position on your feet

**9. (1) I cannot stand to waste my time waiting in line. (2) It hurts my back to stand for so long.**
**In sentence 2, the word stand means:**

Ⓐ tolerate or endure
Ⓑ to undergo
Ⓒ a small rack or table
Ⓓ to maintain an upright position on your feet

**10. Choose the sentence that uses the word loop in the same way.**

The Cub Scout was taught to create a loop as part of the knot-making process.

Ⓐ Tory was taught to create a <u>loop</u> in order to tie her shoes.
Ⓑ On my website, I created a segment <u>loop</u>.
Ⓒ The producer created a <u>loop</u> to be broadcast during the newsreel.

**11. Choose the sentence that uses the word bank in the same way.**

My mother went to the bank to deposit her pay check.

Ⓐ My dad drove to the bank and withdrew some cash.
Ⓑ We went fishing at the bank of the river.
Ⓒ I can bank my passing grades and retake the tests I didn't pass.
Ⓓ I am always right, and you can bank on that!

# CHAPTER 3 → Lesson 17: Context Clues

**1. What is the meaning of the word, "sentiment" in the paragraph below?**

Franklin D. Roosevelt gave his first inaugural address in 1933, during the midst of the Great Depression. He famously said, "The only thing we have to fear is… fear itself." His <u>sentiment</u> helped assuage the fears of many Americans, giving them hope for better days ahead.

- Ⓐ  a person who often cries
- Ⓑ  a view or attitude toward a situation or event
- Ⓒ  a nice piece of jewelry
- Ⓓ  blame

**2. What is the meaning of the word, "assuage" in the paragraph below?**

Franklin D. Roosevelt gave his first inaugural address in 1933, during the midst of the Great Depression. He famously said, "The only thing we have to fear is… fear itself." This sentiment helped <u>assuage</u> the fears of many Americans, giving them hope for better days ahead.

- Ⓐ  to make worse
- Ⓑ  to ease
- Ⓒ  to heighten
- Ⓓ  to strengthen

**3. What is the meaning of the word, "affluent" in the paragraph below?**

The restaurant catered to an <u>affluent</u> crowd. The food was very expensive, the tablecloths were crisp and white, and patrons were expected to dress nicely.

- Ⓐ  practical
- Ⓑ  wealthy
- Ⓒ  honest
- Ⓓ  poor

**4. What is the meaning of the word, "patrons" in the paragraph below?**

The restaurant catered to an affluent crowd. The food was very expensive, the tablecloths were crisp and white, and <u>patrons</u> were expected to dress nicely in order to eat there.

Ⓐ  doctors
Ⓑ  waiters
Ⓒ  cooks
Ⓓ  customers

**5. In the paragraph below, what is the meaning of the word, "miser"?**

In Charles Dickens's classic tale, Ebenezer Scrooge is a <u>miser</u>-- someone who wishes to spend as little money as possible. As a result, his life is devoid of any meaningful relationships with other people. He does not have any true friends to speak of.

Ⓐ  someone who gives gifts often
Ⓑ  someone who wishes to spend as little money as possible
Ⓒ  someone who thinks of others before themselves
Ⓓ  someone who is very old

**6. In the paragraph below, what is the meaning of the word, "devoid"?**

In Charles Dickens's classic tale, Ebenezer Scrooge is a miser-- someone who wishes to spend as little money as possible. As a result, his life is <u>devoid</u> of any meaningful relationships with other people. He does not have any true friends to speak of.

Ⓐ  blooming
Ⓑ  decorated
Ⓒ  filled with
Ⓓ  entirely lacks

**7. What is the meaning of the word, "corridor" in the paragraph below?**

The hospital <u>corridor</u> was long and cold. Door after door opened into room after room of patients in various stages of rest and recovery. Hazel was earnest in her desire to bring some degree of joy to each of them. That's what clowns are for, after all!

Ⓐ  bed
Ⓑ  room
Ⓒ  desk
Ⓓ  hallway

**8. What is the meaning of the word, "earnest" in the paragraph below?**

The hospital corridor was long and cold. Door after door opened into room after room of patients in various stages of rest and recovery. Hazel was <u>earnest</u> in her desire to bring some degree of joy to each of them. That's what clowns are for, after all!

- Ⓐ willing
- Ⓑ excited
- Ⓒ negligent
- Ⓓ serious

**9. In the paragraph below, what is the meaning of the word, "invest?"**

Marcus decided to <u>invest</u> in Mel and Deena's lemonade stand. He gave them twenty dollars to buy fresh lemons, cups, and sugar. In return Mel and Deena will reimburse him with money they earn selling the lemonade plus ten percent of each cup they sell.

- Ⓐ to really enjoy lemonade
- Ⓑ to cheer someone one by clapping and shouting
- Ⓒ to give someone money for fun
- Ⓓ to give someone money with hopes of making money

**10. In the paragraph below, what is the meaning of the word, "reimburse."**

Marcus decided to invest in Mel and Deena's lemonade stand. He gave them twenty dollars to buy fresh lemons, cups, and sugar. In return Mel and Deena will <u>reimburse</u> him with money they earn selling the lemonade plus ten percent of each cup they sell.

- Ⓐ repay
- Ⓑ hit
- Ⓒ shower
- Ⓓ take

## CHAPTER 3 → Lesson 18: The Meaning of Words

1. **Mindy was surprised to discover how disorganized the students had left the books. What is the meaning of the word <u>disorganized</u>?**

   Ⓐ organized
   Ⓑ not organized
   Ⓒ neat
   Ⓓ torn

2. **Which of the following words contains a prefix that means <u>again</u>?**

   Ⓐ preview
   Ⓑ international
   Ⓒ rewind
   Ⓓ disagree

3. **Which of the following words refers to half of the globe?**

   Ⓐ longitude
   Ⓑ hemisphere
   Ⓒ parallel
   Ⓓ latitude

4. **The prefix 'sub' in submarine means:**

   Ⓐ back or again
   Ⓑ above or extra
   Ⓒ under or below
   Ⓓ across or over

5. **The prefix 'hyper' in hyperactive means:**

   Ⓐ within, into
   Ⓑ over or excessive
   Ⓒ lacking or without
   Ⓓ out of or former

6. **If biology is the study of life, which answer choice explains the meaning of the word *geology*?**

   Ⓐ appreciation for the earth
   Ⓑ a science class
   Ⓒ the study of the earth
   Ⓓ the study of life

7. **Choose a word with the prefix below to replace the words <u>came back</u>.**

   Once upon a time, Jane and Jill were best friends. One day, Jane decided that she wanted to travel the world and asked Jill if she could borrow some money. When Jane came back from her vacation she went to see Jill immediately.

   Ⓐ unfair
   Ⓑ returned
   Ⓒ disappear
   Ⓓ replay

8. **Choose a word with the prefix below to replace the words <u>pay back</u>.**

   Jill wanted Jane to pay back the money.

   Ⓐ repay
   Ⓑ unpay
   Ⓒ redo
   Ⓓ undo

9. **Choose a word below that is appropriate for the sentence.**

   The frog _____ grabbed the insect.

   Ⓐ quick
   Ⓑ quickful
   Ⓒ quickly
   Ⓓ quicker

10. **The prefix 're' in returned means:**

    Ⓐ under or below
    Ⓑ before
    Ⓒ back or again
    Ⓓ above or extra

11. What is the root word of understandable? Write your answer in the box below.

12. In the word 'bewailed', the prefix is _____.

## CHAPTER 3 → Lesson 19: For Your Reference

1. **Where would one look to find the definition of a key word when reading a science textbook?**

   Ⓐ  the glossary
   Ⓑ  the thesaurus
   Ⓒ  the dictionary
   Ⓓ  the table of contents

2. **What part of speech is the word, "component," in the thesaurus entry below?**

   **Component.** — n. component; component part, integral part, integrant part; element, constituent, ingredient, leaven; part and parcel; contents; appurtenance; feature

   Ⓐ  adjective
   Ⓑ  verb
   Ⓒ  adverb
   Ⓓ  noun

3. **How many definitions of "silently" are there in the dictionary entry below?**

   **Si.lently,** adv.   [f. SILENT a. + - LY $^2$.]
   **(1)In a silent manner; without speaking, in Silence; without noise or commotion, noiselessly, Quietly; without mention or notice.**
   **1570-6** LAMBARDE *Peramb. Kent* (1826) 157, I could not silently slip over such impieties. 1590 SHAKS. *Mids*. N. III.
   i. 206 Type vp my louers tongue, bring him silently. 1617 MORYSON *Itin*. 1. 246 The Turkey company in London was at this time..silently enjoying the safety and profit of this trafficke.
   **(2)Gradually, imperceptibly. Obs.**$^{-1}$
   **1668** CULPEPPER & COLE *Barthol. Anat*. I. xiii. 30 It goes by little and little straight forward, and is silently terminated towards the spleen.

   Ⓐ  3
   Ⓑ  4
   Ⓒ  1
   Ⓓ  2

## 4. According to the thesaurus entry below, what is a synonym for the word, "veteran?"

**Veteran.**— n. veteran, old man, seer, patriarch, graybeard; grandfather, grandsire; grandam; gaffer, gammer; crone; pantaloon; sexagenarian, octogenarian, nonagenarian, centenarian; old stager.

- Ⓐ veterinarian
- Ⓑ graybeard
- Ⓒ young man
- Ⓓ None of the above

## 5. What is the definition of "skeletal?"

**Skeletal** (ske.l/tal), a. [f. SKELET-ON sb. + -AL.]  Of or belonging to, forming of formed by, forming part of, or resembling, a skeleton.
*Skeletal muscle*, a muscle attached to and controlling a part of a skeleton.
**1854** OWEN in *Orr's Cire. Sci., Org. Nat. I.* 168 The skeletal framework.. does not go beyond the fibrous stage.
**1872** HUMPHRY *Myology* 8 The skeletal formations in the sternal region of the visceral wall.

- Ⓐ A bodily system made of muscle and bones, the most important system in the body.
- Ⓑ Made of bones
- Ⓒ The skeletal region of the visceral wall
- Ⓓ Of or belonging to, forming or formed by, forming part of, or resembling, a skeleton

## 6. Which of the following is not a synonym for "edge?"

**Edge.** — n. edge, verge, brink, brow, brim, margin, border, confine, skirt, rim, flange, side, mouth; jaws, chops, chaps, fauces; lip, muzzle. threshold, door, porch; portal &c. (opening) 260; coast, shore. frame, fringe, flounce, frill, list, trimming, edging, skirting, hem, selvedge, welt, furbelow, valance, gimp. adj. border, marginal, skirting; labial, labiated, marginated.

- Ⓐ brink
- Ⓑ flank
- Ⓒ verge
- Ⓓ rim

**7. Where might one see a sitar?**

**Sitar** (si.tar). *Anglo-Ind*. Also sitarre. [Urdu راتس sitar.] A form of guitar, properly having three strings, used in India.
1845 STOCQUELER *Hdbk*. *Brit*. India (1854) 26 A trio of sitars, or rude violins.
1859 J. LANG *Wand*. *India* 152 Two or three of the company..played alternately on the sitarre (native guitar or violin).

**Si.tarch.** *rare*⁻⁰. [ad. Gr. oiTapxns or oiTapxos, f. oiTos corn, food.]
**1656** BLOUNT *Glossogr*., Sitark, he that hath the Office to provide Corn, and Victuals sufficient.
**1676** COLICS, *Starck*, a Pourveyor.

Ⓐ a hospital
Ⓑ a construction site
Ⓒ an international music festival
Ⓓ at the doctor's office.

**8. Which of the following is not a meaning of the word, "skyscape?"**

**Sky.scape.** [f. SKY sb.¹ after *landscape, seascape.*] A view of the sky ; also in painting, etc., a representation of part of the sky.
**1817** SOUTHEY *Let*. in *Life* (1850) IV. 283 It was the unbroken horizon which impressed me,..and the skyscapes which it afforded.
**1861** C.J. ANDERSON Okavango x. 137
The beautiful and striking skyscapes and atmospheric coruscations attendant on these storms.
**1878** GROSART
*More's Poems* Introd. p. xii, The great ancient Painters, whose backgrounds of portraits..rather than land-scape, or sea-scape, or sky-scape proper, assure us [etc.]

Ⓐ escaping by way of the sky
Ⓑ a view of the sky
Ⓒ a representation of part of the sky in painting, etc.
Ⓓ B & C

**9. Which of the following synonyms for "notch" is a verb?**

**Notch.** — n. notch, dent, nick, cut; indent, indentation; dimple. embrasure, battlement, machicolation; saw, tooth, crenelle, scallop, scollop, vandyke; depression; jag. v. notch, nick, cut, dent, indent, jag, scarify, scotch, crimp, scallop, scollop, crenulate, vandyke. adj. notched &c. v.; crenate, crenated; dentate, dentated; denticulate, denticulated; toothed, palmated, serrated.

Ⓐ nick
Ⓑ embrasure
Ⓒ toothed
Ⓓ palmated

## 10. Which of the following is NOT a definition of the word, "slog?"

Slog (slog), v. colloq. [Of obscure origin. Cf. SLUG v.[4]]

**1. trans. To hit or strike hard ; to drive with blows. Also fig., to assail violently.**

**1853** ' C.BEDE *Verdant Green* xi. 106 His whole person [had been] put in chancery, stung, bruised, fibbed,..slogged, and otherwise ill-treated.

**1884** 'R. BOLDREWOOD' *Melb.*

*Memories* iv. 32 We slogged the tired cattle round the fence.

**1891** *Spectator* to Oct. 487/1 They love snubbing their friends and 'slogging' their enemies.

**b. Cricket. To obtain (runs) by hard hitting.**

**1897** H. W. BLEAKLEY *Short innings* iii. 49 Mr. Dolly slogged sixes and fours until he had made about eighty.

**2. intr. To walk heavily or doggedly.**

**1872** CALVERLEY *Fly Leaves* (1903) 119 Then abiit..off slogs boy. **1876** *Mid-Yorks. Gloss., Slog,* to walk with burdened feet, as through snow, or puddle. **1907** *Westm.*

*Gaz.* 2 Oct. 2/1 Overtaking the guns, we 'slogged' on with them for a mile or more.

**3. To deal heavy blows, to work hard (at something), to labour away, etc.**

**1888** *Daily News* 22 May 5/2, I slogged at it, day in and day out.

**1894** HESLOP *Northumberland Gloss.* s.v., They slogged away at the anchor shank.

Ⓐ to hit or strike hard
Ⓑ to walk heavily or doggedly
Ⓒ to deal heavy blows, to work hard
Ⓓ to jump high and score

# CHAPTER 3 → Lesson 20: Similes and Metaphors

**1. What does the metaphor in the first sentence mean?**

The sky was an angry, purple monster. It roared fiercely as the thunder crashed and the rain poured down.

 Ⓐ The sky had clouds in the shape of a monster.
 Ⓑ The sky was stormy.
 Ⓒ Monsters invaded the town.
 Ⓓ None of the above

**2. What purpose does the author's simile serve in the paragraph?**

In the days after Dad was laid off almost everyone was gloomy. Sam didn't smile, <u>Mom hovered over everyone like a cloud full of rain</u>. It was Sasha who was the ray of sunshine when she declared, "It's alright. Hugs are free!"

 Ⓐ It describes the setting after Dad was laid off.
 Ⓑ It makes the point that mom was gloomy and likely to cry.
 Ⓒ It shows that Sasha was a happy, upbeat presence in the house.
 Ⓓ It reminds us that hugs are free.

**3. By comparing Kevin to a brick wall, what is the speaker trying to say about Kevin?**

The starting goalie was out with an injury, so Kevin was finally getting his chance to prove his worth.  He knew he could do it. He was ready. Kevin was a brick wall.

 Ⓐ He would not allow the opponent to score he'd block the goal posts.
 Ⓑ He was hard-headed.
 Ⓒ He built a wall in front of his soccer goal.
 Ⓓ He threw bricks at his opponent.

**4. What purpose does the author's metaphor serve in the paragraph?**

In the days after Dad was laid off almost everyone was gloomy. Sam didn't smile, Mom hovered over everyone like a cloud full of rain. <u>It was Sasha who was the ray of sunshine when she declared, "It's alright. Hugs are free!"</u>

Ⓐ It describes the setting after Dad was laid off.
Ⓑ It makes the point that mom was gloomy and likely to cry.
Ⓒ It shows that Sasha was a happy, upbeat presence in the house.
Ⓓ It reminds us that hugs are free.

**5. What does the simile in the below paragraph mean?**

<u>Their family was like a patchwork quilt</u> of diversity. Each adopted child added something beautiful to the whole.

Ⓐ Like a patchwork quilt, the family was old and ragged. It was probably time to throw it out.
Ⓑ Their family had old-fashioned traditions, like a patchwork quilt from generations past.
Ⓒ Like a patchwork quilt, the children were adopted by parents who loved them very much.
Ⓓ Like a patchwork quilt that has bits of different fabric stitched together, the family had children of different ethnic origins living together as siblings. The overall effect was beautiful.

**6. Why does the speaker compare ballerinas to swans?**

The ballerinas were like swans gliding over the stage.

Ⓐ to show that they were white
Ⓑ to show that they squawked like birds
Ⓒ to show that they can swim
Ⓓ to show that they are graceful and elegant

**7. Which similes below would be helpful in describing a terrified look on someone's face?**

Ⓐ Her eyes drooped like wilted flowers, and her hands hung limp like wet spaghetti noodles.
Ⓑ Her eyes were as sharp as arrows, and her fists clenched tight like hammers waiting to strike.
Ⓒ Her eyes were soft like a morning dew, and her hands lay still as resting cherubs.
Ⓓ Her eyes were as big as sewer lids, and her hands trembled like tiny earthquakes.

**8. Which metaphor below would be helpful in describing a presentation that went awry?**

Ⓐ   In that moment Alfonso was a lion tamer, and the crowd was a well-trained pride eating from the palm of his hand.

Ⓑ   In that moment Alfonso was the conductor of a train that was steady on its rails and going full steam ahead.

Ⓒ   In that moment Alfonso was a bright flame, and the people gathered like moths around him.

Ⓓ   In that moment Alfonso was the captain of an ill-fated voyage, and he was going down with his ship.

**9. Which simile below would help describe a child's joy in being reunited with a mother returning from a military tour of duty in another country?**

Ⓐ   Hannah's face lit up like fireworks on the Fourth of July when she glimpsed her mother rounding the corner. It was really her!

Ⓑ   Hannah closed up like a locked bedroom door when she saw her mother for the first time.

Ⓒ   Hannah pounded her fist on the counter like it was a judge's ruinous gavel when she saw her mother rounding the corner.

Ⓓ   Hannah's eyes turned down, and her face turned red as a beet when she glimpsed her mother for the first time.

**10. Which metaphor below would be helpful in describing a huge crowd of people at a festival?**

Ⓐ   The people marched through the streets with purpose, like an army marching toward battle.

Ⓑ   The streets were a barren desert, and the music echoed off of empty storefronts.

Ⓒ   A sea of delighted people swept over the sidewalks and into the street as they passed from attraction to attraction.

Ⓓ   I was on an emotional roller coaster on the day of the festival.

# CHAPTER 3 → Lesson 21: Idiomatic Expressions and Proverbs

**1. What is meant by the idiom _hit the ceiling_ in the below sentence?**

If Wendy's dad found out that she took her cell phone to school, he would hit the ceiling.

Ⓐ  Wendy's dad will jump high.
Ⓑ  Wendy's dad will be very angry.
Ⓒ  Wendy's dad will laugh loudly.
Ⓓ  Wendy's dad will congratulate her.

**2. What is meant by the idiom swallow your pride?**

I think that you need to swallow your pride and apologize to your teacher for talking in class.

Ⓐ  to swallow hard
Ⓑ  to deny doing something
Ⓒ  to forget about being embarrassed
Ⓓ  to pretend you are sorry

**3. What does the idiom 'walking on air' mean?**

Mindy was walking on air after she went backstage and met Adam Levine.

Ⓐ  Mindy was floating through the air.
Ⓑ  Mindy was dreaming.
Ⓒ  Mindy was in a state of bliss.
Ⓓ  Mindy was disappointed.

**4. What is the meaning of '_play it by ear_' in the below sentence?**

I am not sure how long I will stay at the dance. I'm going to play it by ear.

Ⓐ  Play a musical instrument without sheet music.
Ⓑ  As you see how things go decide rather than making plans.
Ⓒ  Listen for someone to tell you what to do.
Ⓓ  Think carefully before making a decision.

**5. What does the idiom 'like <u>a chicken with its head cut off</u>' mean?**

After winning a million dollars, Kelly was running around like a chicken with its head cut off.

Ⓐ  to act in a calm manner
Ⓑ  to be bleeding profusely
Ⓒ  to run around clucking and flapping your arms
Ⓓ  to act in a frenzied manner

**6. What does 'down in the dumps' mean in the sentence?**

Jackie was not very happy. Not only did she lose her favorite necklace, but she also learned that her best friend was going to sleep-away camp for the whole summer while she had to go to summer school. Jackie really felt down in the dumps.

Ⓐ  sad
Ⓑ  bringing the garbage to the end of the driveway
Ⓒ  excited
Ⓓ  flabbergasted

**7. What does a 'little white lie' mean in the sentence?**

Amy's aunt spent months knitting a scarf for Amy. When Amy received the present and looked at it, she really didn't like the colors. She couldn't let her aunt know that she was disappointed after all of her aunt's hard work, so she told a little white lie instead.

Ⓐ  huge made up story
Ⓑ  truth
Ⓒ  lie that is told to avoid hurting someone's feelings
Ⓓ  the lie was painted white

**8. What does 'cut corners' mean in the sentence?**

The renovations the Johnsons were making on the house were getting too expensive. The Johnsons wanted the very best, but they didn't have enough money to pay for it. Their architect came to speak with them. "You have some great ideas, but we're going to need to cut corners. We may have to change some of the original plans to save money; otherwise we won't be able to finish the house."

Ⓐ  cut the edges of the play's program
Ⓑ  clip some coupons
Ⓒ  use money wisely and try to save by spending only what is necessary
Ⓓ  mow the lawn

## 9. What does the idiom 'Half a loaf is better than none' mean?

Ⓐ You can't judge a person's character by how he or she looks.
Ⓑ You usually do better than others if you get there ahead of others.
Ⓒ This means having something is better than not having anything at all.
Ⓓ Mind your own business and let others mind theirs.

## 10. What does the idiom 'Beauty is only skin deep' mean?

Ⓐ If something unfortunate happens, it usually won't happen again.
Ⓑ Take care of a small problem before it becomes a big one.
Ⓒ A picture can explain things better than words.
Ⓓ You can't judge a person's character by how he or she looks.

## 11. Which sentence contains an idiom?

Ⓐ It's raining cats and dogs outside!
Ⓑ It's thundering loudly outside.
Ⓒ It rained 6 inches last week.
Ⓓ Wear a raincoat and boots, because it's raining really hard outside.

# CHAPTER 3 → Lesson 22: Synonyms and Antonyms

**1. Choose the correct set of synonyms for "small."**

- Ⓐ enormous, giant
- Ⓑ minute, gargantuan
- Ⓒ small, unseen
- Ⓓ miniature, minute

**2. Choose the correct set of synonyms.**

- Ⓐ unrealistic, believable
- Ⓑ noteworthy, important
- Ⓒ noteworthy, insignificant
- Ⓓ unfair, just

**3. Choose the correct set of antonyms.**

- Ⓐ radiant, dull
- Ⓑ rescue, save
- Ⓒ chortle, laugh
- Ⓓ sparkle, shine

**4. Choose the synonym for "happy."**

- Ⓐ miserable
- Ⓑ ecstatic
- Ⓒ subdued
- Ⓓ wretched

**5. Choose the correct set of antonyms for "pretty."**

- Ⓐ repulsive, unattractive
- Ⓑ lovely, handsome
- Ⓒ enticing, glamour
- Ⓓ appealing, grotesque

6. **What is a synonym for the word, "chaos?"**

   Ⓐ  huge
   Ⓑ  agree
   Ⓒ  disorder
   Ⓓ  famous

7. **Find the correct set of synonyms below.**

   Ⓐ  fat and aged
   Ⓑ  tend and thick
   Ⓒ  fat and thick
   Ⓓ  aged and tend

8. **Find the correct set of antonyms below.**

   Ⓐ  peculiar and general
   Ⓑ  peculiar and common
   Ⓒ  general and included
   Ⓓ  general and common

9. **What would be a good antonym for the word, "recall?"**

   Ⓐ  contend
   Ⓑ  assert
   Ⓒ  forget
   Ⓓ  urge

10. **What is an antonym for the word, "active?"**

   Ⓐ  lazy
   Ⓑ  energetic
   Ⓒ  healthy
   Ⓓ  running

**11. Match the Synonyms for the following words**

Rush.      Error.      Present

| Mistake | |
| Hurry | |
| Gift | |

**12. Pick the Synonyms for the word Peek from the list below and write it in the box given below.**

Stare, Glance, Ogle, glimpse, look, watch

Date of Completion:_____     Score:_____

## CHAPTER 3 → Lesson 23: Academic and Domain Specific 4th Grade Words

**1. Choose the word that best completes the sentence.**

When Jeremy arrived home his mom _____ him about the dance until he could think of no more details to give her.

Ⓐ yelled at
Ⓑ quizzed
Ⓒ praised
Ⓓ waddled

**2. Choose the word that best completes the sentence.**

The woodlands of the Mid Atlantic region are filled with all sorts of interesting _____.

Ⓐ movies
Ⓑ wildlife
Ⓒ colleges
Ⓓ mortar

**3. Choose the word that best completes sentence.**

The _____ John Muir helped preserve our country's natural beauty by helping to establish Yosemite National Park.

Ⓐ antagoinist
Ⓑ pianist
Ⓒ conservationist
Ⓓ statistician

**4. Choose the word that best completes the sentence.**

Sarah was _____ at the news that the giant oak she had worked to protect was going to be removed in order to build a parking lot.

Ⓐ crestfallen
Ⓑ starstruck
Ⓒ jovial
Ⓓ greedy

**5. Choose the word that best completes the sentence.**

When an animal is _____ the government will sometimes place restrictions on hunting it.

Ⓐ rabid
Ⓑ threatening
Ⓒ special
Ⓓ endangered

**6. Choose the word that best completes the sentence.**

"Mommmmm, do I haaaaaave to?" Lester _____ as his mother sat across the table with her eyes trained on his Brussels sprouts.

Ⓐ said
Ⓑ called
Ⓒ shrieked
Ⓓ whined

**7. Choose the word that best completes the sentence.**

"Wha-wha-what was th-that?" Dera _____ as she climbed the creaky stairs in the old house.

Ⓐ commanded
Ⓑ announced
Ⓒ stammered
Ⓓ laughed

**8. Choose the word that best completes the sentence.**

My _____ is that the celery's stalk turned blue because it absorbed the colored water in the vase.

Ⓐ idea
Ⓑ intuition
Ⓒ guess
Ⓓ hypothesis

**9. Choose the word that best completes the sentence.**

Monica _____ Peter's reasoning by referring to an example in the text that did not support the idea he suggested.

Ⓐ agreed
Ⓑ dissed
Ⓒ critiqued
Ⓓ slammed

**10. Choose the word that best completes the sentence.**

When putting forth an idea about what a character is thinking, it is best to use _____ from the text.

Ⓐ characters
Ⓑ evidence
Ⓒ chapters
Ⓓ nonfiction

# End of Language

## Test Taking Tips

1) **The day before the test,** make sure you get a good night's sleep.

2) **On the day of the test,** be sure to eat a good hearty breakfast! Also, be sure to arrive at school on time.

3) **During the test:**

- **Read every question carefully.**
  - Do not spend too much time on any one question. Work steadily through all questions in the section.
  - Attempt all of the questions even if you are not sure of some answers.
  - If you run into a difficult question, eliminate as many choices as you can and then pick the best one from the remaining choices. Intelligent guessing will help you increase your score.
  - Also, mark the question so that if you have extra time, you can return to it after you reach the end of the section.
  - Some questions may refer to a graph, chart, or other kind of picture. Carefully review the infographics before answering the question.
  - Be sure to include explanations for your written responses and show all work.

- **While Answering EBSR questions.**
  - EBSR questions come in 2 parts - PART A and B.
  - Both PART A and B could be multiple choice or Part A could be multiple choice while Part B could be some other type.
  - Generally, Part A and B will be related, sometimes it may just be from the same lesson but not related questions.
  - If it is a Multiple choice question, Select the bubble corresponding to your answer choice.
  - Read all of the answer choices, even if think you have found the correct answer.
  - In case the questions in EBSR are not multiple choice questions, follow the instruction for other question types while answering such questions.

- **While Answering TECR questions.**
  - Read the directions of each question. Some might ask you to drag something, others to select, and still others to highlight. Follow all instructions of the question (or questions if it is in multiple parts)

## Frequently Asked Questions(FAQs)

For more information on 2023-24 Assessment Year, visit
**www.lumoslearning.com/a/maap-faqs**
OR Scan the **QR Code**

# Why Practice with Repeated Reading Passages?

Throughout the Lumos Learning practice workbooks, students and educators will notice many passages repeat. This is done intentionally. The goal of these workbooks is to help students practice skills necessary to be successful in class and on standardized tests. One of the most critical components to that success is the ability to read and comprehend passages. To that end, reading fluency must be strengthened. According to Hasbrouck and Tindal (2006), "Helping our students become fluent readers is absolutely critical for proficient and motivated reading" (p. 642). And, Nichols et al. indicate, (2009), "fluency is a gateway to comprehension that enables students to move from being word decoders to passage comprehenders" (p. 11).

Lumos Learning recognizes there is no one-size-fits-all approach to build fluency in readers; however, the repeated reading of passages, where students read the same passages at least two or more times, is one of the most widely recognized strategies to improve fluency (Nichols et al., 2009). Repeated reading allows students the opportunity to read passages with familiar words several times until the passage becomes familiar and they no longer have to decode word by word. As students reread, the decoding barrier falls away allowing for an increase in reading comprehension.

The goal of the Lumos Learning workbooks is to increase student achievement and preparation for any standardized test. Using some passages multiple times in a book offers struggling readers an opportunity to do just that.

*References*
*Hasbrouck, J., and Tindal, G. (2006). Oral reading fluency norms: A valuable assessment tool for reading teachers. Reading Teacher, 59(7), 636644. doi:10.1598/RT.59.7.3. Nichols, W., Rupley, W., and Rasinski, T. (2009). Fluency in learning to read for meaning: going beyond repeated readings. Literacy Research & Instruction, 48(1). doi:10.1080/19388070802161906.*

# Progress Chart

| Standard | Lesson | Score | Date of Completion |
|----------|--------|-------|--------------------|
| **MS CCRS** | | | |
| RL.4.1 | Finding Detail in the Story | | |
| RL.4.1 | Inferring | | |
| RL.4.2 | Finding the Theme | | |
| RL.4.2 | Summarizing the Text | | |
| RL.4.3 | Describing Characters | | |
| RL.4.3 | Describing the Setting | | |
| RL.4.4 | Describing Events | | |
| RL.4.4 | Figurative Language | | |
| RL.4.5 | Text Structure | | |
| RL.4.6 | Point of View | | |
| RL.4.7 | Visual Connections | | |
| RL.4.9 | Comparing and Contrasting | | |
| RI.4.1 | It's All in the Details | | |
| RI.4.2 | The Main Idea | | |
| RI.4.3 | Using Details to Explain the Text | | |
| RI.4.4 | What Does it Mean? | | |
| RI.4.5 | How is it Written? | | |
| RI.4.6 | Comparing Different Versions of the Same Event | | |
| RI.4.7 | Using Text Features to Gather Information | | |
| RI.4.8 | Finding the Evidence | | |
| RI.4.9 | Integrating Information | | |

| Standard | Lesson | Score | Date of Completion |
|---|---|---|---|
| **MS CCRS** | | | |
| L.4.1.A | Pronouns | | |
| L.4.1.B | Progressive Verb Tense | | |
| L.4.1.B | What's the Verb? | | |
| L.4.1.C | Modal Auxiliary Verbs | | |
| L.4.1.D | Adjectives and Adverbs | | |
| L.4.1.E | Prepositional Phrases | | |
| L.4.1.F | Complete Sentences | | |
| L.4.1.G | Frequently Confused Words | | |
| L.4.2.A | How is it Capitalized? | | |
| L.4.2.B/C | What's the Punctuation? | | |
| L.4.2.C | Conjunctions and Interjections | | |
| L.4.2.D | How is it Spelled? | | |
| L.4.3.A | Word Choice: Attending to Precision | | |
| L.4.3.B | Punctuating for Effect! | | |
| L.4.3.C | Finding the Meaning | | |
| L.4.4 | Same Word Different Meanings | | |
| L.4.4.A | Context Clues | | |
| L.4.4.B | The Meaning of Words | | |
| L.4.4.C | For Your Reference | | |
| L.4.5.A | Similes and Metaphors | | |
| L.4.5.B | Idiomatic Expressions and Proverbs | | |
| L.4.5.C | Synonyms and Antonyms | | |
| L.4.6 | Academic and Domain Specific 4th Grade Words | | |

Grade **4**

Lumos Learning
— Step Up Your Skills —

# MISSISSIPPI
# Math
## MAAP Practice

### Student Copy

((( tedBook )))
**ONLINE**

## 2 Practice Tests
## Personalized Study Plan

**Math Domains**

- Operations & Algebraic Thinking
- Number & Operations in Base Ten
- Number & Operations - Fractions
- Measurement & Data
- Geometry

## Available
- At Leading book stores
- Online www.LumosLearning.com

Made in the USA
Columbia, SC
24 September 2024

42855573R00154